ITSM LIBRARY

*it*SMF
THE IT SERVICE
MANAGEMENT FORUM

Frameworks
for IT
Management

The
Leading
22

TQM
ISO 9000
TickIT
ISO 27001
ISO 20000

ITS-CMM
Six Sigma
eSCM
IT BSC
AS 8015

CoBiT
M_o_R
PrimaVera
ASL, BiSL
ISPL, ITIL®

PRINCE2®
eTOM
MSP
PMBoK
IPMA

VHP

About the ITSM Library

The publications in the ITSM Library cover best practice in IT Management and are published on behalf of *it*SMF Netherlands (*it*SMF-NL).

The IT Service Management Forum (*it*SMF) is the association for IT service organizations, and for customers of IT services. *it*SMF's goal is to promote innovation and support of IT management; suppliers and customers are equally represented within the *it*SMF. The Forum's main focus is exchange of peer knowledge and experience. Our authors are global experts.

The following publications are, or soon will be, available.

Introduction, Foundations and Practitioners books
- Foundations of IT Service Management based on ITIL® / IT Service Management – an introduction, based on ITIL® (Arabic, Danish, German, English, French, Italian, Japanese, Korean, Dutch, Brazilian Portuguese, Russian, and Spanish)
- IT Services Procurement – an introduction based on ISPL (Dutch)
- Project Management based on Prince2 (Dutch, English, German)
- Practitioner Release & Control for IT Service Management, based on ITIL (English)

IT Service Management – best practices
- IT Service Management – best practices, part 1 (Dutch)
- IT Service Management – best practices, part 2 (Dutch)
- IT Service Management – best practices, part 3 (Dutch)

Topics & Management instruments
- Metrics for IT Service Management (English)
- Six Sigma for IT Management (English)
- The RfP for IT Outsourcing (Dutch)
- Service Agreements – A Management Guide (English)
- Frameworks for IT Management (English)

Pocket guides
- ISO/IEC 20000 – a pocket guide (English, German, Italian, Spanish, formerly BS 15000 – a pocket guide)
- IT Services Procurement based on ISPL – a pocket guide (English)
- IT Governance – a pocket guide based on COBIT (English, German)
- IT Service CMM – a pocket guide (English)
- IT Service Management – a summary based on ITIL® (Dutch)
- IT Service Management from hell! (English)

For any further enquiries about ITSM Library, please visit www.itsmfbooks.com, http://en.itsmportal.net/books.php?id=35 or www.vanharen.net.

Frameworks for IT Management

Van Haren
PUBLISHING

Colophon

Title:	Frameworks for IT Management
A publication of:	*it*SMF-NL
Editors:	Jan van Bon (chief editor)
	Tieneke Verheijen (editor)
Publisher:	Van Haren Publishing, Zaltbommel, www.vanharen.net
ISBN(10):	90 77212 90 6
ISBN(13):	978 90 77212 90 5
Edition:	First edition, first impression, September 2006
Design and Layout:	CO2 Premedia, Amersfoort - NL
Printer:	Wilco, Amersfoort -NL

For any further enquiries about Van Haren Publishing, please send an e-mail to:
info@vanharen.net

The International *it*SMF organization, through its International Publications Executive Subcommittee (IPESC), comprised of a council of members from global *it*SMF chapters has given its formal *it*SMF International endorsement to this book.

TRADEMARK NOTICES
PRINCE2™, M_o_R® AND ITIL® ARE REGISTERED TRADE MARKS AND REGISTERED COMMUNITY TRADE MARKS OF THE OFFICE OF GOVERNMENT COMMERCE, AND ARE REGISTERED IN THE U.S. PATENT AND TRADEMARK OFFICE.
COBIT® is a registered trademark of the Information Systems Audit and Control Association (ISACA)/IT Governance Institute (ITGI).
The PMBoK® is a registered trademark of the Project Management Institute (PMI).

Foreword

Providing the best IT services at the lowest cost – this challenge is on most IT managers' agendas nowadays. The solution may be complex, but can't be achieved and sustained without the support of some kind of best-practice framework or quality management system. And, as most of you will have found out by now, in terms of frameworks there is not a single silver bullet for all situations.

However, as we've learned from discussions with our members, there is a huge number of management frameworks in the marketplace and this is confusing for most individual IT managers. Which framework could be – or should be – used in which situation? It's hard to make the right choice all the time. And it's quite impossible just to use all available frameworks, whether they are specially made for IT of IT Management or used as a general management framework, since many of them are overlapping or even conflicting.

So the big question is: how to select the right elements for your quality management system? I am pleased to say that we now have a book that makes it a lot easier for IT managers – who generally have little time to study – to find their way to the required information to make up their mind about the answer.

As for *it*SMF Netherlands, I am very proud to add this book to the ITSM Library. The book has been produced according the high standards we apply for all ITSM Library books, written by well-known experts and severely reviewed by a number of enthusiastic and skilled *it*SMF members. On behalf of *it*SMF Netherlands, I wish to thank this review team for their efforts to support the quality of this book.

I know that you will find this guide informative and a valuable addition to your ITSM library in support of your journey toward service excellence.

Arjen Droog
CEO *it*SMF Netherlands

Endorsement Statement

For many reasons it has been very apparent that IT managers need frameworks to build their service management strategies. Seeing the vast number of management frameworks, it can be hard to choose the right one for IT Management in your own organization. Keeping up to the changes that occur to these frameworks is an added challenge.

I am pleased to say that this *it*SMF book makes it easy to get the necessary information to make the right decisions for your organization and serves our readers well. As the Chair for the *it*SMF International Publications Executive Sub Committee (IPESC), I am very proud to officially add our Committee's formal endorsement of this publication.

The IPESC, through its council of members, their efforts and dedication create added value to the community of ITSM professionals, by endorsing the development of a common global library which supports a uniform understanding of ITSM best practices and knowledge.

Our endorsement process is a rigorous one, with stringent criteria that any ITSM-related publication must meet before it can be endorsed by the IPESC.

On behalf of the *it*SMF global community, I wish to thank the IPESC for their efforts and endorsement of this book.

Sharon Taylor
Chair, International Publications Executive Sub Committee
*it*SMF International

Acknowledgements

*it*SMF Netherlands would like to thank the great number of experts who have been involved in the development of this *Frameworks for IT Management* publication. With the help of 27 authors and a number of additional reviewers, we compiled this book to help IT managers find their way through the 'framework forest'. We owe all the team members our gratitude for supporting *it*SMF-NL in developing this management guide.

With the help of *it*SMF's International Publications Executive Sub Committee (IPESC) we established a list of the frameworks that were considered to be most relevant for IT managers. A uniform structure for all frameworks was defined, to support the interpretation of each framework from the same perspective. For each framework an author was selected, from the *it*SMF community. Authors have been found from all over the world. All authors are experts in the field of the management framework they describe, and in some cases they were the original authors of the framework itself.

We wish to thank them all for contributing to this book and participating in the thorough peer review process *it*SMF-NL applies to all its ITSM Library publications. The authors and reviewers together raised around 500 issues on the initial drafts. All these issues were taken into account by the different authors, revising and improving their chapters. The final results were presented to the Review Team and the Authors Team for a formal final sign-off.

Authors

Samantha Alford (ISO 9000 chapter) is a senior manager with seventeen years' experience in the logistics field. As an ISO 9001:2000 External Quality Auditor she has had responsibility for personnel operating under the ISO 9001:2000 Standard. She is a Director of Herne European Consultancy Ltd (a quality consultancy company) and a published author.

Rolf Akker (Generic Framework for Information Management chapter), a Master of Science in Business Management and certified ITIL Service Manager, participated in several ITIL examination committees for EXIN. Currently he is a consortium member of the Dutch IT Governance Association (ITGA) and one of the two lead authors for the IT Governance Framework developed by the ITGA. He works with Atos Origin Nederland as a Business Consultant

Raul Assatt (PMBOK chapter) is a PMI certified Project Management Professional (PMP) who has managed many projects on the integration of solutions in major companies. As a Director of Programs of Education of Project Management in the Institute of Technology of Buenos Aires (ITBA) he has directed thirty five courses of project management.

Colin Bentley (PRINCE2 chapter) was one of the team that brought PROMPT II, the predecessor of PRINCE2, to the marketplace and wrote the major part of the PRINCE2 manual. He is currently the Chief Examiner in PRINCE2 for the Association for Project Management Group and the UK Office of Government Commerce (OGC), and is responsible for the assessment of new trainers in the method.

Jacqueline van der Bent (TQM chapter) has a PhD in Quality Management, Organizational Learning and Memory. Since 1979 she has been working in industry, sales and non-profit organizations as a management consultant. She assists organizations in adopting business excellence programs, such as EFQM and is a part-time teacher of TQM at an institute for MBA studies.

Paul Breslin (TickIT chapter) has been a practicing TickIT auditor since 1994. Currently he is the e-Business sector leader for DNV Certification, responsible for the commercial and technical development of IT related services including TickIT and BS 15000 certifications. He is also a member of UK IST/15 Software Engineering and the Joint TickIT Industry Steering Committees.

Marghanita da Cruz (AS 8015 chapter) has over twenty five years' experience in implementing IT in the public and private sectors, in large, small and community organizations. She is Principal Consultant of Ramin Communications and chairs the Australian Computer Society's ICT Governance Committee. Marghanita represents the ACS on the technical committee which prepared AS 8015 - 2005 Australian Standard for Corporate Governance of ICT. She would like to thank ACS members Tom Worthington and Tom Cleary for their comments on her chapter.

Ralph Donatz (BiSL chapter, together with Frank van Outvorst) as a management consultant at the business unit TS with Getronics PinkRoccade focuses on how business organizations can improve their control over their information systems. He published many articles in this field and as one of the authors of the BiSL introduction book played a leading role in constructing and promoting the BiSL framework.

Rubina Faber (M_o_R chapter), Director of Regal Training, is involved in consultancy and training, including strategic thinking, implementing risk frameworks, design and presentation. She supports a number of private and public sector organizations raising awareness of risk management at all levels within the organization, delivering accredited courses and helping with the implementation of M_o_R.

Edgar Giesen (Six Sigma chapter, together with Patrick Teters), Business Process Measurement Systems expert within European retail and wholesale banking, makes results sustainable with measurement systems. He developed the Six Sigma Four Step Approach which gives a clear implementation framework for complex Six Sigma programs. Within Capgemini he is one of the trainers for the Six Sigma Green Belt course.

Wim van Grembergen (IT Balanced Scorecard chapter, together with Steven de Haes) is professor and chair of the Information Systems Management Department at the Economics and Management Faculty of the University of Antwerp (Belgium) and executive professor at the University of Antwerp Management School (UAMS). His research focuses primarily on IT governance, strategic alignment and IT performance management. He is also engaged in the continuous development of CoBiT and is academic director of the Information Technology Alignment and Governance Research Institute.

Steven De Haes (IT Balanced Scorecard chapter, together with Wim van Grembergen) is responsible for the Information Systems Management executive programs and research at the University of Antwerp Management School (UAMS). He is engaged in research in the domains of IT governance, strategic alignment and IT performance management. He is involved in the continuous development of CobiT and is currently preparing a PhD in IT governance. He is director and senior researcher of the Information Technology Alignment and Governance Research Institute.

Jon G. Hall (ISO 27001 chapter) is a senior lecturer at the Open University, UK, where he lectures on Information Security Management using BS7799 and ISO 27001. He is Head of Product Research for Tarmin Solutions Ltd, works closely with other industry partners, and has written widely on many aspects of computing.

Bert Hedeman (MSP chapter) is a senior project and program manager and partner of Insights International BV. Bert is an accredited PRINCE2 and MSP trainer and co-author of the books *Project Management based on PRINCE2* and *Programme Management based on MSP*. Since 1995, Bert has also been an accredited assessor for IPMA.

We also wish to thank Bert Hedeman for extending the cross-references of the various project management frameworks in this book.

Jan Hendriks (eTOM chapter) is now working as a consultant for the software services organization of Atos Origin. He started his career in the research laboratories of the Dutch incumbent operator. After switching to internal IT support he became a consultant and worked with diverse areas of interest, such as network administration and management, customer administration and middleware infrastructures.

Peter Hill (CobiT chapter) is an IT governance consultant who started working with CobiT in 1994. He is currently a director of the IT Governance Network, a company specializing in IT governance consulting and training. Peter has extensive experience with CobiT, having used it as the umbrella model to implement IT governance, process improvement, compliance, and management of risk activities for a number of clients. Recently, Peter participated as a member of the CobiT 4.0 development team.

Majid Iqbal (eSCM chapter, together with Mark Paulk) works for Carnegie Mellon University. He is involved in research on best practices in service management and sourcing. He teaches graduate and executive courses on service management. Majid is a member of the ITIL Advisory Group (IAG) and an author of a new ITIL Version 3 volume on service strategies.

Gerrit Koch (IPMA representative for PMI-Netherlands, ICB chapter) was the first IPMA level A-certified Projects Director in the Netherlands. Since 2005, he has been responsible for the competence area of project management for the renowned Dutch management advice office Berenschot. His experience in directing and developing project managers proved to be very useful for his co-authorship of the IPMA Competence Baseline.

Ivor Macfarlane (ISO 20000 chapter) has worked with IT service management best practice for sixteen years and was one of the authors of the original BS15000 standard and the ISO/IEC 20000 assessment workbook. He is working with several major companies on their journey to achieve formal accreditation.

Dr Machteld Meijer (ASL chapter, together with Mark Smalley) is a senior consultant with Getronics PinkRoccade, specializing in the fields of IT process improvement and quality management. She publishes, presents and trains on a regular basis. As an active member of the ASL Foundation, she has contributed considerably to the development of ASL.

Dr Frank Niessink (IT Service CMM chapter) is a principal consultant at CIBIT, a DNV Company. Frank was the primary author of the IT Service CMM, at the Vrije Universiteit of Amsterdam. In his role of consultant, Frank assists clients of CIBIT with assessing their IT service maturity and with improving their IT service processes.

Dr Mark Paulk (eSCM chapter, together with Majid Iqbal) is a Senior Systems Scientist at the IT Services Qualification Center at Carnegie Mellon University, where he works on best practices for sourcing of IT-enabled services. His research interests revolve around quality and process improvement frameworks, high maturity practices, measurement and statistical thinking, and agile methods.

Colin Rudd (ITIL chapter) has been working in the IT industry for over thirty years and is recognized as a leading exponent of service management principles and processes. He has been heavily involved in the development of *New ITIL*, writing or contributing to the production of many of the individual modules. He was also responsible for the design of the overall framework for the new library. Colin now runs his own company, IT Enterprise Management Services Ltd.

Mark Smalley (ASL chapter, together with Machteld Meijer) has twenty years of experience in the field of applications management and has trained hundreds of people in ASL. He works as manager and consultant for Getronics PinkRoccade and is an active member of the ASL Foundation, frequently presenting and publishing on applications management.

Frank van Outvorst (BiSL chapter, together with Ralph Donatz) is as a management consultant with Getronics PinkRoccade involved with professionalizing IT demand organizations by way of coaching, consultancy and training. Frank published many articles in the field of business information management and business information administration. As one of the authors of the BiSL introduction book he played a leading role in constructing and presenting the BiSL framework.

Patrick Teters (Six Sigma chapter, together with Edgar Giesen) is a senior process consultant at Capgemini with eight years of experience in process improvement projects in the telecom and financial markets. In the last two years he specifically focused on the alignment between the business and IT processes, using several methods including Six Sigma.

Dr T.F. (Denis) Verhoef (ISPL chapter) is chair of the ISPG (the Information Services Procurement Group) and partner of the Ordina Group. He is one of the two primary editors of

ISPL. He wrote Requests for Proposal for big and complex IT outsourcings in both the public and private sector and helped with vendor negotiations.

Additional reviewers

Besides the authors, who peer reviewed the chapters of their co-authors, the following people generously offered their time and knowledge to the reviewing process. We owe them our gratitude for giving us and the Authors Team the opportunity to improve the manuscript:

- **Signe-Marie Hernes Bjerke** - Det Norske Veritas, Norway
- **Sophia Klaassen** - Klaassen Interim Management, the Netherlands
- **Ricardo Mansur** - Empreendimentos Mansur, Brazil
- **Maxime Sottini** - Innovative Consulting Srl, Italy

Editorial support

Tieneke Verheijen, the responsible editor for *it*SMF-NL, has done a great job, managing all the authors, supporting them in the authoring process, continuously improving the structure of the book on, making sure that no review issue escaped their attention, and that all issues were carefully processed. Without her dedication to the process and to the quality of the work, this book would have been impossible.

Given the desire for a broad consensus in the IT service management field, new developments, additional material and other contributions from IT service management professionals are welcomed to extend and further improve this publication. Any forwarded material will be discussed by the editorial team and where appropriate incorporated into new editions. Comments can be sent to the chief editor, email: jan.van.bon@itsmf.nl.

Jan van Bon
Chief editor *it*SMF Netherlands

Contents

Introduction

IT management is one of the fastest growing fields of expertise in all management disciplines. High demands of customers, extremely short development cycles and huge costs have made this field one of the most important of all management domains. And in this field of IT management, awareness of the crucial role of IT services has been growing since the early 1990s.

This is the decade of IT service management, but the managers in this discipline have had little opportunity to obtain the training they need. Many managers in IT have learned on the job; some have been trained in one of the very few dedicated training programs available of which ITIL is at the top of the list. The lack of training, which puts a great deal of stress on managers in IT, and in IT related disciplines, needs to be addressed.

Learning on the job

The speed of development of the IT management domain has given public education programs little opportunity to cope with the demands of today's companies. They have not been able to develop curriculae that cover well embedded training in IT (service) management issues, let alone deliver students who have been trained properly as part of their regular educational program. Today higher education programs are starting to offer courses in IT service management. But it is still a long way from being a standard subject in higher education. This means that companies will continue to find a lack of knowledge in recent graduates: they too will have to learn on the job.

The 'framework forest'

This situation has stimulated the development, the import (from other disciplines) and the acceptance of managerial frameworks, methods and methodologies that support the modern IT manager. We have seen a large number of those frameworks in recent magazines and books, at conferences and seminars, and on the Web. No IT service provider can be taken seriously if they do not have a framework of their own. The problem is that there are now too many frameworks - the number has grown so fast that it has become hard to see the forest for the trees.

Gaps

ITSMF, the IT Service Management Forum, is putting a great deal of effort into the development and dissemination of knowledge in the field of IT service management. With over thirty national chapters a huge organization is acting in most corners of the world. Many publications of ITSMF chapters are now finding their way to the practitioners in the field. ITSMF has been greatly influential in developing the globally accepted best practice documentation of ITIL, and continues to do so. Conferences are showcasing the best practices and the latest developments. And websites make the latest information available for all to see.

This information is not just in English: many publications are being translated into ten or more languages. In translating these publications it has become clear that several publications contain material that is new to IT managers, especially in countries that are relatively new to the field of ITIL and IT service management.

More gaps

This is not the only gap that confronts us. We encounter similar problems in small and medium sized enterprises (SMEs). Management in these organizations is often quite unfamiliar with some of the core frameworks and methods (instruments).

Furthermore, we encounter problems in explaining our IT management instruments to business managers: although they frequently encounter the title of an instrument, they often know very little of its content.

Initiative

This situation has led to an initiative to create a publication that covers the most important frameworks we use, in such a way that readers can better understand the potential value of each of these instruments. The instruments are all described by well-known experts in that specific field, in a structured way, to emphasize the specific characteristics of each instrument, and explain how they could be used together:

- **Origin/history.** Where did the instrument come from? Who invented it? When? First publications? Ownership and copyright? Any well-known champions? Current status of development, any important revisions going on or planned?
- **Where is the instrument used?** Target groups or stakeholders? Any specific market sections? Restricted to any layer of management? Quantity details: number of adopting companies, number of certificates, 'installed base'? Acceptance as a standard? Qualification of standard (legal standard, industry standard, *de facto* best practice).
- **Description and core graphics.** Summary of the core characteristics of the instrument, supported by the core graphics. Structure, facts and figures. Objectives? Benefits? Process model? Any certification programs attached (person or company focus)?
- **Approach/how to.** Management guidance: How to apply the instrument? How to implement it? How to position it? Expected outcome? Specific costs? Business case? Frequent pitfalls?
- **Relevance to IT management.** Why is this instrument *specifically* relevant to IT management? What are the main IT management problems that can be solved with it?
- **Strengths and weaknesses.** Where does the instrument prove most of its value? Most successful application? Why consider using it? Established flaws in the instruments. Any acknowledged gaps? Where should/will the instrument be improved?
- **Cross-references/relationships.** Relationships with other frameworks or management instruments.
- **Links and literature.** Where can we find the core information and the most practical information on this instrument? Any user organizations or communities of practice?

Not all of these questions could be answered for each of the selected frameworks. In some cases the information on the number of adopting companies was simply not available, or the framework did not have a certification structure. For others the cross-reference to some of the other frameworks was not available. Each framework was described by an author who was very familiar with the subject, using it in their daily practice. This enabled them to write the chapter from the position of the framework domain, emphasizing the core elements from that very same practice. However, since these domains can vary widely, the resulting chapters will vary as well. The fact that a standard structure was used for each of the chapters will make them comparable.

Scoping

We have created a shortlist of the instruments that are described in this publication, using a number of criteria:
- recognized to be best practice in IT management
- core instrument for many IT managers
- vendor-neutral
- copyright arrangements must be in place
- written in an accessible and plain way.

The shortlist of frameworks in this first edition of the ITSMF Management Frameworks guide contains (in alphabetical order):
- **AS 8015** – The Australian Standard for Governance of IT.
- **ASL** – the Application Services Library
- **BiSL** – the Business Information Services Library
- **CobiT** – Control Objectives in IT and related Technology
- **eSCM** - the eSourcing Capability Model of Carnegie Mellon University
- **eTOM** - the enhanced Telecom Operations Map; the most widely used and accepted standard for business process in the telecom industry
- **Generic Framework for Information Management** – the framework produced in PrimaVera: the Program for Research in Information Management at the University of Amsterdam
- **IPMA Competence Baseline** – a standard for managers of projects, programs and project portfolios
- **ISO/IEC 20000** (former BS15000) - Standard on IT service management
- **ISO 27001** (ISO 17799/BS7799) - Standard on Information Security
- **ISO 9000** (GB/T 19000) - Standard on Total Quality Management
- **ISPL** – the Information Services Procurement Library
- **IT Balanced Scorecard** – the management system for strategic performance and results
- **ITIL** – the IT Infrastructure Library
- **ITS-CMM** – the IT Service Capability Maturity Model
- **PMBoK** – the Project Management Body of Knowledge
- **PRINCE2** – Projects in Changing Environments
- **M_o_R** – Management of Risk
- **MSP** – Managing Successful Programmes
- **Six Sigma** – the Six Sigma Model for Quality Management
- **TickIT** - Quality management for IT
- **TQM** – Total Quality Management: the Fourteen Points of Management of Dr. W. Edwards Deming

Some frameworks that were selected for this book could not be delivered within the development timeframe. These frameworks will be added in a second edition:
- **CMMI** – the Capability Maturity Model Integration (Staged and Continuous)
- **COPC2000** - Customer Operations Performance Center standard on call center operations
- **EFQM** – the European Foundation of Quality Management Model.

The editing team is open to suggestions to add any other core management frameworks that are relevant to the IT manager. Suggestions can be forwarded to the chief editor (jan.van.bon@ itsmf.nl).

Procedure

All draft framework chapters have been peer-reviewed by the other co-authors, and by experts from ITSMF. These reviews revealed further options for improvement of the various chapters, and assured that the chapters were well aligned. The content was managed by expert editors, making sure that the resulting text qualified as 'easy reading'.

Presentation of the chapters

There are many ways to present twenty two management frameworks, but none would contain 'the ultimate truth'. Therefore we do not present an umbrella structure where all presented frameworks fit together. If you are interested in an overall graphic that positions each of the frameworks, see Figure 13.5 in the chapter on the Generic Framework for Information Management.

There is, however, one way of bringing a kind of order to the list, and that is by means of a simple categorization, based on how and where the frameworks are used. This is illustrated in Table 0.1. Several frameworks contain material that could be allocated to more than one category; the frameworks are categorized according to their *main* characteristics.

Category	Type	Frameworks
Quality management	Frameworks that focus on quality standards, applied to specific IT domains (services, security, development, general)	TQM ISO 9000 TickIT ISO 27001/BS17799 ISO/IEC 20000
Quality improvement	Frameworks that focus on improvement of processes, performance or other, not focusing on how-to aspects of operating the IT	ITS-CMM Six Sigma eSCM-SP IT Balanced Scorecard
IT governance	Frameworks that focus on how to organize the IT function in terms of responsibilities, controls, organization	AS 8015 CoBiT M_o_R
Information management	Frameworks that focus on how to perform and organize certain aspects of IT management, such as procurement, service delivery, requirements.	Generic Framework for Information Management BiSL ISPL ITIL eTOM ASL
Project management	frameworks that focus on project, program and portfolio management, not specifically IT	MSP PRINCE2 PMBoK IPMA Competence Baseline

Table 0.1 Categorization of management frameworks

This is the structure that we have applied for this book. It groups the various frameworks into a number of categories that have some coherence, but the reader will still be able to determine which chapters to read first.

Responsible bodies

The frameworks are managed by bodies of various types. The nature of these bodies may be relevant in the selection of frameworks by a specific organization. Table 0.2 provides an overview of the responsible bodies.

Framework	Responsible body	Characterization of the responsible body
AS 8015	Standards Australia	Non-government Australian standards management body standards.org.au
BiSL	ASL Foundation	Public foundation with participants and knowledge partners www.aslfoundation.org
CobiT	ISACA's IT Governance Institute (ITGI)	Research think tank on IT-enabled business systems governance for the global business community, affiliated to ISACA www.itgi.org
eSCM	Carnegie Mellon University, through its IT Services Qualification Center (ITSqc)	University research center www.itsqc.cmu.edu
eTOM	TeleManagement Forum (TM Forum)	Forum for information and communications services, with an open membership of more than 500 companies www.tmforum.org
Generic Framework for Information Management	University of Amsterdam	University
IPMA Competence Baseline	International Project Management Association (IPMA)	International network of national project management societies www.ipma.ch
ISO/IEC 20000 (formerly BS15000)	International Standards Organization (ISO)	ISO is a network of the national standards institutes of 157 countries, on the basis of one member per country, with a central secretariat in Geneva, Switzerland, that coordinates the system. It manages international standards. www.iso.org
ISO 27001 (ISO 17799/ BS7799)	International Standards Organization (ISO)	See text on ISO above
ISO 9000 (GB/T 19000)	International Standards Organization (ISO)	See text on ISO above
ISPL	ISPL Consortium, presided by EXIN	The European Committee has created the ISPL Consortium to develop ISPL to be a *de facto* standard.
IT Balanced Scorecard	None	Copyrights of publications on IT Balanced Scorecard are with the authors of the publications.

Table 0.2 Frameworks and the responsible bodies

Framework	Responsible body	Characterization of the responsible body
ITIL	Office of Government Commerce (OGC), United Kingdom	OGC is an independent office of the UK's HM Treasury and works with public sector organizations to help them improve their efficiency and gain better value for money from their commercial activities. www.ogc.gov.uk
ITS-CMM	-Vrije Universiteit Amsterdam -CIBIT	IT Service CMM is downloadable for free; the Vrije Universiteit Amsterdam and CIBIT contributed to IT Service CMM.
PMBoK	Project Management Institute (PMI®)	The PMI is one of the principal professional non-profit organizations in the project management field. www.pmi.org
PRINCE2	Office of Government Commerce (OGC), United Kingdom	See text on OGC above.
M_o_R	Office of Government Commerce (OGC), United Kingdom	See text on OGC above.
MSP	Office of Government Commerce (OGC), United Kingdom	See text on OGC above.
Six Sigma	None	Six Sigma has an active user community; its most important online community is www.isixsigma.com.
TickIT	Joint TickIT Industry Steering Committee (JTISC)	The Joint TickIT Industry Steering Committee (JTISC) has overall responsibility for the scheme Rules and Procedures (see ecommittees.bsi-global.com/bsi/controller?livelinkDataID=985990 for terms of reference) and is accountable to BSI's Standards Policy and Strategy Committee and each of the three parent bodies: • **British Computer Society** (BCS) – with prime responsibility for professional, educational and technological requirements • **BSI Standards Development** (in their role as TickIT Scheme Manager) with prime responsibility for standardization, international harmonization, certification, accreditation and general public interest requirements • **Intellect** (a trade body for the IT industry) – with prime responsibility for the IT industry commercial requirements.
TQM	None	-

Table 0.2 Frameworks and the responsible bodies (continued)

Additional reading

This Frameworks Guide is intended to help you in finding your way to useful management frameworks that are not always easy to find. Each chapter contains references to additional information sources, to be used if you want to learn more about a specific framework. We hope that it will prove to be a valuable book in the unlocking and demystifying of a number of management frameworks that we consider to belong in our core management toolbox.

1 TQM - Total Quality Management

> *Total Quality Management (TQM) is a complete management vision in which everyone in the organization is continuously incentivized to fulfill the wishes of the internal and external customer, in order to reach a competitive advantage.*

Owner of the copyright:	None
Distribution:	Worldwide
Origin/history:	Evolved from quality improvement philosophies from the early 20th century
When:	From the 1970s
Founding fathers:	A.V. Feigenbaum, W. Edwards Deming, Joseph M. Juran.
Certification bodies?	No certification possible - ISO 9000:2000 certification indicates that an organization is working according to TQM principles. EFQM , MBNQA and INK are evolved from TQM.
Useful tools:	Plan-Do-Check-Act, brainstorming, Pareto analysis, statistical process control, benchmarking, Just-in-time, among others.

By Jacqueline van der Bent

1.1 Origin/history

1.1.1 A long history of quality management

Quality management has a long history. Evidence of the first sign of quality control dates as far back as the building of the pyramids. An example of quality control and inspection closer to home is the Dutch guilds. Rembrandt van Rijn's famous painting 'De Staalmeesters' (in English 'staalmeesters' means something like 'guild masters') is actually a portrait of quality inspectors, which takes its name from the steel pair of tongs used by the 'staalmeesters' to attach a piece of lead on the hallmarked textiles.

1.1.2 Inspection

Industrial development at the end of the 18th and at the beginning of the 19th centuries led to the demand for new methods and techniques to control the quality of the growing number of manufactured products. Tools, such as a rational jig, fixture and a gauging system ensured a certain amount of standardization. This standardization was mainly initiated by the US arms industry at the beginning of the 19th century. The function of quality inspector had begun. This specialist role strengthened the idea that the inspection of products could be done much more efficiently by one person; nowadays products are no longer assessed by the eye but by a more reliable gauging system.

1.1.3 Statistical quality control

When production processes grew more complex and mass production became of significance, the demand for uniformity and standardization grew as well. This gave the initial impetus to the development of statistical quality control.

In 1924 Bell Telephone Laboratories investigated how to manufacture products with a maximum of quality information against a minimum of inspection information.

This was the basis for today's knowledge about statistical quality control, especially on process control and sampling.

The techniques used to control the quality of products were fairly static and focused on tracking problems within the manufacturing process. At the end of the 1950s a new development was announced: quality assurance.

1.1.4 Quality assurance

Tracking problems and inspecting and controlling manufacturing processes is no longer sufficient to guarantee the quality of a product. Other disciplines and management have to play a role. Although quality assurance is mainly concerned with the quality standard ISO 9000, some other elements deserve attention.

- **Costs of quality** - The main exponent of costs of quality is Joseph M. Juran. In 1951 he wrote that one should make a distinction between quality costs that are avoidable and quality costs that are unavoidable. For the first time, managers realized that decisions taken at the beginning of the manufacturing process have far-reaching implications for the level of quality costs that may appear later in the manufacturing process and in the service process. These ideas resulted in the concept of Total Quality Control.
- **Total Quality Control** - A.V. Feigenbaum developed this concept and stated that these products that need to comply with high quality requirements should not be produced in an isolated manufacturing situation. Quality starts with design and ends with service to the customer. Strong co-operation is essential to prevent mistakes in the future. Feigenbaum as well as W. Edwards Deming[1] and Juran was convinced that management is responsible for the system functioning properly.
- **Reliability Engineering** - The arrival of aerospace technology and electronics led the US Department of Defense to draw up a reliability program, which. focuses on a product's performance over time.

1.1.5 The introduction of quality awards

In 1945, at the end of World War Two, Japanese industry had been reduced to ashes. Products still being produced were cheap and of low quality. The Japanese therefore decided to take on as much as possible of the successful production techniques and management methods of the Allied

---

1 Edwards Deming has been inspired by Walter Shewhart, one of his teachers already advocating a 'Learning and Improvement cycle'. The PDCA-cycle of Edwards Deming is also known as the PDSA-cycle, which stands for 'Plan-Do–Study-Act'. In this case, the results are studied instead of checked.

Powers. McArthur encouraged them in this effort and invited experts such as Deming to Japan. Deming visited Japan in 1947 and in 1950 as an advisor in sampling techniques. He trained Japanese managers in statistical quality control. While Deming's ideas on quality were accepted only to a limited extent in his home country, Japanese companies immediately accepted them and adapted them to their own way of working.

To encourage organizations to achieve excellent research in the theory or application of statistical quality control, the Union of Japanese Scientists and Engineers (JUSE) instituted the Deming Prize in 1951. It is named after Deming to honor him for his contribution to the introduction and development of statistical control in Japan. He introduced a new concept to an existing simple diagram of a cycle for quality improvement (see Figure 1.1).

Today the cycle is known as the Plan-Do-Check-Act cycle (in short, the P-D-C-A cycle), also known as the Deming cycle, Deming himself always referred to it as the Shewhart cycle after its originator Shewhart, Deming's former colleague at Bell Laboratories. The cycle proposes a thorough planning of the production of a product (Plan), the production itself (Do), checking whether the production of the product still matches the plan (Check) and taking action when there is a need to adapt the product if the check shows that production is not according to plan and to improve the product (Act). It is a continuous improvement process that is still used in manufacturing companies; it is also applicable to non-profit companies where it is used for the improvement of project outcomes.

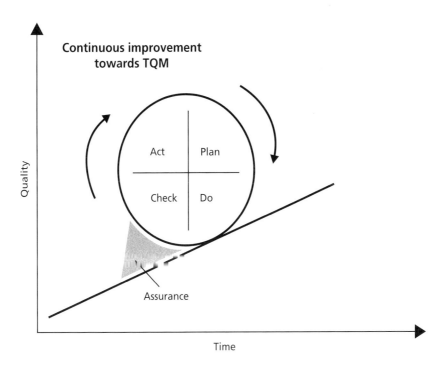

Figure 1.1 The P-D-C-A cycle

1.2 Where is TQM used?

Starting in the European and American industries in order to catch up with Japanese competition in the 1970s and 1980s, Total Quality Management (TQM) is now a world-wide recognized organizational change vision based on quality management. It is used in large and small profit and non-profit organizations.

TQM is not used as a single instrument. It is a collection of views and approaches on organizational change with related methodologies and techniques, all leading to a profound change in the way the organization is managed.

It is possible to use a selection of TQM methodologies and techniques as a company-wide approach or to apply a single technique in a department (e.g. statistical process control in manufacturing).

1.3 Description

Since Taylor[2], TQM is one of the business theories with the most impact on business management. Starting as a new view on product quality in the 1970s and 1980s, it soon became a management tool for gaining a strategic lead on competitors and organizational change. From that time on, many methodologies and techniques were developed to support management.

In general, management strives for a balance between high productivity, low cost and maximum profit. TQM is based upon this fundamental principle. To achieve this, TQM focuses on:
- statistical process control
- process management
- continuous improvement
- zero defects
- education and training
- the role of management
- teamwork.

To keep the improvement process alive, customer and employee satisfaction, communication, deployment and cultural change are essential to achieve business excellence.

Today, quality is no longer an issue for the central quality department manager alone, but for line management in particular. Quality can no longer be delegated. All aspects important to running a business from mission, vision and strategy involvement of employees, entrepreneurship, process management, customer focus, working together with suppliers, continuous learning and business results are part of TQM. These elements are the fundamentals of the management models of EFQM and MBNQA.[3]

---

2 Frederick Winslow Taylor, *Scientific Management - Comprising Shop Management, The principles of Scientific Management and Testimony before the Special House Committee* (New York 1964). Taylor (1856-1917) was an American engineer who introduced scientific methods (time and motion studies) to optimize the way tasks were performed by craftsmen. The results of his studies positively influenced the efficiency of the production process.
3 The European Foundation for Quality Management (EFQM) Excellence Model and the Malcolm Baldridge National Quality Award (MBNQA, USA) and their links to TQM are explained in the cross-reference section 1.7.

At the same time TQM provides management with a set of tools and techniques to support the organization in the change process.

Top management is considered to be the driving force behind the change process, dealing with questions such as the following:
- is our management team ready for this new way of working/thinking?
- is the organization ready for this (cultural) change?
- is competition driving us for a change (survival scenario) or is it something that we, as the management team believe in?
- do we have a vision of the future and is there a clear strategy?
- how do we cope with resistance?
- how do we set up an implementation network?
- do we have funding for education and training?
- how do we reward our employees for their efforts?

When a clear business plan based on TQM is formulated and ready to implement in the organization, a range of methodologies and techniques are available to support the implementation process.
These techniques can be categorized as:
- leading change techniques, such as:
  - policy deployment
  - benchmarking
  - customer satisfaction surveys
  - employee motivation survey
  - managerial audits and self assessments (EFQM/MBNQA)
- process management techniques specifically for:
  - development, for example Taguchi, Shainin
  - manufacturing, e.g. SPC, process capability, Six Sigma
  - logistics and supply management, e.g. Just-in-time, Kan ban
- group dynamics, such as:
  - brainstorming
  - force field analysis
- problem solving:
  - Pareto diagram
  - cause and effect diagram.

1.4   Approach/how to

If the organization is not ready yet for the EFQM or MBNQA approach (see cross- reference section 1.7), it is possible to start on a smaller scale. Whatever improvement program an organization starts with it will always have to work on its mission, vision and strategy, its processes, its customer focus, internally as well as externally, and teamwork to create organizational change. The following five step approach can be applied. The approach is based on the actors gradually become involved in the change process.

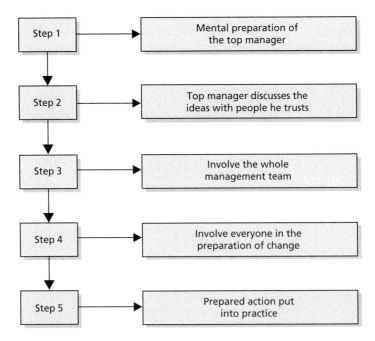

Figure 1.2 The five step approach for change

- **Step 1** - Not everything is clearly developed in the beginning. It is not only the question of whether the top manager has the right skills to act as the champion of change, but also whether his/her ideas will lead to the expected change. Using peers to try out the ideas is very useful. This step is all about mental preparation, knowing what has to be accomplished and how.
- **Step 2** - The still rough ideas are discussed with people who the top manager fully trusts. Feedback is received on how to communicate the new ideas and arguments for pros and cons are discussed. The vision and approach becomes clearer. The framework is ready to be presented to the management team.
- **Step 3** - To involve the management team in the desired changes, the top manager has to explain, argue, convince and motivate his/her colleagues. Honesty, openness and patience are essential values. Pushing to get the ideas across is useless and will lead to resistance. The aim of this step is to prepare a clear image of the changes and a first framework of the implementation plan together with the management team.
- **Step 4** - Once the management team owns the change it is now the task of every individual to act as a champion of change in his/her own department and translate the vision to elements important for this particular department. At the end of this step everyone should be involved in the change process.
- **Step 5** - The central aim of this step is to keep the change process going while stimulating the new initiatives of people who are really driving the change, keeping track of those staying behind and balancing the speed of change. Successes should be communicated and celebrated.

Note that the steps 1 to 5 are not a linear process; unexpected turns will happen.

1.5   Relevance to IT management

The specific TQM methods and techniques based on technical engineering principles were adopted by software engineers in the 1980s. The fast growing importance of software, software development and information technology in industry resulted in a need for software and IT dedicated models, methods and tools. In particular, the efficiency and effectiveness of the software development processes needed to be improved. This was because for an increasing number of products the product development lead-time was determined by the lead-time of the software development (e.g. product in the consumer electronics industry). The TQM principles of 'step-by-step' and continuous improvement were adopted by CMM, for example.

IT policy is never a stand-alone policy, but is part of the policy of the organization. This sets the context for the IT policy, but new developments in IT can lead to other directions in the policy of the organization. They influence each other. When getting the best out of both they add value to the organization by improving efficiency, effectiveness and quality of processes: basic TQM principles.

Improving processes in an organization is impossible when the information on which decisions and subsequent initiatives are based lack accuracy and completeness. The first product whose quality should be ensured is the management information: it serves all the other products and processes. This is why TQM is important for IT: it should ensure that information is reliable and safe.

1.6   Strengths and weaknesses

The management models of EFQM and MBNQA have provided management with a clear structure, supporting material and best practices, but TQM remains disputable. As long as TQM exists there will be supporters and non-believers.

1.6.1   Strengths

Whatever an individual's point of view, TQM has brought the discussion on quality to the agenda of the management board; it is sometimes even seen as a competitive edge. But there are more positive elements to observe:
- it is now widely understood that profound changes take time and that everyone in the organization plays an essential role
- thinking in terms of (business) processes and cross-functional teams is generally accepted
- focus on the customer and gaining business results are very much related,
- employees are a valuable asset with a lot of knowledge about all kinds of processes. They play a key role in improving these processes
- P-D-C-A is a widespread and easy-to-use model (see Figure 1.1)
- continuous learning is a means for survival.

1.6.2   Weaknesses

The abundance of methodologies and techniques makes it difficult to find the best way and it takes some experience to choose the right elements. Some pitfalls include:
- too much focus on internal processes and less on external results
- the idea that standards are not essential

- the development of its own bureaucracy: steering group, working groups, process teams, all with their meeting reports, action plans and lacking focus
- separate plans for business strategy and quality
- 'me too' syndrome starting just because the competition is doing so
- starting too quickly with insufficient thought spent on the implications, preparations and consequences
- once started the organization needs to have the discipline to continue and to put time and effort in the implementation process. If this cannot be managed, it should not start to implement TQM

1.7 Cross-references/relationships

Depending on how the scope of TQM is defined in a particular organization, a number of references can be identified for this subject.

When management is interested in a business-wide general improvement process, it is very likely that they will start with programs that have the basics in place such as ISO 9000:2000.

As well as ISO 9000, TQM strived for overall business improvement. ISO 9000 is seen as the fundamental cornerstone to assure that the organization has the capability to meet its customers' requirements.

Gaining experience on how to organize changes, define and measure process outputs and how to bring the requirements and satisfaction of customers to the fore in the organization will gradually migrate to the EFQM or Malcolm Baldridge models.

The European Foundation for Quality Management Excellence model (Europe) and the Malcolm Baldridge National Quality Award (US, MBNQA) support management teams with an approach that gives structure to the journey to business excellence. They are based upon the TQM concepts and principles.

The EFQM Excellence Model (also referred to as the Business Excellence Model) is the European Foundation for Quality Management's model for TQM. It was introduced as a framework for assessing and improving organizations.

With the importance of IT in modern businesses it is clear that an excellent organization needs robust IT (management) systems. Within the umbrella concept of TQM, IT models such as TickIT, ITS-CMM, CMMI, ITIL and ASL play a part in the ability of an organization to respond to change.

The objective of CMM is measuring and optimizing a software development organization. The methods and techniques used are based on the quality principles of TQM.

TQM, as well as ITIL, focused on the customer and the processes in an organization. The difference is that ITIL is mainly concerned with the IT processes of an organization.

Table 1.1 gives an overview of TQM related models.

	Basics	**Advanced**
General	ISO 9000:2000	EFQM Malcolm Baldridge Award Six Sigma
IT specific	TickIT ISO 27001 ISO 20000 ISPL	ITS-CMM CMMI CobiT ITIL ASL

Table 1.1 TQM related models

1.8   Links and literature

1.8.1   Books on quality
- Bent, B.J. van der (Rotterdam 1999), "Organizatieleren: een zoektocht naar de geheugendragers en de rol van organizatiegeheugen in veranderingsprocessen". Van der Bent.
- Conti, T. (1993), "Building Total Quality. A guide for management". Chapman and Hall.
- Crosby, P.B., "Quality is Free", McGraw-Hill, New York, 1979.
- Deming, W.E., "Out of the Crisis", MIT Center for Advanced Engineering Study, Cambridge, MA, 1986.
- Deming, W.E., "The New Economics for Industry, Government, Education", Second Edition, MIT Center for Advanced Educational Services, Cambridge, MA, 1994.
- Garvin, D. (1988), "Managing Quality. The Strategic and Competitive Edge". The Free Press.
- Hardjono, T, S. ten Have en W. ten Have (1997), "The European Way to Excellence". Directorate-Generale III Industry, European Commission.
- Imai, M. 1986, Kaizen. "The key to Japan's competitive success". Random House Business Division, New York.
- Juran, J. (1988), "Juran on Planning for Quality". The Free Press.
- Van Nuland, Y., G. Broux, L. Crets, W. De Cleyn, J. Legrand, G. Majoor and G. Vleminckx (1999), "Excellent: A guide for the implementation of the EFQM-Excellence model". Comatech.
- Wentink, T. (1999), "Kwaliteitsmanagement en organizatieontwikkeling". Lemma.
- GOAL/QPC publisher of pocket guides:
  – Memory jogger (tools for continuous improvement)
  – The creative tools memory jogger (creative thinking)
  – Memory jogger 9000/2000 (implementing ISO 9001)
  – Project Management Memory jogger

1.8.2   Articles on quality

- MacLeod, A. and L. Baxter (2001), "The Contribution of Business Excellence Models in Restoring Failed Improvement Initiatives", European Management Journal, 4, p.392-403.
- Ross, B. (1986), "W. Edwards Deming: Shogun of Quality Control", F.E., February, pp. 25-31.
- March, A., "A Note on Quality: The Views of Deming", Juran, and Crosby, IEEE Engineering Management Review, Vol. 24, No. 1, Spring 1996, pp. 6-14.

1.8.3   Website references

- **www.deming.org** - Deming Institute
- **www.efqm.com** - European Foundation for Quality Management
- **www.ink.nl** - Quality Institute for the Netherlands
- **www.iso.org** - International Organization for Standardization
- **www.juran.com** - Juran Institute
- **www.kaizen-institute.com** - Kaizen Institute
- **www.kdi.nl** - Dutch Foundation for Quality
- **www.olkk.nl** - On line kwaliteitskring, Dutch quality circle
- **www.vck.be** - Flemish Quality Management Centre

2 ISO 9000 - Quality Management Systems

> *International Organization for Standardization 9000; 2000 (ISO 9000:2000) is a generic name given to a series of standards that have been developed to address the Quality Management Systems (QMS) within an organization to demonstrate its capability to meet its customers' requirements.*

Owner of the copyright:	International Standards Organization (ISO), www.iso.org
Distribution:	Widely used in the international service sector and manufacturing
Origin/history:	Developed from the British Standards Institution's BS 5750
When:	Initial version ISO 9000 released 1987; latest version released 2000
Certification bodies?	Various national accreditation bodies such as UKAS (United Kingdom Accreditation Service) audit the auditors and certify that the registrars are competent and authorized to issue certificates in specified business sectors. They have agreements with each other ensuring that certificates issued by any one of them are accepted worldwide.
Number of certified organizations:	760,900 implementations in 154 countries; the service sector accounts for 31 per cent of the 9001:2000 certificates

By Samantha Alford

2.1 Origin/history

The ISO 9000 standard is maintained by ISO and administered by international accreditation and certification bodies. The standard is widely used in the service sector and manufacturing. However the high costs associated with adopting the Standard and difficulties with implementation have led many companies to use alternatives (e.g. IC 9700, or IC 9200 or an in-house standard). The Standard has evolved over several revisions as detailed below.

ISO 9000 was developed from the British Standards Institution's BS 5750, whose purpose was to provide a common contractual document which demonstrates that industrial production is controlled. Once BS 5750 was produced, key industry bodies adopted this standard in preference to their own. The initial 1987 version of ISO 9000 followed the same structure as BS 5750. This document, while structured like the British Standard, drew heavily from a number of international documents. Even though the Standard has been revised twice since 1987 it retains the core, prevention-oriented, quality assurance requirements.

The 1994 version emphasized quality assurance via preventive actions, and continued to require evidence of compliance with documented procedures. Unfortunately this was implemented within companies through the creation of procedure manuals; companies became burdened with an ISO bureaucracy. Adapting and improving processes could be particularly difficult in this kind of environment.

The 2000 version, ISO 9000:2000, sought to change thinking by putting the concept of process management in the forefront of the Standard. Documents produced by the ISO Technical Committee which drafted the third edition make it clear that they did not see any change in the essential goals of the Standard, which had always been about 'a documented system' not a 'system of documents'. The goal was always to have management system effectiveness via process performance metrics. The third edition makes this more visible and reduces the emphasis on having documented procedures if clear evidence can be presented to show that the process is working well.

Expectations of continual process improvement and tracking customer satisfaction were made explicit at this revision. Unfortunately too many organizations continue to produce unnecessary documents and to write quality systems around the paragraph structures of ISO 9001 rather than analyzing their business processes and building systems around the process flow of the organization.

2.2   Where is ISO 9000 used?

The International Organization for Standardization (ISO) is an international network which identifies and develops International Standards for business, government and society. A broad base of stakeholder groups is involved, from which an international consensus is achieved. The ISO 9000 family of standards is one of ISO's most widely used standards. Through this Standard ISO has sought to become a point of reference for quality management requirements in business-to-business activities. Although ISO standards are voluntary they are widely respected and accepted in both the public and private sectors. ISO 9000 has been implemented on a worldwide basis in 760,900 organizations in 154 countries. The service sector accounts for 31per cent of the 9001:2000 certificates.

ISO 9000 is made up of three sections:
• ISO 9000:2000 - Quality Management Systems - Fundamentals and Vocabulary.
• ISO 9001:2000 - Quality Management Systems - Requirements.
• ISO 9004:2000 - Quality Management Systems - Guidelines for Performance Improvement.

ISO 9000:2000 is a single quality management requirements standard that is applicable to all organizations, products and services. It is not restricted to any particular layer of management and clearly defines the roles of each business area with regard to quality management. Tables 2.1 and 2.2 indicate the responsibilities (as defined in the Standard) of senior management and others within the business for quality management:

Under the ISO international agreement all international standards have to be re-inspected five years after publication. In the case of ISO 9001:2000 a new version should be published during 2008 (i.e. five years after ISO 9001:2000 became the mandatory standard for quality management).

Position	Responsibility
Managing Director	• Establish, document and define organizational policy and objectives • Approve the QMS • Management review • Design control
Quality Manager	• Internal audit • Resolution of QMS discrepancies • Control and maintenance of the QMS • Quality documentation and (quality) change control procedures • Quality training
Financial Director	• Control of budget and finance • Supplier selection and purchasing • Contract management, control and review • Management and co-ordination of sales and support functions

Table 2.1 Organizational responsibilities – senior management

Position	Responsibility
General Managing	• Planning and co-ordination • Design control • Estimating • Project management • Control of contract documentation • Supplier selection and purchasing • Definition of installation, inspection, test and maintenance requirements • Training
Business Development Manager	• Sales • Estimating • New product identification and evaliation • System design
Sales Managers	• Quotations • Contract review and order processing • Sales order processing
Support Manager	• Control of production and measuring equipment • Maintenance of support stores • Processing of sales orders • Purchasing
Engineers	• Installation, repairs, testing and maintenance activities • Control of equipment and materials allocated
Warehouse	• Stock control • Stock replenishment • Protection and preservation of stock • Receiving inspection • Packaging and dispatch
Administration	• Sales database administration • Checking of sales orders • Allocation of order reference numbers

Table 2.2 Organizational responsibilities – others

2.3 Description and core graphics

ISO 9000:2000 certifies that an organization has carried out the correct processes. It does not, however, provide a guarantee of the quality of the end product. Throughout the Standard the need for continuous improvement is heavily emphasized.

Figure 2.1 ISO logo (source: International Organization for Standardization)

ISO 9000:2000 has four major generic business processes covering:
• the management of resources
• the quality of the product
• the maintenance of quality records
• the requirement for continual improvement.

The aim of ISO 9000:2000 is to assist users in producing a Quality Management System that is flexible, structured and customer-orientated. ISO is the only standard that can be used for the certification of a QMS and its generic requirements can be used by any organization to:
• address customer satisfaction
• meet customer and applicable regulatory requirements
• enable internal and external parties (including certification bodies) to assess the organization's ability to meet these customer and regulatory requirements.

ISO 9001:2000 and ISO 9004:2000 have been developed as a consistent pair of QMS standards, based on eight quality management principles with a common process-oriented structure and harmonized terminology. They are designed to be used together, or may be used as standalone documents. These eight principles are of primary concern to any organization, as they will affect that organization's overall approach to quality. These principles:
• reflect best practice
• are designed to enable a continual improvement of the business and its overall efficiency
• are capable of responding to customer needs and expectations.

Figure 2.2 shows the eight quality management principles.

ISO 9000:2000 is compatible with other internationally recognized management system standards, for example those dealing with environmental management, occupational health and safety. ISO 9000:2000 does not include any requirements that are specific to these other management systems. However, it does allow an organization to align and integrate its QMS

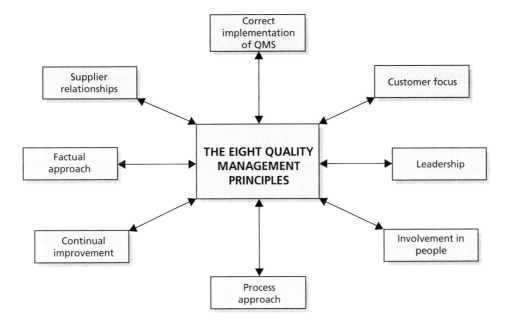

Figure 2.2 The eight quality management principles

with other management system requirements. It may therefore be possible for an organization to adapt its existing health and safety or environmental management system in order to produce a QMS that complies with ISO 9000:2000.

It is intended that by using this Standard, organizations can save time, effort and money by:
• avoiding confusion about the objectives of the audit program
• conducting a combined environmental/quality audit
• ensuring audit reports follow the best format and contain all the relevant information
• evaluating the competence of audit team members against the appropriate criteria.

In terms of the ISO Standard the phrases quality system and quality management system mean one and the same thing. A quality system, however, is neither a manual (i.e. a document) nor a computer program; it is a system that contains all the things that are used to regulate, control, and improve the quality of a product and/or service. It is a network of interrelated processes with each process made up of the people, activities, records, and resources that are required to transform inputs into outputs.

2.4   Approach/how to
The structure of the Standard is as follows:
• Section 1 - Scope
• Section 2 - Normative reference
• Section 3 - Terms and definitions
• Section 4 - Quality Management System

- Section 5 - Management responsibility
- Section 6 - Resource management
- Section 7 - Product realisation
- Section 8 - Measurement, analysis and improvement.

For certification purposes, an organization will have to possess a documented management system that takes the inputs and transforms them into targeted outputs. This is something that (in an effective manner):

- says what is to be done
- does what it was said should be done
- keeps a record of everything that was done (especially if things go wrong).

The basic process to achieve these targeted outputs will encompass:

- the customer requirements
- the inputs from management and staff
- documented controls for any activities that are required to produce the finished article
- delivering a product or service that satisfies the customer's original requirements.

It is important to recognize that it is not possible to be certified to ISO 9000. Although the certification is usually referred to as an ISO 9000:2000 certification, the actual standard to which an organization's quality management can be certified is ISO 9001:2000. For an organization to become registered to the Standard, audit by both an external certification body and by internal staff are required. The aim of this is to demonstrate that a continuous process of review and assessment has been carried out and to show that the system is working as intended, to identify areas for improvement and to correct any problems. There is no difference between being certified and being registered. In some countries organizations will say that they are certified while in others they will say that they are registered. An ISO certificate must be renewed at regular intervals as recommended by the certification body (usually after three years).

In order for an organization to be ISO 9000 certified or registered, an independent registrar will audit the QMS, certify that it meets the requirements of ISO 9001:2000 and provide written assurance that ISO's quality management system standard has been met and that the organization has been registered as certified. On the other hand, for an organization to be ISO 9000 compliant, it must meet ISO's quality system requirements but does not have to be formally certified by an independent registrar (i.e. it self-certifies compliance). While compliance is perfectly acceptable for many organizations, especially smaller ones, an official certificate issued by an independent register tends to carry more weight in the marketplace.

ISO does not itself certify organizations. In many countries accreditation bodies such as UKAS (United Kingdom Accreditation Service), audit the auditors and certify that the registrars are competent and authorized to issue certificates in specified business sectors. These various national accreditation bodies have agreements with each other, ensuring that certificates issued by one of them are accepted worldwide. Both the accreditation bodies and certification bodies require payment for their services.

Under the 2000 Standard auditors are expected to go beyond mere auditing for 'compliance' and to focus on risk, status and importance. They make judgements on what is effective rather than concentrating on what has been formally prescribed. This is to answer the questions; 'Will this process help you achieve your stated objectives? Is it a good process or is there a better one/way to do it better?".

2.5 Relevance to IT management

ISO 9000:2000 is relevant to all organizations, products and services. It is therefore not specifically relevant to IT management. However, if there is a problem with the quality of the system, work will often need to be redone. This leads to a loss of productivity and wasted resources. Incorporation of a quality management system can mitigate against this. Through a focus on customer service and continuous improvement it is possible to ensure that the organization is not perceived to be neglectful or overselling a product. Customer service can also be enhanced by providing support and training and by overcoming errors within systems.

ISO has a set of guidelines to assist in the implementation of ISO 9001:2000 in the software sector (ISO/IEC 90003:2004 Software engineering, Guidelines for the application of ISO 9001:2000 to computer software). These guidelines provide support for organizations in the application of ISO 9001:2000 to the acquisition, supply, development, operation and maintenance of computer software and related support services. ISO/IEC 90003:2004 does not change the requirements of ISO 9001:2000 and its guidelines are not intended to be used as assessment criteria for registration/ certification.

ISO/IEC 90003:2004 is appropriate to software in the following situations:
• part of a commercial contract with another organization
• a product available for a specific market sector
• a product used to support an organization's processes
• a product embedded in a hardware product or related to software services.

Some organizations may be involved in all the above activities; others may specialize in one area. Whatever the situation, the organization's QMS should cover all aspects (software related and non-software related) of the business. ISO/IEC 90003:2004 identifies the issues which should be addressed and is independent of the technology, lifecycle models, development processes, sequence of activities and organizational structure used by an organization.

2.6 Strengths and weaknesses

The greatest strength of ISO 9001:2000 is that it provides a single quality management 'requirements' standard that is applicable to all organizations, products and services. It is the only standard that can be used for the certification of a QMS and its generic requirements can be used by any organization to:
• address customer satisfaction
• meet customer and applicable regulatory requirements

- enable internal and external parties (including certification bodies) to assess the organization's ability to meet these customer and regulatory requirements.

Many companies have found the transition to conforming to IS0 9000 difficult. This has raised many criticisms. The main disadvantages are:
- the process is costly
- there is a lot of administration
- gaining accreditation is time-consuming
- adhering to ISO 9000 makes processes more consistent; however, it also makes it more difficult to improve and adapt processes
- it may not be appropriate to apply a process such as ISO 9000 to a field requiring creativity, such as software engineering
- ISO 9000 can reinforce bad management behavior as audits can become confrontational rather than an opportunity to improve things
- many companies only register to ISO 9000 because they are forced to do so by the marketplace - irrespective of whether the Standard is appropriate to their business
- ISO 9001:2000 does not give much practical advice but instead focuses on general principles.

ISO 9000 is, however, particularly useful as a point of reference in business to business activities. Shantanu Narayen, President and Chief Operating Officer of Adobe claims that 'standards are the engine enabling our industry to develop software in a low risk, cost-effective manner' in an interview in the March 2006 issue of ISO Focus.

2.7 Cross-references/relationships

ISO 9000:2000 is compatible with the ISO 14000 series of Standards (environmental management) as well as national/international health and safety management standards and forms the cornerstone for the integrated management of quality, environment, health and safety. While ISO 9000 family is primarily concerned with quality management the ISO 14000 family is an Environmental Management System (EMS) that is aimed at continually reducing pollution through the more efficient and responsible use of raw materials and the minimization of energy usage and waste.

ISO/IEC 90003:2004 (*Software engineering -- Guidelines for the application of ISO 9001:2000 to computer software*) provides guidance for organizations using ISO 9001:2000 to purchase, supply, develop, operate and maintain computer software and related support services.

Cross-reference to other sections of this book:
- **TQM** ISO 9000:2000 is aimed at improving an organization's overall quality performance and provides a stepping stone to Total Quality Management
- **TickIT** procedures relate directly to the requirements set out in ISO 9001:2000 and similarly to this Standard, certification is conducted by an independent third party certification body using specialist auditors trained by the International Register of Certificated Auditors (IRCA) with the support of the British Computer Society

- **ISO 27001** (ISO 17799/BS7799) - Standard on Information Security ISO/IEC 27001:2005 is designed to ensure the selection of adequate and proportionate security controls that protect information assets and give confidence to interested parties
- **ISO/IEC 20000** promotes the adoption of an integrated process approach to effectively deliver managed services to meet the business and customer requirements. ISO/IEC 20000-2 is a code of practice, and describes the best practices for service management. These can both link in to the ISO 9000:2000 customer service mandate
- **Six Sigma** – the Model for Quality Management Six Sigma is a process-focused methodology designed to improve business performance through improving specific areas of strategic business processes
- **ITIL** - if an organization has intentions to become ISO 9000 certified, the ITIL processes can speed up the process to reach the desired and mandatory levels of quality
- **ASL** - when ASL processes (at maturity level 2 to 3) are implemented within an application management organization, this organization should be close to being able to achieve ISO 9000 certification
- **PRINCE2** has a section covering quality. Although ISO 9000:2000 is not specifically mentioned it is implied that a project management system must have a quality bias as the industry standard ISO 9000:2000 would be the method to achieve this quality
- **PMBoK** fits into the process philosophy of modern quality management in project -oriented companies
- **IPMA** Competence Baseline is based on the EFQM Model and fits better into the process philosophy of modern quality management in project-oriented companies.

2.8   Links and literature

More detailed information on ISO 9000:2000 and its sector specific guidance documents can be obtained from national ISO member bodies. Other standards in the *ISO Catalogue* associated with the software lifecycle can be found in the ISO online catalogue classified under ICS 35.080 *Software* (e.g. ISO/IEC 14598 - software product evaluation).

The following books and websites may also be useful:
- Ray Tricker and Bruce Sherring-Lucas, "ISO 9001:2000 in Brief" (Oxford 2001).
- Ray Tricker, "ISO 9001: 2000 Audit Procedures" (Oxford 2002).
- Ray Tricker, "ISO 9001:2000 The Quality Management Process" (VHP, Zaltbommel 2006).
- www.iso.org
- en.wikipedia.org
- emea.bsi-global.com
- www.aslfoundation.org

Details of courses can be obtained from www.iqms.co.uk.

.

3 TickIT - Software Quality Management

TickIT was designed with and for the IT industry and includes practical guidance for both software development and service, as the TickIT guide's subtitle states: 'Using ISO 9001:2000 for software quality systems construction, certification and continual improvement.'[4] A major element of TickIT is the scheme for certification of an organization's software quality management system to ISO 9001. TickIT is fully described in a public guide which contains detailed commentary on how to apply ISO 9001:2000 to software.

Owner of the copyright:	Joint TickIT Industry Steering Committee (JTISC)
Distribution:	Globally, but especially in the UK
Origin/history:	Launched after a report was published by the British Department of Trade and Industry showing there was a strong reluctance among software producers to adopt ISO 9000, because they felt it to be too general.
When:	1991
Participants in the committee:	British Computer Society (BCS), Intellect (a trade body for the IT industry), British Standards Publications (BSI) and certification bodies.
Certification bodies?	Like ISO 9000, each country has certification bodies of its own; see www.tickit.org.
Number of certified organizations:	1093 certificates in 44 countries (74 per cent of the certificates are currently in the UK). *Source:* www.tickit.org/cert-org.htm

By Paul Breslin

3.1 Origin/history

The TickIT initiative was launched in 1991 after a report was published by the British Department of Trade and Industry reviewing the state of software quality and development in industry.

The outcome of the report showed there was a strong reluctance among software producers to adopt ISO 9000, because they felt it to be too general. They found that a large number of elements were hard to interpret for the software industry and the guidance notes were unclear.

As a result of this report the British Government appointed the British Computer Society (BCS) to lead the TickIT initiative. The main aim was to define the organization, rules and procedures for a Software Sector Certification Scheme. This scheme was to cover the assessment and certification of an organization's software quality management system to ISO 9001.

---

4 **The TickIT Guide** 'Using ISO 9001:2000 for software quality management system construction, certification and continual improvement' Issue 5.0, January 2001.

The scheme is owned and managed by its stakeholders through the Joint TickIT Industry Steering Committee (JTISC). This includes representation from the British Computer Society (BCS), Intellect (a trade body for the IT industry), British Standards Publications (BSI) and certification bodies. The TickIT Industry Committee has overall responsibility for the scheme Rules and Procedures (see ecommittees.bsi-global.com/bsi/controller?livelinkDataID=985990 for terms of reference). It is supported by other committees e.g. SWETIC committee to coordinate Swedish interests.

A wide range of organizations have adopted the TickIT model including major software services companies. See www.tickit.org for a full list.

3.2   Where is TickIT used?

The TickIT Scheme was designed with and for the IT industry and covers software development, maintenance and service. At the core of TickIT is the third party certification scheme that is essentially a software sector implementation of ISO 9001 certification. TickIT also includes a published guidebook with the scheme rules, notes for purchasers and suppliers of software as well as audit guidance to TickIT auditors.

Globally, but especially in the UK, there has been good demand from the market for specialized software management quality assurance. This is due to software development being a complex design process that demands reliable and continuous controls. ISO 9001/TickIT certificates are issued to many different organizations and are not limited by size or location. Some 1090 companies are certified (Q4 2005) of which approximately 75 per cent are UK based. The TickIT market is now generally stable and can be considered mature; however, the governing committee for the scheme is actively pursuing an update and development program to maintain the scheme's relevance to the industry.

3.3   Description and core graphics

The certification aspects of the scheme are operated under the TickIT Uniform Arrangements which are based on well established national accreditation procedures. They are defined in the TickIT Guide and include the overall management of the scheme. The scheme is essentially ISO 9001 certification under long established and well known national accreditation arrangements. At present national accreditation bodies in the UK (UKAS) and Sweden (SWEDAC) offer accreditation to certification bodies who want to offer TickIT services. As part of these uniform arrangements, TickIT auditors have to be registered with the International Register of Certificated Auditors (IRCA). Registration is by resume, training and examination and must be renewed every three years. Full details are at www.irca.org.

Figure 3.1 shows an example of the TickIT graphic that is used on certificates and marketing material.

Figure 3.1 TickIT graphic (source: TickIT)

3.4 Approach/how to

Organizations seeking certification adopt and implement the ISO 9001 quality management system model using the TickIT Guidance. The management system is then reviewed and assessed using third party audits by a TickIT registered certification body who issues a formal certification of compliance. As is normal for management systems certification, the organization is subject to surveillance audits following initial certification to ensure ongoing compliance with the standard.

TickIT certification is relevant where software is developed and where the software is incorporated into the organization's delivered product or service. The scope of TickIT is described on the website www.tickit.org. Some examples of where it is used are:

- development of software products, whether application software, system software or embedded software
- delivery of systems/products where software is only a part of the included product
- internal software development for an organization's administrative systems
- facilities management and/or computer operations services where software development is part of the contract
- software replication services.

There are direct costs involved in achieving certification through the need to contract with a third party certification body and also in purchasing any training or consultancy support the organization may require. However, there are also indirect costs of implementing an ISO 9001 process model, which is normally done through an internal implementation project. As it is an organizational process model, the project has to be inclusive of all affected staff. This can involve considerable internal effort but results in increased awareness and commitment in working to more efficient and effective processes.

3.5 Relevance to IT management

TickIT directly tackles the problems of poor quality and poor quality management in software.

The ISO 9001 Standard has specific requirements to monitor and measure processes and customer satisfaction. Once an organization has implemented these requirements, it should be able to assess the costs of poor software quality with a good degree of accuracy. This in turn will allow the quantification of benefits to be more easily expressed as the costs of poor software quality are driven down over time.

Successfully realizing a modern software quality management system means that the organization has defined, implemented and is managing a set of processes that are specifically suited for its purpose and goals. IT management thus gains increased visibility of the software development process; there is better management and control of the processes and improved traceability between the processes and the associated quality controls.

3.6 Strengths and weaknesses

The main benefits for software quality management systems are similar to those for quality systems in general. These are the need to demonstrate a clear understanding of customer requirements and to show that the organization's products and services consistently meet those requirements.

The opportunities for continual improvement that result from effective use of a modern quality system can lead to:
• improved and consistent software product quality
• more efficient processes
• reduction in failure costs due to defects and/or cost and schedule overruns
• increased staff satisfaction.

Certification of the quality system provides a marketing advantage to organizations, reduces the number of client (second party) audits, provides increased motivation to meet the Standard's requirements and gives a more objective basis for implementing improvements.

There are some extra benefits that are specific to the TickIT Scheme:
• use of software-specific guidance to the ISO 9001 model
• application of formally registered auditors who have specific experience and competence in the software sector.

The certification process is designed to guide organizations towards compliance but problems can occur if there is insufficient understanding within the organization of the role and goals of the ISO 9001 process model. The need is for a management system that meets the organization's purpose as well as being compliant. Too often the focus is on compliance only and this can lead to implementations that are too 'heavy' with complex prescriptive procedures. The affected staff then often sees them as overly bureaucratic and not actually adding to the quality of the software. A 'heavy' quality system is also expensive to maintain as it will require regular and careful update to account for changes and to ensure any internal impacts are fully worked out.

The TickIT scheme is planned to be improved as the Guide is somewhat dated, being published in 2001, and the scheme is still perceived as being UK-centred. The improvements are aimed at maintaining the scheme's relevance to modern software development approaches such as RAD, Agile Programming and to account for other established process models such as the CMM-I.

3.7   Cross-references/relationships

- **ISO 9000** - TickIT certification is ISO 9001 certification for the software sector so it is highly coupled to the quality model and certification approach used for that standard. Although it is not a mandatory requirement to use TickIT, it provides software-sector specific guidance to ISO 9001.
- **ISO/IEC 27001** - Similarly, certification schemes for TickIT and ISO 27001 can be integrated to achieve certification.
- **ISO/IEC 20000** - Certification schemes for TickIT and ISO 20000 are both management systems certification involving third party assessments using a common approach. Hence they can be easily integrated to achieve certification of both the software development processes and the IT service management processes.
- **CMMI** - An earlier version of the CMMI process model, the SW-CMM, is highlighted in the TickIT Guide as a good means of meeting the process improvement requirements in the 9001 Standard. This is due to the staged nature of these capability maturity models providing a clear roadmap for software development organizations. There is, however, no formal relationship between TickIT and the CMMI assessment schemes at the time of writing.

3.8   Links and literature

Reference	Notes
www.tickit.org	Website for the TickIT scheme.
www.irca.org	Website for the organization that manages the registration of TickIT Auditors.
"The TickIT Guide 'Using ISO 9001:2000 for software quality management system construction, certification and continual improvement' Issue 5.0, Jan 2001	"Soft bound A4 book, 220pp. Overview of scheme; guidance for customers, suppliers and auditors; software specific interpretation of ISO 9001 and software process definitions. Essential reference for any and all stakeholders.
"TickIT Scheme Procedures and Guidance, Issue 5, May 2003"	Collection of rules and procedures for certification bodies; includes the TickIT Uniform Arrangements. Held only by accredited Certification Bodies units.
"ISO/IEC 12207/1995, AM1:2002, AM2:2004 'Information Technology – Software lifecycle processes'"	Long established Standard defining software processes and used as a base reference by the scheme. The 12207 processes are elaborated further in the TickIT Guide.
ISO/IEC 90003:2004 'Software engineering. Guidelines for the application of ISO 9001:2000 to computer software.	Published after the TickIT Guide so not yet formally referenced. Replaces ISO 9000-3:1997 which is now withdrawn. Uses extensive referencing to other software related Standards.

EN 45012:1998 'General requirements for bodies operating assessment and certification/registration of quality systems'

Base Standard for accreditation of certification bodies. This Standard plus requirements in theTickIT Uniform Arrangements are the framework for operating TickIT certification.

ISO 19011:2002 'Guidelines for quality and/or environmental management systems auditing'

Base Standard for auditing quality systems Applicable to TickIT audits.

"Certification as a TickIT 2000 Auditor, IRCA/162/05/1, May 2005"

Full details on the process and requirements for becoming a TickIT auditor.

4 ISO 27001 - Information Security Management Systems

> *ISO 27001 provides a model and detailed guidance for reducing an organization's exposure to information security risk, as implemented through an Information Security Management System (ISMS). Organizations will, in their lifetime, experience many changing information security risk profiles in the environment of their operations. An ISMS implemented under the ISO 27001 series of Standards grows with the organization through planned maintenance and improvement cycles.*

Owner of the copyright:	International Standards Organization (ISO): www.iso.org
Origin/history:	The ISO 27001 series springs from BS7799, a British Standard derived from the UK DTI CCSC (Commercial Computer Security Centre) 'User's Code of Practice' (first published in 1989). The latest 1999 version was accepted as the International Standard for Information Security Management, ISO/IEC 17799:2000, which after revisions, was republished in 2005 as ISO/IEC 17799:2005 (likely to become ISO/IEC 27002).
When:	Latest version: 2005
Participants in the committee:	International Standards Organization (ISO)
Certification bodies?	ISO

By Jon Hall

4.1 Origin/history

The genesis of ISO 27001 series of Standards is BS7799, a British Standard derived from the UK DTI CCSC (Commercial Computer Security Centre) 'User's Code of Practice' (first published in 1989). BS7799, published in 1995 as BS7799:1995, was reissued as BS7799:1999 after major revisions. After minor revisions, this document was accepted as the International Standard for Information Security Management, ISO/IEC 17799:2000, which after revisions, was republished in 2005 as ISO/IEC 17799:2005 (likely to become ISO/IEC 27002).

A second part of the Standard, BS7799-2, published in 1998, was added to provide guidance on the creation of and requirements for Information Security Management Systems. To bring it into line with other management system Standards (ISO/IEC 9001:2000 and ISO/IEC 14001:1996), BS7799-2 was revised to include the Plan-Check-Do-Act (PDCA) cycle, which extended its reach to include establishing, implementing, operating, monitoring, reviewing, maintaining and improving an organization's information security management system. This was published as BS7799-2:2002 and, again after revision, was accepted as a full international Standard ISO/IEC 27001:2005.

There has been a curious interplay between the two parts of the Standard: although introduced as a support document to the original code of practice, the second part of the Standard quickly became the more important of the two documents, providing guidance for building and maintaining an organization's ISMS. Hence, what was Part 2 is now ISO/IEC 27001, and what was Part 1 will become ISO/IEC 27002.

4.2   Where is ISO 27001 used?

An Information Security Management System (ISMS) is the instrument by which the value of each of an organization's information assets are protected on an ongoing basis.

Today's organizational environment places great value in the information assets that an organization holds. There are business imperatives to share these information assets so that they can be used for greatest value creation. Due to regulation, legislation and the protection of competitive advantage, there are competing forces that require information assets to be protected.

4.3   Description and core graphics

The ISO 27001 series of Standards recognizes that many facets of information security management should be expressed through the implementation and operation of an ISMS: there are technical, human, system, organizational and societal factors, each of which contributes to the complexity of the topic, and a sophisticated and holistic approach is necessary to produce a fit-for-purpose system.

ISO 27001 has two parts:

1.   ISO 27001:2005, Information technology – Security techniques – Information Security management Systems – Requirements
2.   ISO 17799:2005, Information technology – Security techniques – Code of practice for information security management

ISO 27001:2005 provides a management approach to the synthesis of an information security management system that is fit for purpose, measured by the information security requirements and expectations of all interested parties.

ISO 17799:2005 is a code of practice, organized as 11 areas and 39 security control objectives, each of which is directed at a particular area of information security concern facing an organization. For each area, the code of practice describes high level information security objectives and the control by which risks in the scope of the objective are treated. Also included is implementation guidance.

ISO 27001:2005 includes a summary of ISO 17799:2005 in its Appendix A.

4.4   Approach/how to

Information security management under ISO 27001 is achieved through the systematic assessment of the risks facing an organization's information assets, implemented through the

Security area	High-level objective
Access Control	To control access to information.
Asset Management	To achieve and maintain appropriate protection of organizational assets.
Business Continuity Management	To counteract interruptions to business activities and to protect critical business processes from the effects of major failures of information systems or disasters and to ensure their timely resumption.
Communications and Operations Management	To ensure the correct and secure operation of information processing facilities.
Compliance	To avoid breaches of any law, statutory, regulatory or contractual obligations, and of any security requirements.
Human Resources Security	To ensure that employees, contractors and third party users: • understand their responsibilities and liabilities before during and after employment • are aware of security issues facing the organization and are equipped to deal with them in their normal duties; • reduce the risk of theft, fraud, misuse of facilities, and human error.
Information Security Incident Management	To ensure information security events and weaknesses associated with information systems are: • communicated in a manner allowing timely corrective action to be taken • dealt with in a consistent and effective manner.
Information Systems Acquisition, Development and Maintenance	To ensure that security is an integral part of installed information systems technology base.
Organizing Information Security	To manage information security within the organization.
Security Policy	To provide management direction and support for information security in accordance with business requirements and relevant laws and regulations.

Table 4.1 Security areas and high level objectives

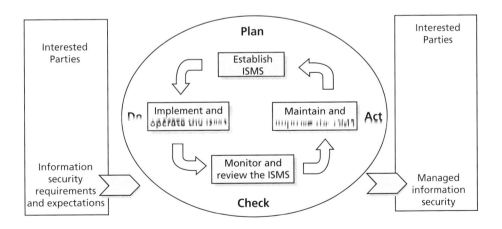

Figure 4.1 the PDCA cycle (source: BS ISO/IEC 27001:2005 BS 7799-2:2005, BSI)

treatment by controls of the vulnerabilities that exist in the systems, technologies and media used to hold them.

ISO 27001 has as its basis the Plan-Do-Check-Act (PDCA) cycle to structure the iterative creation, development, operation and maintenance of the ISMS. The PDCA cycle consists of the four iterated stages as shown in Figure 4.1. The figure also shows the input parameters to the PDCA cycle, which are the information security requirements and expectations of the interested parties. Each completed iteration of the PDCA cycle closes the gap between these requirements and expectations and the performance of the operated ISMS.

According to the Organization for Economic Co-operation and Development's *(OECD) Guidelines for the Security of Information Systems and Networks*[5], organizations should adopt a comprehensive approach to security management as a process which includes the prevention, detection and response to incidents, ongoing maintenance, review and audit of the system, and which applies to all policy and operational levels that govern the security of information systems and networks. Through the PDCA cycle, ISO 27001:2005 provides an information security management system framework for implementing the following OECD principles:
- awareness
- responsibility
- response
- risk assessment
- security design and implementation
- security management
- reassessment.

4.4.1 Planning the ISMS

ISO 27001 organizes the planning of the information security management system into four parts.

At an organizational level, there is the preparation of the **ISMS documentation**, in which is captured the context and scope of the ISMS, and the policies under which it will operate. The documentation is the interface of the ISMS to the executive of the organization. It should be developed with the full support of the board, and reflect the board's attitude to Information Security Management.

The ISMS documentation defines:
- the organization's *Information Security Policy* which begins the documentation process by setting the overall direction for Information Security within the organization
- the *Statement of Applicability* which concludes the documentation process, by detailing the organization's implementation of its defined ISMS.

---

5   Available from www.ftc.gov/bcp/conline/edcams/infosecurity/popups/OECD_guidelines.pdf

Between these two is the hard work of developing the ISMS. The requirements of the Information Security Policy are described first; the Statement of Applicability will be described in section 1.3.3.

The Information Security Policy

The Information Security Policy should contain a clear statement of management's commitment to and intent for information security, consistent with the organization's business goals and all appropriate regulation and legislation. It briefly explains the choices made in the development of the ISMS with respect to security policy, principles (including OECD Guidelines), Standards, compliance requirements, organizational security learning, responsibilities and motivation, business continuity and incident reporting. It gives criteria against which security risks to information assets can be evaluated. It underpins the ISMS and contributes to the traceability and repeatability of its processes.

The Information Security Policy documents the meaning of information security for the organization, in terms of its boundaries, context, scope, and security goals. It should define the framework for the organization's systematic approach to risk assessment – a process for evaluating the likelihood and impact of a breach of an asset's security requirements – along with a definition of what constitutes acceptable risk, and how unacceptable risk should be mitigated.

The Information Security Policy should be written in an accessible way, and brought to the attention of those whose behavior comes within the scope of the ISMS or, more generally, are affected by it.

From the Information Security Policy, an external assessor will also wish to gain an understanding of the meaning of information security for the organization, in terms of the security policies, principles, Standards, and compliance requirements that influence its approach to information security. An external assessor will wish to know:
• which legislation, regulation, and contractual requirements the ISMS is designed to deal with
• how the ISMS will be disseminated through the organization
• the responsibilities of the individuals involved and the reporting structures for information security incidents
• the consequences of information security policy violations.

Information Security Policy Review

The Information Security Policy will define a schedule for the management review of the ISMS – including the Information Security Policy itself – to ensure that changes in the organizational environment, business circumstances, legal conditions, or technical environment do not diminish its suitability, adequacy and/or effectiveness.

Asset identification, risk assessment and risk treatment

For the purposes of the Standard, an organization is characterized by the business or service area in which it exists and operates, its location, its assets and its technology. These variables determine the information security threats that are faced by the organization. The context of the ISMS is the relationship that the protected areas hold to the remainder of the organization and its business environment. Within the context of the ISMS, the scope of the ISMS determines the information assets that need protecting under the ISMS.

After the definition of the Information Security Policy can begin three tasks, which take place sequentially within all organizational units that fall within the context and scope of the ISMS:
• asset identification
• risk assessment
• risk treatment.

The components of the separate stages are shown in Figure 4.2.

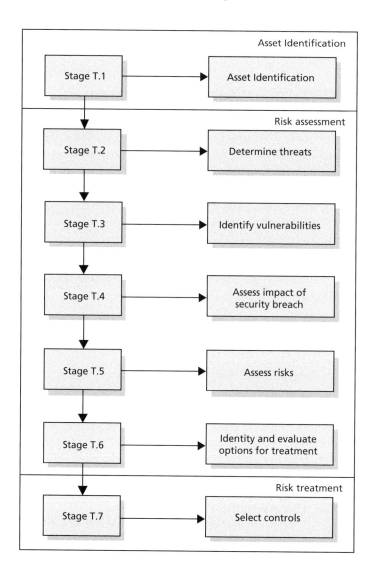

Figure 4.2 Asset identification, risk assessment and risk treatment process

Asset identification

Stage T.1: identify the assets at risk. For each asset that falls within the context and scope of the ISMS, its security requirements – in terms of the need to preserve its confidentially, integrity and availability – are analyzed. Each asset should be assigned an owner, within whose responsibility that asset's information security falls. An asset inventory or register should be constructed and maintained, in which is recorded its owner, value, information security requirements (in terms of confidentiality, integrity and availability) and location; any processes that protect the asset should be defined, including what constitutes its acceptable use.

Risk assessment

The goal of risk assessment is to identify, quantify, and prioritize risks as they apply to the identified assets so to as be consistent with the organization's approach to risk, as documented within its Information Security Policy.

Stage T.2: Threat analysis. There should be a systematic approach to determine the possible threats to information assets. A threat is an opportunity, not always taken, that exists for breaching an information asset's information security requirements.

Stage T.3: Vulnerability analysis. A vulnerability provides a vector for a threat to become a successful attack on the assets. A vulnerability is a weakness in the defenses of an asset that should be covered by the application of controls.

Stage T.4: Assess the impact. Should the information security requirements of an asset be breached by a successful attack, damage will be done to the asset. For each of the asset's information security requirements, the impact of the breach should be determined.

Stage T.5: Assess the risks. Should the information security requirements of an asset be breached by a successful attack, damage will be done to the asset. This can be characterized in two dimensions:
- **impact:** the cost to the organization of the breach, based on the impact of the breach to the asset determined in the previous stage
- **likelihood:** the probability of the attack being successful.

The risk to the organization is the product of the likelihood and the impact.

Stage T.6: identify and evaluate options for the treatment of risks. From the stated attitude to risk, recorded in the Information Security Policy, the risks to information assets that are acceptable can be determined. Also, for those for which the risk is not acceptable, the options for the treatment of risks can be assessed. The choices are to:
- **avoid or transfer the risk:** for instance, by disposing of the asset to which the risk applies or insuring against it – clearly, asset disposal may not be possible
- **control the risk:** that is to lower the risk to the asset by taking measures to reduce the asset's vulnerabilities. In this case the risk is assigned a priority level for treatment.

Documents generated in the risk assessment task should present evidence that every real risk has been assessed, along with a justification for the outcome – acceptance, avoidance, transfer or control – of each individual assessment.

Risk treatment

Stage T.7: select control objectives and controls. In risk treatment, for each prioritized risk for which the risk should be lowered, a choice of the control objective is made: the control objective states how the vulnerability underpinning the risk will be 'patched'.

For each control objective, a control (a countermeasure) is chosen that will implement it. There are 39 control objectives and over 150 controls to choose from in ISO 27001:2005. Controls should be chosen from this set, or may be chosen from elsewhere. The risks should be treated in order of priority.

As part of the choice of control, there should be determined a review maintenance schedule and criteria by which the performance of the control can be assessed. Management should sign off the results of asset identification, risk assessment and risk treatment phases; special attention must be given to the assessment of residual risks. Management authorization for implementation and operation of the ISMS should be sought.

The Statement of Applicability

The Statement of Applicability formally documents:
- the decisions reached on which control objectives and controls have been chosen together with a justification of why they were selected
- which controls are currently implemented and functioning
- which controls of the Standard have not been implemented, together with the reasons for each decision.

The wording of the Statement of Applicability should, for each control, be a form of the description of the control requirement, sufficiently detailed to enable a third party auditor to understand what the organization has decided to do and why. It may also be appropriate that reasoning and/or background material be included; references to the underlying documentation that contains the reasoning/background should be made.

4.4.2 The Do stage

The Do stage of the PDCA cycle can now be entered. At exit of this stage, the organization will have an implemented an ISMS that is reducing risk to critical information assets. Here, the theory that is detailed in the Statement of Applicability is put into practice.

To do this, the organization will formulate and implement a risk treatment plan that identifies the appropriate management action, resources, responsibilities and priorities for managing information security risks, by implementing the controls selected in the Service Oriented Architecture (SOA) to meet the control objectives.

The organization will need to define how to monitor the effectiveness of the risk treatment. This feeds into the Check stage of the PDCA cycle. The organization will need to implement training and awareness programs in all areas that the implementation of controls impinge on. The organization will implement procedures and other controls capable of enabling prompt detection of security events and response to security incidents (see 4.4.3).

4.4.3 The Check stage
At the end of the Check stage, a report on the results of the performance and fitness-for-purpose of the ISMS in operation (from the Do stage) will be given to management for review of the effectiveness of the system. The process performance of the system is assessed and measured against the ISMS policy, objectives and, after iteration under the PDCA cycle, against practical experience of how the system behaves.

4.4.4 The Act stage
After management review, corrective and preventive actions are taken, based on the results of the internal ISMS audit and management review or other relevant information, to achieve continual improvement of the ISMS (adapted from ISO 27001, page vi).

4.5   Relevance to IT management
The ISO 27001 series of Standards is a key factor in IT management for any organization. Through the Standard is recognized the value of information that an organization uses. Many of those information assets that are of value to an organization will be held on IT equipment, and many of the vulnerabilities that threaten to decrease their value exist because of IT equipment. Indeed, many of the controls chosen to manage the risks will impinge on IT management.

However, Information Security Management is not just an IT management issue and treating it as such would be an error, because many of the information security vulnerabilities that are faced by organizations do not reside in the IT infrastructure but in the social side of the organization's socio-technical system. Asset identification and risk assessment stages should thus be organization-wide.

On the control of risks side, many of the controls in the Standard affect the management of IT, and their review and maintenance – a necessary component of the ISMS – will properly come within that function.

4.6   Strengths and weaknesses
The ISO 27001 series of Standards provides detailed guidance for the synthesis of a fit-for-purpose Information Security Management System, measured by an organization's risk profile. The system is built by iteration through the PDCA cycle, each cycle improving the effectiveness of the system. There is excellent depth of guidance in the code of practice for the ISMS, and the breadth of implemented systems is very good.

It may appear that the Standard's focus on confidentiality, integrity and availability is rather limiting, given the complexity of modern computer systems. In fact, confidentiality, integrity and availability are precisely the right level to begin an analysis of an asset's information security needs; they cover in scope the need to make best use of the asset within the scope of the ISMS, and to keep it scarce outside that scope. Issues such as authentication are actually part of the controls for the vulnerabilities that protect an asset's information security requirements.

One of the main problems with implementing an ISMS is the large numbers of assets that are available to an organization. In the order of a thousand assets is not unusual; the Standard indicates that all such assets should be assessed for their information security requirements, against each applicable threat. The large numbers of asset/threat combinations provide a great challenge for the first iteration through the PDCA cycle.

Modern organizations need to share information outside their physical boundaries, with partner organizations. Defining the scope and context of the ISMS becomes difficult given that it is possible that two or more organizations will be subject to it. External assessment of all party organizations against the Standard may reduce this problem, and agreement on a relatively small number of details — such as information security levels — will help more.

4.7   Cross-references/relationships

ISO 27001 is closely aligned with (in terms of document structure and intent) both ISO 9001:2000 (ISO 9001:2000, *Quality management systems – Requirements*) and ISO 14001:2004 (*Environmental management systems – Requirements with guidance for use*). The intention is to support consistent and integrated implementation and operation with those management Standards so that a single organizational management system can satisfy each of these three Standards.

4.8   Links and literature

- ISO 27001:2005, Information technology – Security techniques – Information Security management Systems – Requirements
- ISO 17799:2005, Information technology – Security techniques – Code of practice for information security management

There is a **Management Guide on ISO 27001/ISO 17799** available from Van Haren Publishing:

Alan Calder, *Information Security based on ISO 27001/ISO 17799 - A Management Guide* (Van Haren Publishing 2006).
ISBN: 90 77212 70 1

Further information on ISO/IEC 27000 series of Standards is available via many national Standards organizations, for example www.bsi-global.com for the UK.

More information on ISO Standards in general: www.iso.org.

5   ISO/IEC 20000 - ITSM Standard

> *ISO/IEC 20000 is the formal Standard for IT service management.*

Owner of the copyright:	International Standards Organization (ISO): www.iso.org
Distribution:	Formal certification against the Standard grows rapidly. Although the original Standard was developed in the UK, take up has been international with only about thirty per cent of the initial tranche of achievers being UK based.
Origin/history:	Initially developed as a British Standard, BS15000, before adoption by the International Standards Organization (ISO) and International Electrotechnical Commission (IEC), it was also adopted by Standards bodies in Australia (AS 8018), Hungary, South Africa and Korea.
When:	Version 1 published 2000, Version 2 published 2002.
Participants in the committee:	The committee of the British Standards Institution comprised IT service management experts from vendor and user organizations, ITSMF and from relevant UK public sector bodies, such as CCTA (now part of OGC) and the national Audit Office. This same committee worked with a group of 'early adopter' service providers who effectively trialled Version 1.
Certification bodies?	The formal certification scheme for organizations wishing to demonstrate their conformance to the requirements of ISO IEC 20000 is currently owned and administered by ITSMF.
Number of certified organizations:	Over seventy organizations have achieved certification in the first eighteen months of the scheme's operation from the first existence of BS15000.

By Ivor Macfarlane

5.1   Origin/history

The Standard was originally developed – and published in 2000 as BS15000 – by a committee of the British Standards Institution. This group comprised IT service management experts from vendor and user organizations, ITSMF and from relevant UK public sector bodies, such as CCTA (now part of the UK Office of Government Commerce) and the National Audit Office. This same committee worked with a group of 'early adopter' service providers who effectively trialled Version 1. From this exercise the committee went on to develop and produce Version 2 in 2002.

ISO/IEC 20000 will fall due for renewal by SC7, the responsible ISO committee within three years, but is likely to remain substantively unaltered until then.

5.2   Where is ISO/IEC 20000 used?

ISO/IEC 20000 is appropriate to IT service provider organizations. It is appropriate to all industry sectors and to all sizes of organization except the very smallest (where a wide ranging ISO 9000 certification is probably more sensible).

Although the traditional use of a formal Standard is to achieve formal certification, the product is also helpful as a benchmark and guide to implementing best practice processes. The inherent nature of a Standard – unambiguously expressed requirements – allows meaningful period-by-period comparisons, which can deliver a measure of improvement in a service provider's processes.

Formal certification against the Standard grows rapidly with over seventy organizations achieving certification in the first eighteen months of the scheme's operation from the first existence of BS15000. Although the original Standard was developed in the UK, take-up has been international with only about thirty per cent of the initial tranche of achievers being UK based.

5.3   Description and core graphics

ISO 20000 is a management Standard, addressing the establishment and maintenance of processes and the mechanisms to ensure their relevance and improvement.

The core content of the Standard is owned and maintained by the International Standards Organization, but national Standards bodies publish this content directly with additional nationally relevant content like bibliography and references. For example in the UK it is published as BS ISO/IEC 20000.

The Standard comprises two parts:
- Part 1 - Specification. This is the documented requirements that an organization must comply with to achieve formal certification against ISO/IEC 20000
- Part 2 - Code of Practice: Expansion and explanation of the requirements in section 1.

Both parts share a common structure:
1.   Scope
2.   Terms and definitions
3.   Requirements for a management system
4.   Planning and implementing service management
5.   Planning and implementing new or changed services
6.   Service delivery processes
7.   Relationship processes
8.   Resolution processes
9.   Control processes
10. Release processes.

The relationships of the key processes set out in the later sections are illustrated in Figure 5.1.

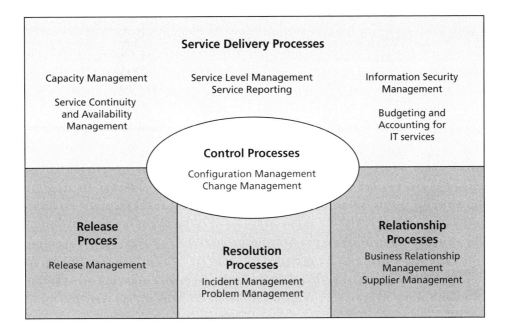

Figure 5.1 Service management processes

As Figure 5.1 shows, there are four kinds of key processes that are all related to the fifth kind of processes, the control processes. For all processes there is a defined objective and specifications.

The service delivery process consists of:
• service level management
• service reporting
• service continuity and availability management
• budgeting and accounting for IT services
• capacity management
• information security management.

The relationship processes are:
• business relationship management
• supplier management.

The resolution processes are:
• incident management
• problem management.

The control processes are:
• configuration management
• change management.

The last process, the release process, is defined as just the release management process.

Like any standard, ISO 20000 is primarily used as a demonstration of compliance to accepted best practice. In addition to the central elements of good IT service management best practice, it also requires service providers to implement the 'Plan-Do-Check-Act' methodology (Deming's quality circle) and apply it to their service management processes. This enshrines 'Continual Service Improvement' into the service provider, ensuring that the organization's processes develop, mature and adapt to their customers' requirements and errors and omissions are avoided and those that have been dealt with do not recur.

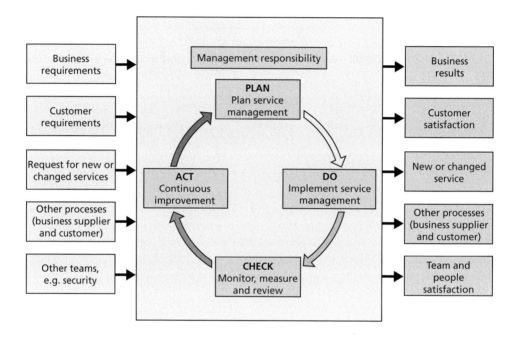

Figure 5.2 Plan-Do-Check-Act for Service Management processes

5.3.1 Benefits

Organizations' major purpose is the demonstration that a service provider complies with the requirements set out in the Standard. This, in turn, may be for one or more reasons, such as:

- **a focus for internal achievement** – a concrete demonstration of relevant and appropriate processes and approach within the service provider
- **demonstrating compliance** to show credibility to existing and/or potential customers
- **formal requirement set down by customers** – requiring their service provider to comply with formally accepted best practice
- **corporate policy** that the organization as a whole complies with all appropriate international Standards.

In addition to the formal demonstration of compliance, many organizations use ISO/IEC 20000 internally to identify targets of performance to measure themselves against. In this case, although compliance to all elements within the Standard is not yet achieved, nonetheless improvements in compliance can be measured, either internally or by use of external consultants, and demonstrates period-on-period improvement.

The main elements of ISO/IEC 20000 (Parts 1 and 2 of the Standard) are supported by several British Standards Institution (BSI) published documents, including:

- **BIP0015** – Self-assessment workbook. This book contains some guidance on assessing an organization for its compliance with the Standard, and effectively sets out the elements of ISO/IEC 20000 in the form of questions
- **Manager's guide to service management** – an introductory book aimed at making managers aware of the importance and elements of IT service management
- **Achieving ISO/IEC 20000** – a series of books giving specific guidance on the implementation and maintenance of processes that conform with the Standard.

5.3.2 Certification program

A formal certification scheme exists for organizations wishing to demonstrate their conformance to the requirements of ISO/IEC 20000. This scheme is currently owned and administered by ITSMF.

To be entitled to the ISO/IEC 20000 certification status, a service provider must comply with all the requirements within Part 1 of the Standard. The area of application for the Standard can, however, be scoped by any other factor, restricting the entity certified in terms of, for example:

- **geography** – limited to services provided by or for a specific office, group of offices, city and so on
- **customer/logical** – limited to services provided for one or more customer groups, or to a single division within the organization
- **language** or other delineating element.

5.3.3 Individual qualifications and training available

Experienced ISO 9000 auditors who wish to carry out formal ISO/IEC 20000 audits or a Registered Certification Body (RCB) under the ITSMF scheme must attend an ITSMF approved training course.

Those wishing to advise organizations (as internal or external consultants, or who may be working directly on a project to achieve ISO/IEC 20000 certification within an organization) can attend an ITSMF approved training course that will allow them to sit an examination leading to a formal qualification. This course is usually three days, including the examination. Many people in the industry have already obtained this qualification, and the training is available from many IT service management training providers. Details of the current scheme can be found from the websites (see below).

5.4   Approach/how to

ISO/IEC 20000 can be applied by any service provider who wishes to demonstrate conformance with best practice in IT service management. The degree and scale of application ranges from through a spectrum of formality, cost and visibility:

- internal **comparison**, an informal comparison of actual practices against ISO/IEC requirements and adoption of some of those practices, making use of he guidance and supporting ideas set out in Part 2 (Code of Practice) and the supporting documentation
- **internal benchmarking** – using the Standard, and its supporting documentation, especially the assessment workbook, to identify the degree of compliance. Then through an improvement exercise, a higher degree of compliance can be shown at a repeat assessment, thus demonstrating improvement
- **formal certification** – via the official scheme – demonstrating adherence to best practice.

Although ISO/IEC 20000 does contain some guidance, especially in the Code of Practice and supporting documentation, it is primarily a measure of process conformance to be achieved by an organization, rather than setting out a means of achieving that process conformance. At a minimum, organizations seeking formal ISO/IEC 20000 certification will require an effective Service Improvement Program which addresses weak areas and improves the processes to conform with the requirements of the Standard.

The costs to an organization of achieving conformance would include:

- **training of staff** – typically in awareness of IT service management (often in practice delivered as ITIL awareness or ITIL foundation or managers level training)
- **costs of the improvement** – for example contract staff to cover for those identifying and implementing improvements, external consultancy
- **assessment** by a registered certification body for formal audit against the Standard.

5.5   Relevance to IT management

The Standard is wholly concerned with service management and thus is centrally relevant. It does not depend upon any specific approach, rather assessments are made against the processes in place, irrespective of what methods, guidance or techniques have been adopted by the service provider to develop and maintain the processes.

5.6   Strengths and weaknesses

It is still early in the life of this Standard family but already take-up is significant and growing. With significant world-wide adoption, ISO/IEC 20000 offers the community an agreed and accepted core of best practice.

In order to achieve wide and comprehensive coverage, the Standard addresses only the generically valid core elements of the service management processes, and so can never describe the full set of processes/procedures that any specific service provider will require in order to deliver effective and efficient, customer focused services.

5.7   Cross-references/relationships

As mentioned above, ISO/IEC 20000 judges the implemented processes, not the means of achieving them, and is therefore fully compatible with all and any mechanism.

There is however considerable historical synergy with the ITIL guidance. The original version of BS15000 was developed alongside the development of ITIL Version 2, with an overlap of authors between the two products. Leading industry opinion has declared that the proposed structure, approach and content of ITIL Version 3, to be published in early 2007, will be consistent with the requirements of ISO/IEC 20000.

The relationship between ISO/IEC 20000 and ITIL, showing the ITIL guidance delivering the detail that underpins the Standard, is illustrated in Figure 5.3.

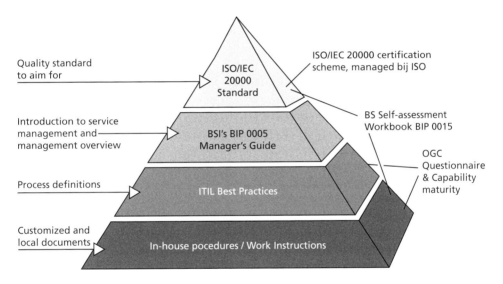

Figure 5.3 Relationship between ISO/IEC 20000 and ITIL

5.8   Links and literature

Further information on ISO/IEC 20000 is available via many national Standards organizations, for example www.bsi-global.com for the UK.

Details of the certification scheme can be found on the Web at www.bs15000certification.com.

Information about BSI's supporting publications can be found from www.bsi-global.com, or can be obtained through many ITSMF bookstores, as can the Standard itself.

More information on ISO Standards in general: www.iso.org.

There is an **ITSMF endorsed Pocket Guide on ISO 20000** available:

Jan van Bon (chief editor) and others, *ISO/IEC 20000, a pocket guide* (Van Haren Publishing 2006).
ISBN: 90 77212 79 5.

6 IT Service CMM - the IT Service Capability Maturity Model

The IT Service Capability Maturity Model (IT Service CMM) is a maturity model aimed at organizations that provide IT services. Its purpose is twofold: to assess the current maturity of IT service providers and to provide direction for improvement of the organization's IT service processes.

Owner of the copyright:	Vrije Universiteit Amsterdam and CIBIT. The IT Service CMM is free to download and use.
Distribution:	The IT Service CMM is used primarily by Dutch, companies.
Origin/history:	IT Service CMM originates from a multi-partner research projects, partly supported by the Dutch Ministry of Economic Affairs, called 'Kwintes' (1997-1999). The Kwintes project aimed at developing methods for specifying and controlling IT services. Level Two of the IT Service CMM was developed during the Kwintes project. After the Kwintes project ended, development of the IT Service CMM continued in an open source fashion. The further development of the model was coordinated by CIBIT and involved participants from several universities and companies. The development activities ended in January 2005 with the release of the IT Service CMM Version 1.0 (see www.itservicecmm.org).
When:	January 2005
Participants in the committee:	CIBIT, several Dutch universities and companies

By Frank Niessink

6.1 Origin/history

The IT Service CMM described in this document originates from a multi-partner research project, partly supported by the Dutch Ministry of Economic Affairs. Partners in this project – 'Kwintes (1997-1999) – were two Dutch companies (Cappemini and Twijnstra Gudde), the Tax and Customs Computer and Software Centre of the Dutch Tax and Customs Administration, and three Dutch universities (the Technical Universities of Delft and Eindhoven, and the Vrije Universiteit Amsterdam).

The Kwintes project aimed at developing a method to specify and control IT services. Level Two of the IT Service CMM was developed during this project. After the Kwintes project ended in 1999, a new project was initiated to specify levels three, four and five of the IT Service CMM. This project – DOCIS, which stands for Development of an Open-Content IT Service Maturity Model – was coordinated by CIBIT and involved participants from several universities and companies. The DOCIS project ended in January 2005 with the release of the IT Service CMM Version 1.0 (see www.itservicecmm.org).

Authors of the IT Service CMM are Frank Niessink, Viktor Clerc, Ton Tijdink (all three working for CIBIT) and Hans van Vliet (Vrije Universiteit Amsterdam).

No major changes to the IT Service CMM itself are expected. The Software Engineering Institute has started a project to develop a CMMI[1] for Services constellation that will extend the current CMMI for Product Development to the service arena. CIBIT, currently the main custodian of the IT Service CMM, is participating in the CMMI for Services project. The CMMI for Services constellation is expected to supersede the IT Service CMM when it is released in the first quarter of 2007.

6.2   Where is the IT Service CMM used?

The IT Service CMM is targeted at organizations that provide IT services. IT services are services that enable users of IT to effectively use their IT to perform their business processes. Examples of IT services include the maintenance of software systems, operation of information systems, the management and maintenance of workstations, networks or mainframes and the provision of contingency services. The IT Service CMM does not distinguish between IT service providers that are internal, such as an IT department within a bank, and IT service providers that deliver services to external customers, such as Application Service Providers (ASPs).

The IT Service CMM is used by different companies as the basis for assessing the current maturity of their IT service organization(s) and for improving the process maturity of these IT service organization. Examples include the Rabobank Group, the Informatie Beheer Groep (IB Groep), ING Direct, ISC (ICT-Service Organization Police and Justice Department), ICT Services DJI (Correctional Institutions Agency) and Essent.

6.3   Description and core graphics

The objective of the IT Service CMM is twofold:
• to enable IT service providers to assess their capabilities with respect to the delivery of IT services
• to provide IT service providers with directions and steps for further improvement of their service capability.

The IT Service CMM aims to fulfill these goals by measuring the capability of the IT service processes of organizations on a five-level ordinal scale. Each level prescribes certain key process areas that have to be in place before an organization resides on that level. Key process areas implement a set of related activities that, when performed collectively, achieve a set of goals considered important for enhancing service process capability. Hence, organizations can improve their service capability by implementing these key process areas.

---

1   CMMI (Capability Maturity Model Integrated) is a maturity model aimed at organizations that develop hardware and/or software products. It is the successor of the original CMM for Software, integrating different disciplines such as software engineering, systems engineering and supplier sourcing.

The service process maturity of organizations is measured on a *five-level ordinal scale*.

1. **Initial** - this is the level where all IT service organizations reside that have not implemented the Level Two key process areas.
2. **Repeatable** - organizations that have reached Level Two will be able to repeat earlier successes in similar circumstances. Thus the emphasis of Level Two is on getting the IT services right for one customer.
3. **Defined** - the service organization has defined its processes and is using tailored versions of these standard processes to deliver the services. By using common organization-wide standard processes, the process capability to deliver services consistently is improved.
4. **Managed** - organizations gain quantitative insight into their service processes and service quality. By using measurements and an organization-wide measurement database they are able to set and achieve quantitative quality goals.
5. **Optimizing** - the entire organization is focused on continuous process and service improvement. Using the quantitative measurements the organization prevents problems from recurring by changing the processes. The organization is able to introduce new technologies and services into the organization in an orderly manner.

Table 6.1 gives an overview of the key process areas by level. The key process areas are grouped into *three process categories*:

- **management** is concerned with the management of services
- **enabling** deals with enabling the delivery process by means of support processes and standardization of processes
- **delivery** consists of the processes that result in the consistent, efficient delivery of services according to appropriate quality levels.

6.3.1   Level One: Initial

An organization that has not implemented the Level Two key process areas operates at Level One. There are no key process areas defined for Level One.

6.3.2   Level Two: Repeatable

The key process areas for maturity Level Two are concerned with establishing the processes that enable the organization to repeat earlier successful services in similar situations. The IT Service CMM distinguishes between two kinds of processes that an organization has to implement on this level. The first category deals with service management: the planning, specification, tracking and evaluation of services. The second category is concerned with service support: processes that support the activities that actually deliver the services.

The management processes on this level look as follows. First, the IT service provider and the customer draw up an agreement about the services to be delivered, the quality of the services – specified in terms of service levels– and the costs of the services (Service Commitment Management). To ensure that the service levels are realistic, the IT service provider draws up a service delivery plan that shows the feasibility of the service levels (Service Delivery Planning). During service delivery, the IT service provider tracks the realized service levels and reports these to the customer on a regular basis to demonstrate that the provider has indeed delivered the services against the promised service levels (Service Tracking and Oversight). After a period of service provision, the customer and the IT service provider review the service level agreement

	Management	Enabling	Delivery
5. Optimizing		Technology Change Management	
	Process Change Management		Problem Prevention
4. Managed	Quantitative Process Management		Service Quality Management
	Financial Service Management		
3. Defined	Integrated Service Management	Organization Process Focus	
		Organization Service Definition	Service Delivery
		Organization Process Definition	
		Training Program	
		Intergroup Coordination	
		Resource Management	
		Problem Management	
2. Repeatable	Service Commitment Management	Configuration Management	
	Service Delivery Planning	Service Request and Incident Management	
	Service Tracking and Oversight	Service Quality Assurance	
	Subcontract Management		
1. Initial	Ad hoc processes		

Table 6.1 Key process areas

to see whether it still conforms to the IT service needs of the customer (Service Commitment Management). Just like the organization draws up a service level agreement with its customer, the organization should also use service level agreements when it delegates parts of the service delivery to third parties (Subcontract Management).

The IT Service CMM identifies three support processes that a Level Two organization needs to implement. First, almost all IT services concern the management, operation or maintenance of IT components. Therefore, where necessary for consistent service delivery, these components are put under configuration control. This ensures that at all times the status and history of these components is known, and that changes are controlled (Configuration Management). Second, during the period that the services are delivered, service requests and incidents can occur that need to be resolved by the IT service provider. These service requests and incidents can range from simple requests for a new laptop to serious incidents that prevent the customer from using its IT. All these service requests and incidents need to be identified, tracked, resolved and reported to the customer (Service Request and Incident Management). To handle the service requests and to resolve incidents, changes to the configuration may be necessary. The change requests are evaluated by the configuration control board with respect to the service level agreement and risk for the integrity of the configuration. Only after a change request has been approved by the configuration control board, will the configuration be changed (Configuration Management).

Finally, to ensure the quality of the services and service processes, the IT service provider deploys quality assurance techniques, such as reviews and audits (Service Quality Assurance).

6.3.3 Level Three: Defined

At Level Three, an organization standardizes its processes and uses tailored versions of these standard processes to deliver the IT services. This results in more predictable performance of the processes and hence it increases the ability of the organization to draw up realistic service level agreements. The Level Three key process areas each fall into one of the three process categories: management, enabling or delivery.

The first category – service management – is concerned with the tailoring of the standard service processes to the customer and the service level agreement at hand. Also, the actual service processes need to be integrated with each other and with third party service processes (Integrated Service Management).

The second category – enabling – deals with making standard processes available and usable. The organization develops a set of standard services and describes these services in the service catalog (Organization Service Definition). The organization develops and maintains standard processes for each of these standard services. Usually, organizations will provide several services to one customer at the same time. Hence, not only the service processes themselves, but also the integration of these processes has to be standardized as much as is feasible (Organization Process Definition). To coordinate process efforts across services and organizational units and over time, organizational support is institutionalized (Organization Process Focus). Also, to teach people how to perform their roles and how to work with the standards, a training program needs to be put in place (Training Program). Furthermore, means are established for the different groups involved in the service delivery to communicate efficiently and effectively (Intergroup Coordination). Underlying problems of service requests and incidents occurring during different service delivery are analyzed (Problem Management) and resources are negotiated before making service commitments, and monitored during the service delivery (Resource Management).

The third category – service delivery– concerns the actual delivery of the services to the customer using the tailored service processes (Service Delivery).

6.3.4 Level Four: Managed

At Level Four, organizations gain a quantitative understanding of their standard processes by taking detailed measures of service performance and service quality (Quantitative Process Management) and by using these quantitative data to control the quality of the delivered services (Service Quality Management). The quantitative data is also used to develop a cost model of the IT services and provide a charging system tailored to the customer and IT services delivered (Financial Service Management).

6.3.5 Level Five: Optimizing

At Level Five, service providers learn to change their processes to increase service quality and service process performance (Process Change Management). Changes in the processes are triggered by improvement goals, new technologies or problems that need to be resolved. New technologies are evaluated and introduced into the organization when feasible (Technology

Change Management). Problems that occur are prevented from recurring by changing the processes (Problem Prevention).

6.4 Approach/how to

Since the IT Service CMM has two main goals, there are two main ways to applying the model: as a guide for the implementation of IT service processes and as a means to assess the current state of the IT service organization. In the latter case, a process assessment is done to investigate the current state of affairs and to generate improvement actions.

Usually, an organization that wants to improve its IT service processes will start with an assessment to determine its strong and weak points. An assessment team will perform interviews and study documents to gather findings. These findings are compared with the IT Service CMM to determine which of the requirements of the model have been met by the organization, and which requirements haven't been met. Typically, an assessment (interviews, documentation study, workshops) takes one or two weeks to perform.

With the assessment results as a starting point, the organization establishes an improvement program. Depending on the culture of the organization, the ambition level, and organization size, the improvement program can be processed in a blueprint fashion or more incrementally. The IT Service CMM does not prescribe how the improvement activities should be organized. Preferably, the goals of the improvement program are not stated in terms of a specific maturity level, but rather in terms of measurable business goals.

6.5 Relevance to IT management

The IT Service CMM is specifically relevant to IT management since it provides an instrument that can be used to obtain an objective measurement of the maturity of the organization. In addition, the IT Service CMM can provide strong guidance in improving the organization.

6.6 Strengths and weaknesses

The main strength of the IT Service CMM is its strong focus on process improvement. Due to its different levels of maturity it lays out a path of improvement for organizations to follow, which is one of the purposes of the model. The other purpose of the IT Service CMM is to be used as a reference framework. Therefore, the model specifies little about how a certain maturity level should be reached; it merely specifies the characteristics of organizations at each maturity level. Consequently, organizations still have a lot of freedom on how to organize their processes and internal structure. The IT Service CMM does not provide much guidance on that subject.

6.7 Cross-references/relationships

Since the IT Service CMM was based on the Software CMM (Version 1.1) there are many similarities between the two models. Also, the IT Service CMM covers many of the same process areas as the IT Infrastructure Library (ITIL). However, there are a few important differences:

- at Level Two, the IT Service CMM contains process areas for Service Delivery Planning and Service Quality Assurance. These processes are not present in ITIL
- at Levels Three, Four and Five, the IT Service CMM contains many process areas targeted at improving the IT service processes and organization. These process areas cover areas such as process standardization, quantitative process management, training, intergroup coordination and problem prevention. In comparison with the ITIL, the IT Service CMM offers more specific guidance on process improvement.

6.8   Links and literature

The IT Service CMM is freely available from www.itservicecmm.org. The model, White Papers, a questionnaire and other support materials can be downloaded from the website.

In addition, a **Pocket Guide** is available that gives a more extensive overview of the model than this chapter, but still is much briefer than the model itself:

Viktor Clerc and Frank Niessink, *IT Service CMM, a pocket guide* (Van Haren Publishing 2004).
ISBN: 90-77212-35-3.

7   Six Sigma

> *Six Sigma (6σ) is a branding term, given to a structured, disciplined, rigorous approach to process improvement. It is a methodology that provides businesses with the tools to improve the capability of their business processes and/or IT processes. This increase in performance and decrease in process variation leads to defect reduction (Six Sigma literally means only 3.4 defects per million opportunities occurring) and vast improvement in profits, employee morale and quality of product.*

Owner of the copyright:	None
Distribution:	While its origins lie in the manufacturing industry, Six Sigma is now used in more than ten industry sectors worldwide, among them IT.
Origin/history:	The roots of Six Sigma lie with the invention of the normal curve by Carl Frederick Gauss (1777-1855). After the rise of Total Quality Management (TQM), in the early 1980s Motorola engineer Bill Smith coined the term 'Six Sigma'.
When:	Early 1980s
Founding fathers:	Carl Frederick Gauss, Total Quality Management guru Walter Shewhart, and Bill Smith, among many others.
Certification bodies?	Individual training and examination for Yellow Belts, Green Belts, Black Belts, Master Black Belts, Champions and Executives available.
Number of certified organizations:	None

By Edgar Giesen and Patrick Teters

7.1   Origin/history

The web site isixsigma.com gives the following overview of the history of Six Sigma.

> *The use of Six Sigma as a measurement standard can be traced back to Carl Frederick Gauss (1777-1855). He introduced the concept of the normal curve. The use of Six Sigma as a measurement standard originates in the 1920s. Then, Walter Shewhart showed that three sigma from the mean is the point where a process requires correction. Many measurement standards (Cpk, Zero Defects, etc.) later were adopted but Motorola engineer Bill Smith coined the term 'Six Sigma'.*
>
> *In the early and mid-1980s with Chairman Bob Galvin at the helm, Motorola engineers decided that the traditional quality levels—measuring defects in thousands of opportunities—did not provide enough granularity. They started measuring the defects per million opportunities and this helped the company realize more than $16 billion in savings.*
>
> *Since then, hundreds of companies around the world have adopted Six Sigma as a way of doing business. This is also a result of many of America's leaders openly praising the benefits of Six Sigma,*

such as Larry Bossidy of Allied Signal (now Honeywell), and Jack Welch of General Electric Company.

source: www.isixsigma.com/library/content/c020815a.asp

7.2 Where is the Six Sigma methodology used?

While its origins lie in the manufacturing industry, Six Sigma is now used in more than ten industry sectors worldwide, such as defense, finance, food and ICT. Table 7.1 shows a selection of the major companies that are now using Six Sigma. This is not an exhaustive list, but it gives an overview of the diversity of the usage of this methodology.

Company Name	Year Six Sigma was implemented
Motorola	1986
Allied Signal (Merged With Honeywell in 1999)	1994
GE	1995
Honeywell	1998
Ford	2000
LG Philips	> 2000
Boeing	> 2000
Citibank	> 2000
JP Morgan	> 2000
Nokia	> 2000
Sarah Lee	> 2000

Table 7.1 Major companies and the year they implemented Six Sigma

As Six Sigma was invented by Motorola and was later optimized by General Electric it was always perceived as a methodology used for the operations and manufacturing industries. Over the past five to six years this has rapidly changed. Financial companies, energy and utilities related industries have found Six Sigma as a rigorous improvement method for their processes (this includes both their business and IT processes).

A good example is the adoption of the Six Sigma methodology by ABN AMRO NV in the Netherlands as their quality and process improvement method. At the beginning of 2004 ABN AMRO NV did a pilot project with the help of Capgemini Consulting Services, which led to a cost reduction of 1.2 million Euros in three months. Besides the financial benefit, ABN AMRO NV saw that the Six Sigma approach helped the organization to work together globally and to quantify the process KPIs and improvements. ABN AMRO NV adopted not just the Six Sigma methodology but also the mindset, more widely known as the Six Sigma philosophy.

Another example is the use of Six Sigma in the utilities industry. Six Sigma is now used for the optimization of processes and for the analysis of root cause of problems. Because of the technical nature of this industry a large amount of data is being kept in the databases. For example, Essent, a major provider of electric power in the Netherlands, is able to analyze this data for operations improvement with the help of Six Sigma. Essent has chosen to use Six Sigma as a powerful toolbox with robust tooling for its purposes.

Both success stories are based on the Six Sigma approach that has been optimized by General Electric, but in a completely different way and with a completely different approach. The next section provides a description of the three levels of Six Sigma.

7.3   Description and core graphics

The term Six Sigma refers to the statistical notion of having 99.99 per cent confidence of achieving specified results. A greater sigma implies a lower expected Defects per Million Opportunities (DMO) for defect or error.

The fundamental objective of the Six Sigma methodology is the implementation of a measurement-based strategy that focuses on process improvement and variation reduction through the application of Six Sigma improvement projects.

The practical goal of this is to increase profits by eliminating variability, defects and waste that undermine customer loyalty. This can be achieved in many industries and for many purposes such as operational excellence (process), IT development and IT maintenance.

Six Sigma relies on tried-and-true methods that have been available for decades and combined these to create a new and structured methodology. It discards a great deal of the complexity that characterizes total quality management (TQM) there are more than 400 TQM tools and techniques.

Six Sigma takes a small subset of these methods and trains a small cadre of in-house technical leaders, known as Six Sigma Black Belts, to a high level of proficiency in the application of these techniques. Some of the methods used by Black Belts, including up-to-date IT, are highly advanced.

Given the impact on customer satisfaction of even one error, many organizations are incentivized to aspire to Six Sigma level DMO to ensure better customer retention.

7.3.1   The three levels of Six Sigma

Six Sigma can be perceived at three levels.

1. **Metric:** 3.4 Defects Per Million Opportunities (DPMO). DPMO takes the complexity of product/process into account. This should be measured in Critical to Quality (CTQ) characteristics, and not the characteristics of the whole unit.

2. **Methodology:**
   – **DMAIC** (Define-Measure-Analyze-Improve-Control) - structured problem solving roadmap and tools. This is an improvement system for existing processes falling below specification and looking for incremental improvement.
   – **DMADV** (Define-Measure-Analyze-Design-Verify) - data driven quality strategy for designing product and processes. This is an integral part of a Six Sigma Quality Initiative.

- **DFSS** (Design For Six Sigma). Unlike the DMAIC methodology, the phases or steps of DFSS are not universally recognized or defined — almost every company or training organization will define DFSS differently. A company might tailor to suit its business, industry and culture or it might implement the version of DFSS used by the consulting company assisting in its deployment. DFSS is more of an approach than a defined methodology.

Since DMAIC is the most universally used and most standard methodology, this chapter will only focus on that specific methodology.

3. **Philosophy:** reduce variation in the business and take customer-focused, data- driven decisions. The philosophy of Six Sigma is to use the framework not only for the process improvement projects, but also for the complete operation of the business. One of the companies that has used Six Sigma in this way is General Electric.

Six Sigma, as understood by many organizations, simply means a measure of quality that strives for near perfection. Six Sigma is a disciplined, data-driven approach and methodology for eliminating defects (driving towards six standard deviations between the mean and the nearest specification limit) in any process - from manufacturing to transactions and from product to service.

The statistical representation of Six Sigma describes quantitatively how a process is performing. To achieve Six Sigma, a process must not produce more than 3.4 defects per million opportunities.

A Six Sigma **defect** is defined as anything outside customer specifications. A Six Sigma **opportunity** is the total number of chances for a defect to occur. Process at Six Sigma level can easily be calculated using a Process Sigma calculator, which calculates the DPMO, the defects percentage, the Yield percentage and the process sigma after entering the number of opportunities and defects in a process. An example can be found at the Six Sigma website (www.isixsigma.com).

7.3.2 The DMAIC approach

The tools used are applied within a simple performance improvement framework known as DMAIC, which is an acronym for five interconnected phases: Define, Measure, Analyze, Improve and Control. This is analogous to the earlier TQM model known as plan-do-study-act.[2] Anyone with a little knowledge of Six Sigma is familiar with the DMAIC cycle (see Figure 7.1).

DMAIC is almost universally used to guide Six Sigma process improvement projects. Radical improvement in quality requires transformation the management philosophy and organizational culture. Projects are the means through which processes are systematically changed; they are the bridge between planning and implementation. However, DMAIC is not a method of planning projects, but a grouping (group) to optimize tooling for Six Sigma projects.

---

2 Walter Shewhart invented this 'Learning and Improvement cycle'. It was refined by W. Edwards Deming, who turned it into a Plan-Do-Check-Act (PDCA)- or Plan-Do-Study-Act (PDSA)-cycle. In the latter case, the results are studied instead of checked. *The Deming management method* by M. Walton and W.E. Deming (New York 1986).
Statistical Method from the Viewpoint of Quality Control by W.A Shewhart (Washington DC 1939)

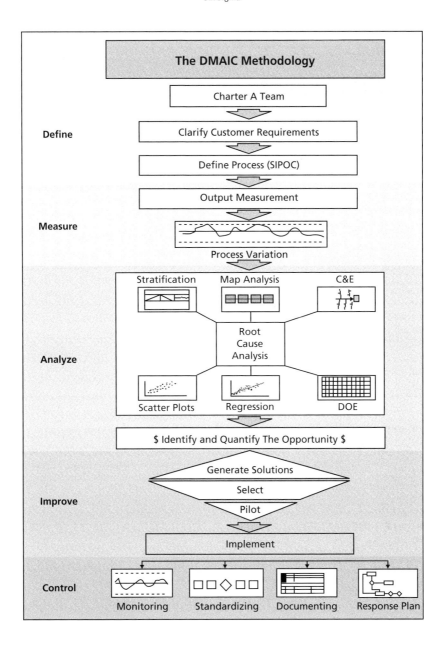

Figure 7.1 The DMAIC framework

7.4 Approach/how to

DMAIC refers to a data-driven quality strategy for improving processes, and is an integral part of a Six Sigma Quality Initiative. Figure 7.2 shows the DMAIC project cycle with questions that should be addressed in any Six Sigma operation and/or project.

The Six Sigma Project DMAIC Cycle

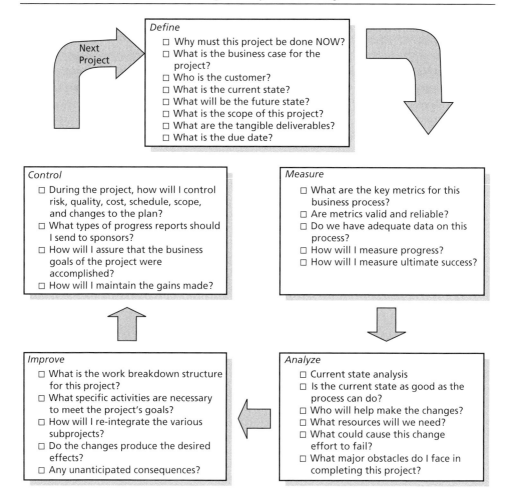

Figure 7.2 The Six Sigma Project DMAIC Cycle

7.4.1 DMAIC steps in helicopter view

Each step in the cyclical DMAIC Process is required to ensure the best possible results. The process steps are:

- *Define* the Customer, their Critical to Quality (CTQ) issues, and the core business process involved:
  - define who the customers are, their requirements for products and services, and their expectations
  - define project boundaries: the start and end of the process
  - define the process to be improved by mapping the process flow
- *Measure* the performance of the core business process involved:
  - develop a data collection plan for the process
  - collect data from many sources to determine types of defects and metrics
  - compare to customer survey results to determine shortfall

- *Analyze* the data collected and process map to determine root causes of defects and opportunities for improvement:
  - identify gaps between current performance and goal performance
  - prioritize opportunities to improve
  - identify sources of variation
- *Improve* the target process by designing creative solutions to fix and prevent problems:
  - create innovate solutions using technology and discipline
  - develop and deploy implementation plan
- *Control* the improvements to keep the process on the new course:
  - prevent reverting back to the old way
  - require the development, documentation and implementation of an ongoing monitoring plan
  - institutionalize the improvements through the modification of systems and structures (staffing, training, incentives).

7.4.2 Six Sigma quality tools and templates overview

Six Sigma has gathered many quality improvement tools beneath one umbrella; this is one of its significant strengths. Below is a list of tools that are widely used with the Six Sigma methodology. This list is not exhaustive, but gives an overview of the most powerful tools:[3]

- Affinity Diagram
- brainstorming
- calculators
- Cause and Effect/Ishikawa/Fishbone
- charters
- Control Charts
- contract management software
- Creativity/Out-of-the-Box Thinking
- Design Of Experiment
- Document Control
- Flow Chart/Flow Charting
- FMEA/risk assessment
- histogram
- Kano analysis
- Organizing Data
- Online Statistics Textbooks
- Pareto
- Poka Yoke (Mistake Proofing)
- Process Map/Process Mapping
- Project Charters
- Quality Function Deployment/House of Quality
- Scatter Diagram/Plot
- SIPOC Diagram
- Six Sigma Report Templates

---

3 A complete list is described in Implementing Six Sigma, written by Forrest Breyfogle. (2003).

- Software
- Support and Restraint
- surveys
- Taguchi diagram.

7.5 Relevance to IT management

Six Sigma is a method that can be used to deliver tooling to optimize IT management. In this context Six Sigma is not used as a philosophy, but as a tool kit to solve IT management issues.

In IT management, many issues have a cause and effect relationship. Six Sigma can help with optimizing areas important to IT management, such as problem management, change management (for software) and software testing. To illustrate what Six Sigma can mean for IT management, some examples are provided below.

7.5.1 Problem management – structured root cause analysis

Six Sigma can be used to detect the root cause of repeatable problems and optimize problem management by making sure that all the problems occurring are new and unique instead of repeatable problems.

7.5.2 Software change management

The purpose of change management in software is to guarantee the security of the operational software and/or platform by managing the implementation of new and/or changed code.

It is important to define a clear relationship between the changed and/or added code and the running code and to make sure that this list of relationships is exhaustive. This makes it easier and faster to identify the impact; this way of working helps an organization to be more flexible and faster.

With the help of some of the Six Sigma tools such as the Taguchi diagram a change manager can see the real impact of software, it can also help developers at an early stage with the process of delivering high quality software.
Six Sigma is used as a toolbox from which a change manager can select tools for the specific task of doing change management.

7.5.3 Software test – managing the tension between time and quality

Software testing is one of the most challenging parts of the development cycle. It is always under time pressure and the testers always need to make choices. Testing everything would take too long and testing a selection brings great risks. A tester has to deal daily with this tension.

Six Sigma helps to manage this tension by delivering a structure and the tools to transfer intuition to facts. Testers can identify relationships and see the impact on specific code areas; they can use the root cause analysis tools to identify the most impact and the areas of highest risk. With the help of these tools a tester can make an 80/20 analysis: which 20 per cent of the configuration is responsible for 80 per cent of the issues. This leads to a highly efficient and rapid way of testing; the tension of time pressure and quality can be managed better.

7.6   Strengths and weaknesses

When someone has a hammer, he sees everything as a nail

This is the most important concern with Six Sigma. It is a rigorous improvement method or philosophy, which is fast to implement, has a high success rate due to the structure of the methodology and consists of one language worldwide. However, Six Sigma is not a one-size-fits-all methodology. It is best used when a process has the following characteristics: high volume process and/or high risk process, large data sets available and/or measurable and repeatable process (non-innovative processes).

Table 7.2 shows some of the benefits and concerns that can be used to identify candidate Six Sigma projects.

Benefit	Concern
Secure	Only reliable for repeatable processes
Rigorous and structured method	High volumes needed
A statistical approach instead of intuition (fact based approach)	Process data needed for Six Sigma analysis
Trained and internationally recognized resources with appropriate skills	Extensive training needed for correct usage
Fast to implement	Statistical knowledge and/or affinity needed

Table 7.2 Benefits and concerns of using Six Sigma

Six Sigma can be used in many situations, but not always in the same way. Although Six Sigma can be used as a thinking framework and a toolbox in almost every situation, use of the complete Six Sigma cycle should be carefully considered and examined. Before an organization decides to start using Six Sigma as a philosophy it should really understand the impact of implementation on the organization and the resources required, as these are substantial.

In conclusion, Six Sigma can benefit an organization, if used in the right way and for the right purpose. Its toolbox should be used in a structured way like DMAIC; then its benefits should outweigh the concerns.

7.7   Cross-references/relationships

Six Sigma can be linked to many methodologies for process improvement. The links to TQM, CMMI (Capability Maturity Model) and SCOR (Supply-Chain Operations Reference-model (SCOR) are described in this section.

Six Sigma is linked with the TQM methodology. Most of the TQM tooling has been incorporated within the Six Sigma methodology. Most of the 400 TQM tools, have been reviewed by Six Sigma and about a hundred tools have been adopted.

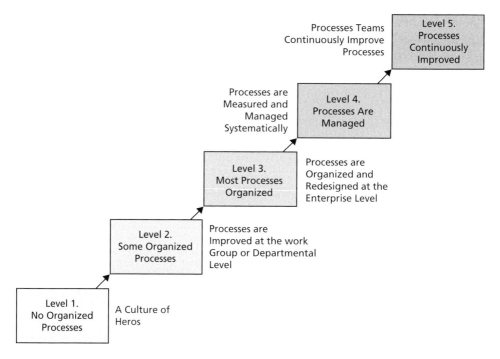

Figure 7.3 SEI's CMMI model of the steps in an organization's growth in process maturity

Looking at CMMI, the Software Engineering Institute (SEI) considers that most organizations go through a development process that includes five levels of maturity. (Figure 7.4).

Most organizations are somewhere between Level 2 and Level 3. That is, they are somewhere between defining and redesigning individual processes and assembling a process architecture that defines how all the organization's major processes work together to generate value.

There are some differences between Six Sigma's DMAIC and the Supply Chain Council's SCOR methodology. DMAIC focuses on a single, narrowly defined process - usually a sub-process or part of it. The team measures the process and proceeds to focus on improving the quality of the output of the process. There is little focus on how this process fits within the larger context of the organization's value chains, or how the process is managed or measured by senior management.

The SCOR methodology begins by defining the organization's entire supply chain. Once the organization's supply chain is defined, measures and benchmarks are applied to determine which specific processes within the supply chain would yield the greatest performance improvement for the organization as a whole.

This makes the SCOR model a top-down approach to reach for Level 3-4: from the complete supply-chain it focuses on a specific process. Six Sigma is better used bottom-up to achieve CMM level 2: it starts with a focus on a specific process and has little focus on how this process fits within the larger context of the organization's value chains. DMAIC is very much a Level 2, bottom-up approach, while SCOR is a Level 3-4 top-down approach.

IT management frameworks such as ITIL categorize IT's activities into processes, but mostly lack tangible quality measures and improvement techniques. Six Sigma is complementary to those IT management frameworks. For example, Six Sigma provides an excellently structured root cause analysis that can help ITIL's Problem Management in finding the root causes of problems.

7.8 Links and literature

7.8.1 Books
- Boer, Sven den, et. al., "Six Sigma for IT management" (Van Haren Publishing 2006).
- Breyfogle III, Forrest W., "Implementing Six Sigma – Smarter Solutions Using Statistical Methods", Second Edition (Wiley, New Jersey 2003). The bible for Six Sigma experts.
- Brue, Greg, "Six Sigma For Managers" (McGraw-Hill 2005).
- Brussee, Warren, "Statistics for Six Sigma Made Easy" (McGraw-Hill 2004).
- Chen, Chris and Hadley M. Roth, "The Big Book of Six Sigma Training Games: Proven Ways to Teach Basic DMAIC Principles and Quality Improvement Tools" (McGraw-Hill 2004).
- Chowdhury, Subir, "Power of Six "Sigma (Kaplan Business 2001).
- George, Michael L., "Lean Six Sigma for Service : How to Use Lean Speed and Six Sigma Quality to Improve Services and Transactions" (McGraw-Hill 2003).
- George, Michael L., David Rowlands and Bill Kastle, "What is Lean Six Sigma" (McGraw-Hill 2003).
- George, Michael L., "Lean Six Sigma : Combining Six Sigma Quality with Lean Production Speed", (McGraw-Hill 2003).
- Harry, Mikel and Richard Schroeder, "Six "Sigma (Campus Fachbuch 2000).
- Keller, Paul A., "Six Sigma Demystified : A Self-Teaching Guide (Demystified)" (McGraw-Hill 2004)
- Pande, Peter S. et. al., Robert P. Neuman Roland R. Cavanagh, "The Six Sigma Way: How GE, Motorola, and Other Top Companies are Honing Their Performance" (McGraw-Hill 2000).
- Pande, Peter S., Robert P. Neuman and Roland R. Cavanagh, "The Six Sigma Way Team Fieldbook: An Implementation Guide for Process Improvement Teams" (McGraw-Hill 2001).
- Pyzdek, Thomas, "The Six Sigma Handbook: The Complete Guide for Greenbelts, Blackbelts, and Managers at All Levels, Revised and Expanded Edition", 2nd revised edition (McGraw-Hill 2003).
- Pyzdek, Thomas, "The Six Sigma Project Planner : A Step-by-Step Guide to Leading a Six Sigma Project Through DMAIC" (McGraw-Hill 2003).
- Sheehy, Paul et. al., "The Black Belt Memory Jogger: A Pocket Guide for Six Sigma Success" (Goal/QPC 2002).

7.8.2 Websites
- **www.BPtrends.com** - a BPM knowledge database, source for the links to other methodologies.
- **www.isixsigma.com** - a Six Sigma knowledge database website.

8 eSCM-SP v2: eSourcing Capability Model for Service Providers, Version 2

The eSourcing Capability Model for Service Providers, Version 2 – eSCM-SP v2 or SCM-SP – is a best practice framework that providers of IT-enabled services can use to develop and improve their ability to consistently deliver high-quality services while minimizing costs and risks to their customers. The framework consists of a reference model, capability determination methods, and a certification scheme.

Owner of the copyright:	Carnegie Mellon University, through its IT Services Qualification Center (ITSqc): www.itsqc.cmu.edu
Distribution:	The consortium actively supporting ITSqc's work now has fourteen members, and the number is growing. Over twenty pilots have been performed. The eSCM SP is available on the ITSqc website for any service provider to use for internal process improvement.
Origin/history:	It was developed by a research consortium led by the IT Services Qualification Center (ITSqc) at Carnegie Mellon University [Hyder 2004a, Hyder 2004b].
When:	First version released 2001. Current Version 2 released in 2004.
Participants in the committee:	Members of research consortium. See ITSqc website for details: www.itsqc.cmu.edu
Certification bodies?	Carnegie Mellon University.
Number of certified organizations:	Six official certifications are listed on the ITSqc web site. Numerous self-appraisals have been done in the USA, Europe, Asia, and South America.

By Mark C. Paulk and Majid Iqbal

8.1 Origin/history

The need for a capability model such as eSCM-SP was first established in 2000 during a time which sourcing was emerging as a key strategy for organizations worldwide. However, as with any new idea, sourcing successes were accompanied by a large number of failures.

A knowledge gap between the vision of successful sourcing and its realization through effective implementation and practice existed, because there was no neutral, non-proprietary, and rigorous basis for evaluating the sourcing capabilities of the providers of IT-enabled services. Such evaluations were desired not only by the customers of service providers, but also the management of service providers themselves when making strategic decisions about their business. The leadership at Carnegie Mellon University accepted the challenge of providing a framework for effectively reducing the risks from sourcing and increasing the benefits.

An industry consortium led by the *IT Services Qualification Center* (ITSqc) at Carnegie Mellon was established to develop a reference model and methods for evaluating the capabilities of service providers. The first version of the eSCM-SP was released in 2001. After integrating feedback from pilot implementations and consultations with industry leaders and practitioners, Version 1.1 was released a year later in 2002. After further feedback and piloting, the current Version 2 was released in April 2004.

Ownership for the ongoing development, distribution and maintenance of the eSCM-SP is held by ITSqc. All intellectual property related to the eSCM-SP is owned by Carnegie Mellon University which, as a non-profit academic institution, is committed to the mission of creating knowledge for the public domain. The technical reports describing the eSCM-SP and its use are freely available on the ITSqc website for use by the community. The consortium supporting this work, which has an open membership, advises ITSqc on how to appropriately address the needs of the community. The eSCM-SP has been endorsed or adopted for implementation by some of the leading providers of IT-enabled services.

The eSCM-SP is currently going through the adoption and growth phase in the product lifecycle. Extensive data is being collected by ITSqc for analysis that will lead to the formal validation and improvement of future versions of the model. The next major revision of the model is expected to start in 2008.

8.2   Where is eSCM-SP v2 used?

At the time of writing, the consortium actively supporting ITSqc's work has fourteen members, and the number is growing. Over twenty pilots have been performed, numerous self-appraisals have been done, and six certificates have been issued by Carnegie Mellon University. The eSCM-SP is available on the ITSqc website for any service provider to use for internal process improvement; official certifications are listed on the ITSqc web site. Appraisals have been carried out in the USA, Europe, Asia and South America.

The guidance provided in the eSCM-SP can be applied by providers of IT-enabled services in practically all market sectors and service areas with no particular restrictions. The usefulness and relevance of the guidance will vary depending on the critical issues for different markets and services. Within a given market sector and service area, the guidance of eSCM-SP can be applied in many types of sourcing arrangements. The types of sourcing relationships may determine the business objectives for both the customer and service provider, and ultimately the form of value expected. The types of sourcing relationships fall broadly into categories such as co-sourcing, multi-sourcing, alliances, joint ventures and in-sourcing.

The eSCM-SP is not limited to any particular level of management or control perspective, although parts may directly relate to particular roles and responsibilities. The applicability of the eSCM-SP is best described by the set of critical issues that it seeks to address [Hyder 2004a]. The original set of 23 critical issues can be summarized in six categories of items that are critical for success:

- good relationships between the service provider and the customer, the end users, suppliers, and all stakeholders
- selecting, hiring, and retaining a motivated workforce
- well defined and delivered services that satisfy commitments and meet customer needs
- managing common business threats, such as security issues, risk management, disaster recovery, and statutory and regulatory requirements
- providing world-class services that are always improving
- managing service transitions well at engagement, initiation and completion.

8.3   Description and core graphics

The eSCM-SP is expected to serve the following purposes:
- give service providers guidance that will help them improve their capability across the sourcing lifecycle
- provide customers with an objective means of evaluating the capability of service providers
- offer service providers a standard to use when differentiating themselves from competitors.

The eSCM-SP is a capability model that defines the sourcing capabilities that service providers should develop and improve in order to be viewed by their current and prospective customers as capable and reliable partners. The sourcing capabilities are defined in terms of best practices that contribute to successful sourcing. These best practices are grouped into Capability Areas and structured into Capability Levels that describe the organizational capability of the service provider. The long-term proposition of the eSCM-SP is that sourcing relationships can be systematically managed to be more effective in delivering value and more resilient to business risks resulting from changes in economic and social conditions. The eSCM-SP Capability Determination Methods offer service providers a comprehensive and flexible approach to demonstrating value to both internal and external stakeholders.

The structure and contents of the eSCM-SP v2 are based on extensive consultations with stakeholders in industry and government from across the world, academic research, and feedback from pilot implementations of an earlier version of the model. The eSCM-SP v2 is composed of 84 Practices that are considered useful and relevant to achieving success in sourcing relationships. Each Practice has coordinates in a space defined by three dimensions, as shown in Figure 8.1:
1. Sourcing Lifecycle
2. Capability Area
3. Capability Level.

Note that Capability Levels 1 and 5 are not defined in terms of implementing Practices in the figure; this is discussed later in this chapter.

In the first dimension, Sourcing Lifecycle, a Practice can be one of the following types, also shown in Figure 8.1:
- Ongoing
- Initiation
- Delivery
- Completion.

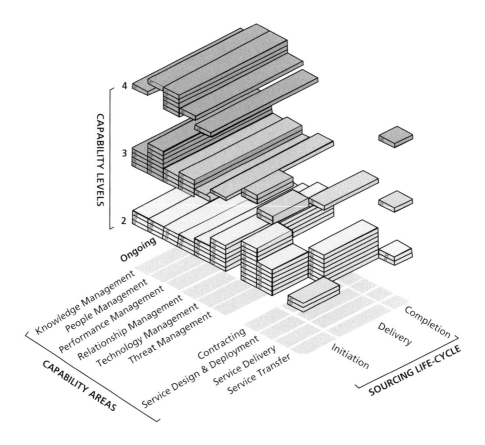

Figure 8.1 The structure of the eSCM-SP v2

Ongoing Practices are considered to be effective across the entire sourcing lifecycle. Practices belonging to the Initiation, Delivery, and Completion phases are effectively applied in the specific phases of that lifecycle. During the *Initiation* phase, negotiations take place between customers and service providers, leading to agreements on requirements, the design of services to be provided, and the deployment (transitions) of such services. Initiation may also include the transfer of ownership or control over critical assets such as personnel, technology infrastructure, and intellectual property. During the *Delivery* phase the service provider is expected to execute the ongoing delivery of services based on well-defined contracts and service level agreements. During *Completion* the service provider is expected to transfer the ownership or control of specific sets of resources, and the responsibility for service delivery, back to the customer, or to another organization specified by the customer.

The second dimension of the eSCM-SP is defined in terms of Capability Areas that are logical groupings of Practices to help users of the model better remember and intellectually manage its content. These groupings allow service providers to build or demonstrate capabilities in each critical sourcing function and map to the critical sourcing issues previously identified. The ten Capability Areas of eSCM-SP are:

- Knowledge Management (knw)
- People Management (ppl)
- Performance Management (prf)
- Relationship Management (rel)
- Technology Management (tch)
- Threat Management (thr)
- Contracting (cnt)
- Service Design and Deployment (sdd)
- Service Delivery (del)
- Service Transfer (tfr).

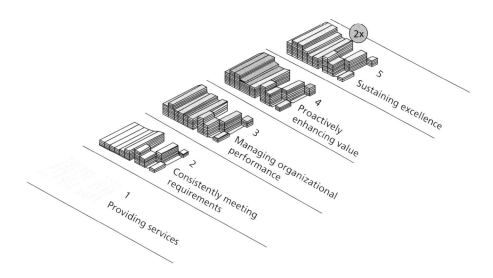

Figure 8.2 The Capability Levels

The third dimension of the eSCM-SP is defined in terms of Capability Levels (shown by Figure 8.2). The five Capability Levels of the eSCM-SP describe an improvement path that customers should expect service providers to follow.

- At *Capability Level 1, Providing services,* a service provider is able to provide services but has not implemented all of the Level 2 Practices, and may be at a higher risk of failure. As Figure 8.2 suggests, Capability Level 1 is not defined in terms of Practices implemented but rather in terms of failing to implement all of the Level 2 Practices.
- At *Capability Level 2, Consistently meeting requirements,* a service provider is able to consistently meet requirements and has implemented, at a minimum, all 48 of the Level 2 Practices.
- At *Capability Level 3, Managing organizational performance,* a service provider is able to deliver services according to stated requirements, even if the required services differ significantly from the provider's experience, and has, at a minimum, implemented all 74 of the Level 2 and 3 Practices.
- At *Capability Level 4, Proactively enhancing value,* a service provider is able to continuously

innovate to add statistically and practically significant value to the services it provides. To achieve Level 4 the service provider has successfully implemented all 84 of the eSCM-SP Practices.

- At *Capability Level 5, Sustaining excellence,* a service provider has demonstrated measurable, sustained, and consistent performance excellence and improvement by effectively implementing all of the Level 2, 3, and 4 Practices for two or more consecutive Certification Evaluations covering a period of at least two years. There are no additional Practices to be implemented at Level 5.

8.4 Approach/how to

8.4.1 Evaluating service provider capabilities

ITSqc provides four Capability Determination methods that service providers (and their customers) can use to determine the capability of the provider relative to the eSCM-SP. All four methods determine this capability by systematically analyzing evidence of the provider's implementation of the eSCM-SP v2 Practices. These methods allow providers to determine their current capabilities and to define targets for self-improvement.

Applying any of these methods results in a report, which includes the service provider's strengths, its opportunities for improvement, and the status of its improvement efforts relative to the eSCM-SP. This information can support, guide, and encourage a service provider's commitment to continuous self-improvement.

The methods also provide a consistent way for customers to evaluate their current service providers or to compare multiple potential providers. Information from a capability determination may be used to assess risks and provide decision inputs for a customer when it is selecting a service provider.

The four Capability Determination methods that are available from ITSqc are:
- full evaluation
- full self-appraisal
- mini evaluation
- mini self-appraisal.

Capability Determinations are usually conducted for a single service provider and will include in their scope any critical pieces of the sourced service that may be under the control of third-parties such as suppliers and partners. The time and effort required to conduct a Capability Determination varies greatly depending on the size and organizational span of the service provider to be evaluated, the model scope, and the size of the determination team.

8.4.2 Certification

The eSCM-SP certification program represents an independent and credible means to determine compliance of a service provider with the eSCM-SP. Certification can be used by customers to evaluate potential service providers, and by service providers to differentiate themselves from their competitors. Evaluations may only be performed by Lead Evaluators and Evaluators from

		Evaluation	Self-appraisal
Full	**Purpose**	For certification	To prepare for a Full Evaluation or launch or validate an improvement effort. No certification.
	Team	External, trained and authorized by Carnegie Mellon University	Internal, external, or combination
	Lead evaluator	Required	Strongly recommended
	Sponsor	Customer or service provider	Service provider
	Model scope	All eSCM-SP Practices	All eSCM-SP Practices
Mini	**Purpose**	To prepare for a Full Evaluation or as part of a provider selection process. No certification.	To launch or validate an improvement effort. No certification.
	Team	External, trained and authorized by Carnegie Mellon University	Internal, external, or combination
	Lead evaluator	Required	Recommended
	Sponsor	Customer or service provider	Service provider
	Model scope	Subset of eSCM-SP Practices	Subset of eSCM-SP Practices

Table 8.2 Capability Determination methods

ITSqc-authorized organizations while adhering to a Code of Professional Practice. A Certification Board composed of senior ITSqc professionals conducts a rigorous review of all Full Evaluation plans and results before deciding on a certification.

Certificates last for at most two years. Certificates may be revoked or suspended before they expire for a number of reasons. Major changes in the service provider's ownership, staffing, or processes may trigger some form of confirmation by ITSqc to verify the provider's continued eSCM-SP compliance.

The certificate provides proof of the service provider's compliance with the eSCM-SP at a particular Capability Level. It also contains important information about the boundaries of the certification, including who is certified and what is the organizational span of the certification. It also lists any qualifications on the Practice Ratings.

At the time of writing, six certificates have been issued in South Korea and India. The ITSqc web site (itsqc.cs.cmu.edu) contains the official list of the certified service providers, and the authorized Evaluators, Lead Evaluators, and Authorized Organizations that provide Capability Determination services.

8.5 Relevance to IT management

By definition, the eSCM-SP focuses on the work of service providers of IT-enabled services, where IT is a key component of service delivery or an enabler for delivering services. These services are often provided remotely, using telecommunication or data networks. They range from routine and non-critical tasks that are resource-intensive and operational in nature to strategic processes that directly affect revenues. The eSCM-SP will be useful to service organizations seeking to evaluate, develop and improve their capabilities in the design, deployment, and delivery of

IT-enabled services as well as helping them manage risks associated with sourcing contracts during the initiation and completion phases. Due to its focus on sourcing contracts, phases, relationships, and operations, the eSCM-SP chooses to emphasize certain challenges and issues that, while faced by most organizations, are particularly critical for organizations that are engaged in the sourcing and provision of IT-enabled services.

8.6   Strengths and weaknesses

Unlike most other best practice frameworks, the eSCM-SP covers the lifecycle of service provision from initiation to completion of a relationship. It addresses enterprise-level issues that are crucial for business success, yet outside the scope of more focused frameworks.

The long-term benefit expected from the use of the model is to make sourcing relationships durable and beneficial for all parties involved as the result of greater effectiveness and efficiency in providing services. Success of the sourcing relationship depends on both sides of the customer-supplier relationship performing effectively. The eSCM-SP addresses best practices for the supplier side; a partner model, the eSourcing Capability Model for Client Organizations, addresses the customer side of the relationship.

As is true of all best practice frameworks, the eSCM-SP captures those practices that are generally held to provide a significant return on investment for the service provider. The Practices in the model are described at an abstract level so as not to constrain the implementation for different markets and services. However, as a consequence, the service provider must choose an appropriate implementation for its business environment. Guidance for implementing the Practices in a particular environment may come from more focused frameworks such as ITIL or from selection of specific methodologies and tool suites.

It is expected that the eSCM-SP will be improved as a result of feedback from its use. New releases of the model are expected on roughly a five-year cycle, depending on the feedback received from pilots, certifications, service providers and customers. Since the model has already undergone a fairly comprehensive set of pilots and reviews during its development, the degree of change to address the objectives of the model are anticipated to be relatively minor.

8.7   Cross-references/relationships

The eSCM-SP is a best practice framework that is gaining world-wide adoption, which is expected to lead to the status of a *de facto* standard. Based on detailed comparisons of the eSCM-SP with a variety of other frameworks, there are no known conflicts with other commonly used process improvement and quality management frameworks. Many service providers use multiple frameworks, and the synergy with previous work can accelerate implementation of the model. There may be many reasons for adopting a multiple improvement framework, such as aptness for a particular kind of work done by the organization, customer requirements, and market expectations.

A variety of comparisons of the eSCM-SP to related frameworks have been published:

- ISO 9001 (Quality management systems) [Guha 2005a]
- BS 15000/ISO 20000/ITIL (IT service management) [Iqbal 2004]
- Control Objectives for Information and related Technology (CoBiT) [Iqbal 2005]
- Capability Maturity Model for Software (Software CMM) [Paulk 2005a]
- Capability Maturity Model Integration (CMMI) [Paulk 2005b]
- COPC (Customer operations performance center) [Guha 2005b].

These comparisons are in both directions. Service providers may wish to leverage existing investments in other frameworks when implementing the eSCM-SP and vice versa.

Other comparisons are under development, such as for ISO/IEC 17799 (Information security management). The eSCM-SP has emerged as a framework that can be used to align and integrate (for the purpose of successful sourcing) the guidance from several other frameworks. Organizations that have implemented other frameworks can leverage their investment in those frameworks towards implementing the eSCM-SP.

8.8   Links and literature

Information on the eSCM-SP and related work by ITSqc is freely available on the ITSqc website. Working drafts are made available for public review on the website as appropriate. ITSqc provides training courses and workshops that are open to the public, as well as events that support the needs of the consortium members.

8.8.1 Links

The website of ITSqc at Carnegie Mellon University is:
www.itsqc.cmu.edu

ITSqc technical reports are available at:
www.itsqc.cmu.edu/downloads

8.8.2 References

[Guha 2005a]   S. Guha, W.E. Hefley, E.B. Hyder, M. Iqbal, and M.C. Paulk, "Comparing the eSCM-SP v2 and ISO 9001:2000: A comparison between the eSourcing Capability Model for Service Providers v2 and ISO 9001:2000 (Quality Management Systems-Requirements)," Carnegie Mellon University, IT Services Qualification Center, CMU-ITSQC-05-001, March 2005,

[Guha 2005b]   S. Guha, W.E. Hefley, E.B. Hyder, M. Iqbal, and M.C. Paulk, "Comparing the eSCM-SP v2 and COPC-2000 CSP Gold Standard: A comparison between the eSourcing Capability Model for Service Providers v2 and Customer Operations Performance Center (COPC)-2000 CSP Gold Standard, Release 3.4," Carnegie Mellon University, IT Services Qualification Center, CMU-ITSQC-05-003, June 2005.

[Hyder 2004a] E.B. Hyder, K.M. Heston, and M.C. Paulk, "The eSourcing Capability Model for Service Providers v2: Model Overview," Carnegie Mellon University, Institute for Software Research International, CMU-ISRI -04-113, April 2004.

[Hyder 2004b] E.B. Hyder, K.M. Heston, and M.C. Paulk, "The eSourcing Capability Model for Service Providers v2: Practice Details," Carnegie Mellon University, Institute for Software Research International, CMU-ISRI -04-114, April 2004.

[Iqbal 2004] M. Iqbal, J. Dugmore, S. Guha, W.E. Hefley, E.B. Hyder, and M.C. Paulk, "Comparing the eSCM-SP v2 and BS 15000: A Comparison Between the eSourcing Capability Model for Service Providers v2 and BS 15000-1: 2002 (IT Service Management)," Carnegie Mellon University, Institute for Software Research International, CMU-ISRI-04-129b, October 2004.

[Iqbal 2005] M. Iqbal, S. Guha, W.E. Hefley, E.B. Hyder, and M.C. Paulk, "Comparing the eSCM-SP v2 and CoBiT: A Comparison Between the eSourcing Capability Model for Service Providers v2 and Control Objectives for Information and Related Technology, 3rd Edition," Carnegie Mellon University, IT Services Qualification Center, CMU-ITSQC-05-004, December 2005.

[Paulk 2005a] M.C. Paulk, S. Guha, W.E. Hefley, E.B. Hyder, and M. Iqbal, "Comparing the eSCM-SP v2 and Software CMM v1.1: A comparison between the eSourcing Capability Model for Service Providers v2 and the Capability Maturity Model for Software," Carnegie Mellon University, IT Services Qualification Center, CMU-ITSQC-05-002, August 2005.

[Paulk 2005b] M.C. Paulk, S. Guha, W.E. Hefley, E.B. Hyder, and M. Iqbal, "Comparing the eSCM-SP and CMMI: A comparison between the eSourcing Capability Model for Service Providers v2 and the Capability Maturity Model Integration v1.1," Carnegie Mellon University, IT Services Qualification Center, CMU-ITSQC-05-005, December 2005.

9 IT Balanced Scorecard

> *The IT Balanced Scorecard is an instrument that can be leveraged to measure and manage IT performance and to enable alignment between the business and IT.*

Owner of the copyright:	Copyrights of publications on IT Balanced Scorecard are with the authors of the publications.
Distribution:	The IT Balanced Scorecard is becoming a popular tool with its concepts widely supported and disseminated by international consultant groups such as Gartner, IDC and others. Recent research by ITGI on *Measuring and demonstrating the value of IT* in 2005 in fourteen countries in the Americas, Asia-Pacific and Europe, demonstrated that about thirty per cent of IT managers use the IT Balanced Scorecard as an instrument to measure and manage the performance of IT investments, projects and departments.
Origin/history:	The Balanced Scorecard was developed in the early 1990s by Kaplan and Norton at enterprise level. The Balanced Scorecard can also be applied to the IT function and its processes, as was conceptually described by researchers such as Gold and Willcocks. This has been further developed and described by authors such as Van Grembergen and De Haes.
When:	Late 1990s, first decade of the second millennium.

By Wim Van Grembergen and Steven De Haes

9.1 Origin/history

The Balanced Scorecard (BSC) was developed in the early 1990s at enterprise level by Kaplan and Norton at enterprise level. Many organizations have built on the concepts promoted by Kaplan and Norton to create organization-specific business Balanced Scorecards. Many researchers and practitioners also leveraged the Balanced Scorecard concepts to create a measurement instrument in other domains, such as for corporate governance and human resources. The Balanced Scorecard can also be applied to the IT function and its processes. This was conceptually described by researchers such as Gold and Willcocks and has been further developed and described by authors such as Van Grembergen and De Haes.

9.2 Where is the IT Balanced Scorecard used?

The Balanced Scorecard is a performance management system that enables businesses to drive strategies based on measurement and follow-up. It was initially developed at enterprise level by Kaplan and Norton. The Balanced Scorecard can, however, easily be applied to information technology (IT) investments, projects or departments as an IT performance management and alignment instrument.

The IT Balanced Scorecard is becoming a popular tool with its concepts widely supported and disseminated by international consultant groups such as Gartner, IDC and others. As a result of this interest, many real-life applications have been developed and are supported by software tools. Recent research by the IT Governance Institute (www.itgi.org) on *Measuring and demonstrating the value of IT* in 2005 in fourteen countries in the Americas, Asia-Pacific and Europe, demonstrated that about thirty per cent of IT managers use the IT Balanced Scorecard as an instrument to measure and manage the performance of their IT investments, projects and departments (see Figure 9.1 and 9.2).

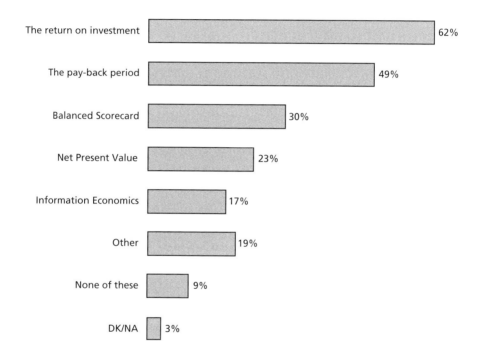

Figure 9.1 Use of performance measurement techniques for IT projects and investments (*Van Grembergen W., De Haes S., "Measuring and demonstrating the value of IT", in IT Governance Domain Practices and Competencies (series of IT Governance Institute), 2005.*)

9.3 Description and core graphics

In the early 1990s, Kaplan and Norton introduced the Balanced Scorecard at enterprise level. Their fundamental premise is that the evaluation of an organization should not be restricted to a traditional financial evaluation but should be supplemented with objectives and measures concerning customer satisfaction, internal processes and the ability to innovate. Results achieved within these additional perspective areas should assure future financial results and drive the organization towards its strategic goals while keeping all four perspectives in balance.

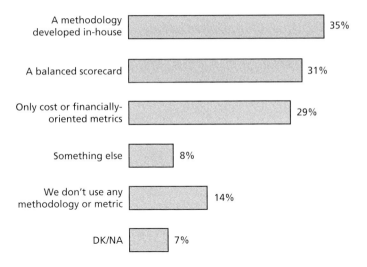

A methodology developed in-house — 35%

A balanced scorecard — 31%

Only cost or financially-oriented metrics — 29%

Something else — 8%

We don't use any methodology or metric — 14%

DK/NA — 7%

Figure 9.2 Measurement techniques for the IT department (*Van Grembergen W., De Haes S., "Measuring and demonstrating the value of IT", in IT Governance Domain Practices and Competencies (series of IT Governance Institute), 2005.*

For each of the four perspectives of the business Balanced Scorecard, Kaplan and Norton propose a three layered structure, as shown in Figure 9.3:
1. mission (for example to become the customer's preferred supplier)
2. objectives (for example to provide the customers with new products)
3. measures (for example the percentage of turnover generated by new products).

The Balanced Scorecard can be applied to the IT function, its processes and projects. To achieve that, the focus of the four perspectives of the business Balanced Scorecard need to be translated, as shown in table 9.1. The *User Orientation* perspective represents the user (internal or external) evaluation of IT. The *Operational Excellence* perspective represents the IT processes employed to develop and deliver the applications. The *Future Orientation* perspective represents the human and technology resources needed by IT to deliver its services over time. The *Corporate Contribution* perspective captures the business value created from the IT investments.

Again, each of these perspectives has to be translated into corresponding goals and metrics that assess the current situation. These assessments need to be repeated periodically and aligned with pre-established goals and benchmarks. Example metrics for the four perspectives are[4]:

*   **corporate contribution:**
    *   *control of IT expenses*
        *   percentage over or under IT budget
        *   allocation to different budget items
        *   IT budget as a percentage of turnover

4 Van Grembergen, W. "The Balanced Scorecard and IT governance", Information Systems Control Journal, Volume 2, 2000, pp.40-43.

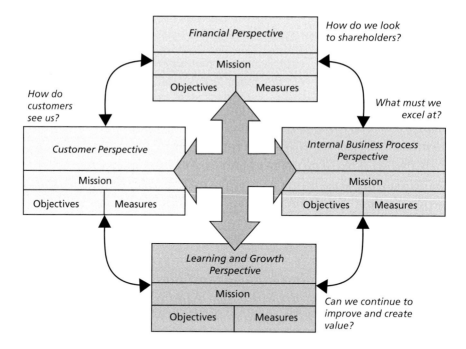

Figure 9.3 Generic business Balanced Scorecard (*Kaplan, R. and Norton, D. "The Balanced Scorecard – measures that drive performance", Harvard Business Review, January-February 1992, pp. 71-79.*)

USER ORIENTATION How do the users view the IT department?	CORPORATE CONTRIBUTION How does management view the IT department?
Mission To be the preferred supplier of information systems	**Mission** To obtain a reasonable corporate contribution to IT investments
Objectives • Preferred IT supplier • Partnership with users • User satisfaction	**Objectives** • Control of IT expenses • Business value of the IT function • Business value of new IT projects
OPERATIONAL EXCELLENCE How effective and efficient are the IT processes?	FUTURE ORIENTATION How well is IT positioned to answer future challenges?
Mission To deliver effective and efficient IT applications and services	**Mission** To develop opportunities to answer future challenges
Objectives • Efficient software development • Efficient computer operations • Efficient help desk function	**Objectives** • Training and education of IT staff • Expertise of IT staff • Research into emerging information technologies

Table 9.1 Generic IT Balanced Scorecard (*Van Grembergen, W. "The Balanced Scorecard and IT governance", Information Systems Control Journal (previously IS Audit and Control Journal), Volume 2, 2000, pp.40-43.*)

- IT expenses per staff member
– *business value of the IT function*
  - percentage of the development capacity engaged in strategic projects
  - relationship between new developments/infrastructure investments/replacement investments
– *business value of new it projects*
  - financial evaluation based on ROI, NPV, IRR, PB
  - business evaluation based on Information Economics
- **user orientation:**
  – *preferred IT supplier*
    - percentage of applications managed by IT
    - percentage of applications delivered by IT
  – *partnership with users*
    - index of user involvement in generating strategic applications
    - index of user involvement in developing new applications
  – *user satisfaction*
    - index of user friendliness of applications
    - index of user satisfaction
- **operational excellence:**
  - *efficient software development*
  - average days late in delivering software
  - average unexpected budget increase
  - percentage of projects performed within SLA
  - percentage of maintenance activities
  – *efficient computer operations*
    - percentage unavailability of network
    - response times per category of users
    - percentage of jobs done within time
  – *efficient help desk function*
    - average answer time of help desk
    - percentage of questions answered within time
- **future orientation:**
  – *training and education of staff*
    - number of educational days per person
    - education budget as a percentage of total IT budget
  – *expertise of the IT staff*
    - number of years of IT experience per staff member
    - age pyramid of the IT staff
  – *research into emerging technologies*
    - percentage of budget spent on IT research.

To leverage the IT Balanced Scorecard as a management and alignment instrument, it should be enhanced with cause-and-effect relationships between measures. These relationships are articulated by two types of measures: outcome measures (lag indicators) and performance drivers (lead indicators). A well developed scorecard should contain a good mix of these two metrics. Outcome measures without performance drivers do not communicate how they are to be achieved. And performance drivers without outcome measures may lead to significant investment without a measurement indicating whether the chosen strategy is effective.

A good example of a cause-and-effect relationship, defined throughout the whole scorecard is illustrated in Figure 9.4: more and better education of IT staff (future perspective) is an enabler (performance driver) for a better quality of developed systems (operational excellence perspective). This in turn is an enabler for increased user satisfaction (user perspective), which eventually must lead to a higher business value of IT (corporate contribution perspective). This implies that an outcome measure in a specific perspective becomes a performance driver for a higher perspective. For example: average answer time of the help desk is an outcome measure in the operational excellence perspective, but is at the same time a performance driver for elements in the user perspective such as index of user satisfaction (a lower average answer time of the help desk will lead to higher user satisfaction).

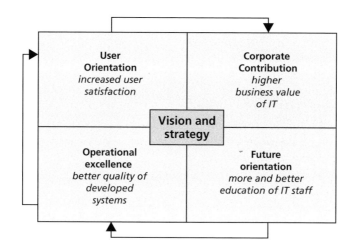

Figure 9.4 Cause-and-effect relationships within the IT Balanced Scorecard (*Van Grembergen W., Saull R., De Haes S., "Linking the IT Balanced Scorecard to the Business Objectives at a major Canadian Financial group", Journal for Information Technology Cases and Applications (JITCA), vol. 5, no. 1, 2003.*)

The proposed IT Balanced Scorecard links with the business, mainly through the Corporate Contribution perspective. The relationship between IT and business can be more explicitly expressed through a cascade of scorecards. In Figure 9.5 the relationship between IT scorecards and the business scorecard is illustrated. The IT Development Balanced Scorecard and the IT Operational Balanced Scorecard both are enablers of the IT Strategic Balanced Scorecard that in turn is the enabler of the Business Balanced Scorecard. This cascade of scorecards becomes a linked set of measures that will be instrumental in aligning IT and business strategy and that will help to determine how business value is created through IT.

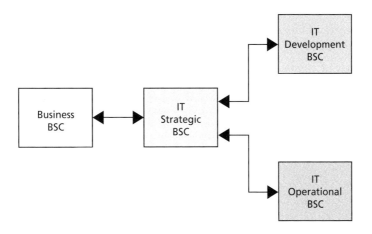

Figure 9.5 Cascade of Balanced Scorecards *(Van Grembergen W., Saull R., De Haes S., "Linking the IT Balanced Scorecard to the Business Objectives at a major Canadian Financial group", Journal for Information Technology Cases and Applications (JITCA), vol. 5, no. 1, 2003.)*

9.4 Approach/how to

Implementing an IT Balanced Scorecard requires, as is the case with many methodologies, support from senior management. A generic high-level roadmap to introduce the Balanced Scorecard consists of four steps:
- presentation of the concept to senior and it management
- establishing a project team
- data-gathering phase where information is collected on:
  - corporate and IT strategy
  - IT metrics already in use for performance measurement
- developing the organization-specific IT Balanced Scorecard.

The CIO of a large Canadian financial organization summarized the following lessons learned after his IT Balanced Scorecard implementation project:
- start small with only key objectives and measures
- consider the scorecard technique as a supportive mechanism for IT/business alignment and IT governance
- consider the construction and implementation of an IT Balanced Scorecard as an evolutionary project
- provide a formal project organization
- provide best IT practices supporting the IT Balanced Scorecard
- regularly revisit the dynamic measures
- focus first on the establishment of appropriate objectives and measures and after that on automation via tools and software.

To drive the development of the IT Balanced Scorecard, it could be leveraged as a maturity model. This enables the organization to identify the as-is and to-be situation of the IT Balanced Scorecard in its organization, to analyze the gaps between as-is and to-be and to translate those gaps into pragmatic improvement projects. The maturity model for IT Balanced Scorecard implementation contains the following five levels[5].

- **Level 1 - Initial:** There is evidence that the organization has recognized a need for a *measurement system* for its IT division. There are ad hoc approaches to measure IT with respect to the two main IT processes, for example operations and systems development. This measurement process is often an individual effort in response to specific issues.

- **Level 2 - Repeatable:** Management is aware of the concept of the *IT Balanced Scorecard* and has communicated its intent to define appropriate measures. Measures are collected and presented to management in a scorecard. Linkages between outcome measures and performance drivers are generally defined but are not yet precise, documented or integrated into strategic and operational planning processes. Processes for scorecard training and review are informal and there is no compliance process in place.

- **Level 3 - Defined:** Management has standardized, documented and communicated the IT Balanced Scorecard through formal training. The scorecard process has been structured and *linked to the business planning cycle*. The need for compliance has been communicated but compliance is inconsistent. Management understands and accepts the need to integrate the IT Balanced Scorecard within the alignment process of business and IT. Efforts are underway to change the alignment process accordingly.

- **Level 4 - Managed:** The IT Balanced Scorecard is fully integrated into strategic and operational planning and review systems of the business and IT. Linkages between outcome measures and performance drivers are systematically reviewed and revised based upon the analysis of results. There is a full understanding of the issues at all levels of the organization, which is supported by formal training. Long term stretch targets and priorities for IT investment projects are set and linked to the IT scorecard. A business scorecard and *a cascade of IT scorecards* are in place and are communicated to all employees. Individual objectives of IT employees are connected with the scorecards and incentive systems are linked to the IT Balanced Scorecard measures. The compliance process is well established and levels of compliance are high.

- **Level 5 - Optimized:** The IT Balanced Scorecard is fully aligned with the business's strategic management framework and the vision is frequently reviewed, updated and improved. Internal and external experts are engaged to ensure industry best practices are developed and adopted. The *measurements* and results are part of management reporting and *are systematically acted upon* by senior and IT management. Monitoring, self-assessment and communication are pervasive within the organization and there is optimal use of technology to support measurement, analysis, communication and training.

9.5   Relevance to IT management

Getting business value from IT and measuring that value are important governance domains. These are responsibilities of both the business and IT and should take both tangible and

---

5   Van Grembergen W., Saull R., De Haes S., "Linking the IT Balanced Scorecard to the Business Objectives at a major Canadian Financial group", Journal for Information Technology Cases and Applications (JITCA), vol. 5, no. 1, 2003.

intangible costs and benefits into account. In this way, good IT performance management should enable both the business and IT to fully understand how IT is contributing to the achievement of business goals, in the past and in the future. Measuring and managing IT performance, for which the Balanced Scorecard is an ideal instrument, should provide answers to questions such as:

- if I spend extra funds on IT, what do I get back?
- how does my IT benchmark against competitors?
- do I get back from IT what was promised?
- how do I learn from past performance to optimize my organization?
- is my IT implementing its strategy in line with the business strategy?

9.6 Strengths and weaknesses

"Use of an IT Balanced Scorecard is one of the most effective means to support the board and management in achieving IT and business alignment."

In these words, the IT Governance Institute promotes the IT Balanced Scorecard as a best practice for performance measurement and alignment. This is supported by testimonials from several executives, such as those shown below.

"The major advantage of the IT Balanced Scorecard is that it provides a systematic translation of the strategy into critical success factors and metrics, which materializes the strategy."
(CIO of a Belgian financial organization, 2006).

"The Balanced Scorecard gives a balanced view of the total value delivery of IT to the business. It provides a snapshot of where your IT organization is at a certain point in time. Most executives, like me, do not have the time to drill down into large amounts of information."
(Vice president of a Canadian insurance organization, 2003).

Kaplan and Norton identified important barriers and pitfalls of an effective Balanced Scorecard implementation, which need to be taken into account and monitored:

- visions and strategies that are not actionable
- strategies that are not linked to departmental, team and individual goals
- strategies that are not linked to long- and short-term resource allocation
- feedback that is tactical, not strategic.

9.7 Cross-references/relationships

The IT Balanced Scorecard is one of the core concepts that is integrated in the CobiT4.0 framework. CobiT 4.0 defines 34 IT processes grouped into four domains: planning and organization (PO), acquisition and implementation (AI), delivery and support (DS), and monitor and evaluate (ME). For each IT process, CobiT 4.0 describes control objectives, inputs/outputs, roles and responsibilities and maturity models. Next to that, each of the IT processes contain a list of IT goals they support, goals of the IT process itself and goals of the activities within the process. For all these goals, corresponding outcome measures are defined. This entails that CobiT defines outcome measures at IT level, IT process level and activity level. An important difference to mention is that CoBiT discusses key goals indicators instead of outcome measures and also key performance indicators instead of performance drivers. An example of IT goals, process goals and activity goals is shown in Figure 9.6, for CoBiT Process DS5 – Ensure Systems Security.

Again, as in the Balanced Scorecard, important cause-and-effect relationships between measures can be defined. In the example of Figure 9.6, the KGI (outcome measure) *'number and type of suspected and actual access violations'* is identified on IT process level for the IT process goal *'permit access to critical and sensitive data only to authorized users'.*

Goals and Metrics

Activity Goals	Process Goals	IT Goals
• Understanding security requirements, vulnerabilities and threats • Managing user identities and authorisations in a standardised manner • Defining security incidents • Testing security regularly	• Permit access to critical and sensitive data only to authorised users. • Identify, moniter and report security vulnerabilities and incidents. • Detect and resolve unauthorised access to information, applications and infrastructure. • Minimise the impact of security vulnerabilities and incidents.	• Ensure critical and confidential information is withheld from those who should not have access to it. • Ensure automated business transactions and information exchanges can be trusted. • Maintain the integrity of information and processing infrastructure. • Account for and protect all IT assets. • Ensure IT services and infrastructure can resist and recover from failures due to error, deliberate attack or disaster.

are measured by · *are measured by* · *are measured by*

Key Performance Indicators	Process Key Goal Indicators	IT Key Goal Indicators
• # and type of security incidents • # and type of obsolete accounts • # of unauthorised IP addresses, ports and traffic types denied • % of cryptographic keys compromised and revoked • # of access right authorised, revoked, reset or changed	• # and type of suspected and actual access violations • # of violation in segregation of duties • % of users who do not comply with password standards • # and type of malicious code prevented	• # of incidents damaging reputation with the public • # of systems where security requirements are not met • Time to grant, change and remove access privileges

Figure 9.6 Goals and metrics for BiT process DS5 – ensure system security

(ITGI, 2005, CoBiT 4.0, on-line available at www.itgi.org)

In order to reach this goal, several activity goals within the process must be executed, such as *'managing user identities and authorization in a standardized manner'* (Figure 9.6).

This goal can be measured by a KGI (outcome measure) on activity level, which is also a KPI (performance driver or lead indicator) for goals at IT process level, such as *'number and type of obsolete accounts'.* It is assumed that a lower score for this metric implicates a better indication for reaching the IT process goal. A similar cause-and-effect relationship can be defined between process goals and IT goals and their corresponding metrics.

This implies that COBIT provides all the essential components to build up a Balanced Scorecard for an IT process, a specific function (for example development) within IT or for the IT department as a whole. Mapping the COBIT process domains (PO, AI, DS, ME) on the above cascade of scorecard (see Figure 9.7) reveals that the DS processes provide input to build up a scorecard for the operations department (IT operational Balanced Scorecard) the AI processes provide input to build up a scorecard for the IT development function (IT development Balanced Scorecard) and the PO processes provide input for an IT strategic Balanced Scorecard. The ME processes finally provide goals and metrics encompassing all other domains.

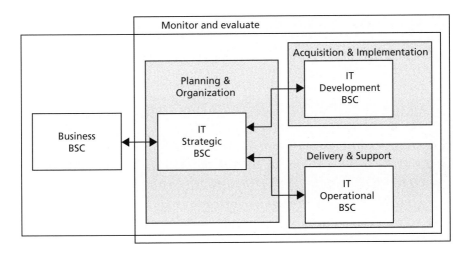

Figure 9.7 Balanced scorecard and COBIT (*Van Grembergen, W. "The Balanced Scorecard and IT governance", Information Systems Control Journal (previously IS Audit and Control Journal), Volume 2, 2000, pp.40-43.*)

9.8 Links and literature

9.8.1 Articles, papers and books
- De Haes S., Van Grembergen W., "IT Governance Best Practices in Belgian Organizations", in Proceedings of the Hawaii International Conference on System Sciences (HICSS), 2006.
- ITGI, 2005, COBIT 4.0, on-line available at www.itgi.org.

- Kaplan, R. and Norton, D. "The Balanced Scorecard – measures that drive performance", *Harvard Business Review*, January-February 1992, pp. 71-79.
- Kaplan, R. and Norton, D. "Putting the Balanced Scorecard to work", *Harvard Business Review*, September-October 1993, pp. 134-142.
- Van Grembergen W., Saull R., De Haes S., "Linking the IT Balanced Scorecard to the Business Objectives at a major Canadian Financial group", Journal for Information Technology Cases and Applications (JITCA), vol. 5, no. 1, 2003
- Van Grembergen, W. and Van Bruggen, R. "Measuring and improving corporate information technology through the Balanced Scorecard technique", Proceedings of the Fourth European Conference on the Evaluation of Information technology", Delft, October 1997, pp. 163-171.
- Van Grembergen, W. "The Balanced Scorecard and IT governance", Information Systems Control Journal (previously IS Audit and Control Journal), Volume 2, 2000, pp.40-43.
- Van Grembergen W., De Haes S., "Measuring and demonstrating the value of IT", in IT Governance Domain Practices and Competencies (series of IT Governance Institute), 2005.
- Willcocks, L. Information management. The evaluation of information systems investments, Chapman and Hall, London, 1995.

9.8.2 Websites

- Balanced Scorecard Institute: www.balancedscorecard.org
- IT Governance Institute: www.itgi.org
- Information Technology and Alignment (ITAG) Research Institute: www.uams.be/itag

10 AS 8015-2005 - Australian Standard for Corporate Governance of IT

> *The Australian Standard Corporate Governance of Information and Communication Technology (AS 8015-2005) provides a model, principles and vocabulary to assist those seeking to implement effective governance of the use of IT within their organizations.*

Owner of the copyright:	AS 8015 is published by Standards Australia.
Distribution:	Anecdotal evidence indicates wide interest in the Standard. However, figures of formal adoption are not available.
Origin/history:	In response to the lack of guidance to those seeking to implement effective governance of the use of IT within their organizations, Standards Australia committee IT-030 was established. Thirteen organizations were represented on IT 030, which consulted widely before recommending the publication of the AS 8015-2005. Input from over thirty other organizations and individuals is acknowledged in the publication.
	The author of this chapter represented the Australian Computer Society (ACS) on IT-030.
	Around this time, related Australian Corporate Governance Standards were published - Good Governance Principles (AS 8000-2003), Fraud and Corruption Control (AS 8001-2003), Organizational Codes of Conduct (AS 8002-2003), Corporate Social Responsibility (AS 8003 2003) and Whistle Blower protection programs (AS 8004-2003).
	The well established and internationally recognized Risk Management Standard AS/NZ 4360-2004 was revised and published by Standards Australia. BS15000 also came to the attention of IT-030 and it was adopted as AS 8018-2004 IT Service Management.
	Building on these existing Standards, AS 8015-2005 Corporate Governance of IT was published with the intention to provide guidance on corporate governance of IT. IT-030 envisages that two subsequent governance Standards will provide detailed linkages to project management and AS 8018 service management of IT.
When:	First published in January 2005.
Certification bodies?	Certification is yet to be determined. Some Australian Standards are legislated.

By Marghanita da Cruz

10.1 Origin/history

Enthusiasm for new technology has made the objective evaluation of IT difficult. During the dom.com heyday of the late 1990s, it seemed no longer necessary to justify any investment in IT.

While many of these investments in IT returned very little, the use of IT has become intrinsic to business operations. Increasingly, customers and suppliers expect to do business over the Internet. New business practices continue to be driven by developments in IT. The risks to organizations from these new business processes cannot be ignored.

Successful business models, laws and social norms sometimes only become apparent some time after a new technology emerges. New risks often emerge as IT initiatives develop and business practices mature.

The corporate collapses and associated financial losses in the first few years of the new millennium made investors and regulators more cautious and the response was to demand a greater level of disclosure and accountability.

Broad-scale outsourcing demonstrated that service providers' interests do not always align with those of a user organization. The failure of some IT initiatives have not only cost organizations strategic opportunities; they have also led to protracted legal disputes and costly court cases.

Analysis of costly failures of IT initiatives have consistently indicated poor corporate governance and a lack of guidance to those whose role it was to manage the risks associated with achieving the benefits and value from investments in IT.

Corporate governance has become a popular, if misused term. While the usual emphasis is to equate it with conformance and compliance with legal and regulatory requirements, it has a much broader meaning. For an organization the other critical components of corporate governance are performance and ongoing viability.

The titles of Standards in the set of Australian Corporate Governance Standards help define the scope of the term. They are as follows:
• Good Governance Principles (AS 8000-2003)
• Fraud and Corruption Control (AS 8001-2003)
• Organizational Codes of Conduct (AS 8002-2003)
• Corporate Social Responsibility (AS 8003-2003)
• Whistle Blower protection programs (AS 8004-2003).

These Standards along with AS 4360-2004 Risk Management and the adoption of BS15000 as: **AS 8018-2004 IT service management** provided a context for the drafting and subsequent publication of AS 8015-2005.

Australian Standards are prepared by committees of experts from industry, governments, consumers and other relevant sectors. The requirements or recommendations contained in published Standards are a consensus of the views of representative sources and take account of comments received from other sources.

The following organizations were represented on the committee responsible for AS 8015:

- Australian Computer Society (ACS) www.acs.org.au/governance
- Australian Bankers Association www.bankers.asn.au
- Australian Institute of Company Directors www.companydirector.com.au
- Project Management Institute www.pmi.org.au
- Society of Consumer Affairs Professionals Australia (SOCAP) www.socap.org.au
- Australian Chamber of Commerce and Industry www.acci.asn.au
- Australian Electrical and electronic Manufacturers Association www.aeema.asn.au
- Australian Institute of Project Management www.aipm.com.au
- Consumers' Federation of Australia www.consumersfederation.com
- Department of Defence (Australia) www.defence.gov.au
- Information Systems Audit and Control Association www.isaca-canberra.org.au
- University of New South www.unsw.edu.au
- Royal Melbourne Institute of Technology (RMIT) www.rmit.edu.au.

Over thirty other organizations contributed to the drafting of the Standard.

As Principal Consultant of Ramin Communications, the author of this chapter co-coordinated initial market research to scope and position the Standard. Later as the ACS representative on the committee, she ran seminars across Australia to obtain comments from ACS members and the wider community on the draft Standard.

The ACS is the recognized Australian association for Information and Communication Technology (IT) professionals. Its members work in all areas of business and industry, government and academia, and are qualified and experienced IT professionals who have a commitment to the wider community to ensure the beneficial use of IT.

10.2 Where is AS 8015 used?

AS 8015 is a brief and concise twelve-page document. Its objective is to provide a framework, which the directors of any organization can use to govern the use of IT.

The Standard defines corporate governance as the system by which entities are directed and controlled, a director as a member of the most senior governing body of an organization and an entity as a legally constituted organization.

The Standard also provides useful guidance to those to whom directors turn to for advice or to whom they delegate responsibilities for managing the operations of the organization, such as senior managers, consultants, technical specialists, vendors and service providers.

An organization could be a company listed on a stock exchange, a small business owned and operated by one or two people, an association, a charity or a government agency.

10.3 Description and core graphics

AS 8015 Corporate Governance of Information and Communication Technology provides a framework for effective governance of the use of IT by an organization.

The Standard uses the term 'directors' to include owners, members of supervisory boards, partners, council members, senior executives, officers authorized by Acts of Parliament - in short, anyone responsible for the activities of an organization.

The framework described in AS 8015 comprises:
• a model
• guiding principles
• vocabulary.

Figure 10.1 reproduces the AS 8015 model.

In the model, directors monitor and evaluate the organization's use of IT against the pressures and needs acting on it. They should then direct the development and implementation of policies and plans to address any gaps.

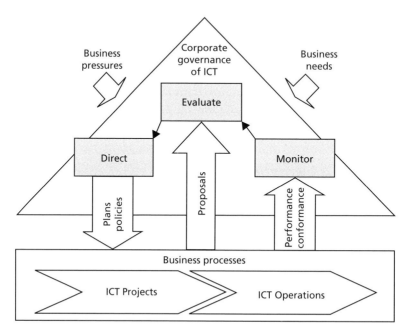

Figure 10.1 Model for corporate governance of IT (source: AS 8015-2005 Australian Standard for Corporate Governance of Information and Communication Technology, Standards Australia)

The Standard provides six guiding principles:
1. Establish clearly understood responsibilities for IT
2. Plan IT to best support the organization
3. Acquire IT validly
4. Ensure that IT performs well, whenever required
5. Ensure IT conforms with formal rules
6. Ensure IT respects human factors.

The third component of the Standard is a vocabulary drawn from and complementing terms defined and used in the other Australian Standards for corporate governance and risk management.

10.4 Approach/how to

AS 8015 provides a prudent approach to investment in IT, an approach which recognizes that there are risks associated with the operational and planned use of IT and ensures these are managed effectively.

The Standard provides guidance to directors to help them meet their responsibilities in regard to IT and meet their obligations in relation to:
• privacy legislation
• record keeping
• financial reporting
• prudent management of organizational resources.

In the model directors monitor, evaluate and direct the use of IT against the business pressures and needs of the organization.

The principles provide guidance to directors, and those advising them, on the risks associated with IT. The Standard elaborates on what directors should do to implement each principle.

> *IT is defined as the resources required to acquire, process, store and disseminate information. Resources are in turn defined as the people, procedures, software, information, equipment, consumables, facilities, capital and operating funds and time.*

The Standard elaborates on each principle to provide guidance on the tasks directors should undertake.

In the case of the first principle – **Establish clearly understood responsibilities for IT** – directors should:
• **evaluate** options for assigning responsibilities
• **ensure** that those assigned responsibilities are competent
• **monitor** the performance of those assigned responsibilities.

The options for assigning responsibilities for IT arise from the business models and organizational structures through which it is used. For example, some equipment could be owned and managed in-house, advice can be sought from external consultants and other IT could be procured from vendors and service providers who specialize in website hosting or even provide integrated business support such as payroll management.

To implement the second principle – **Plan IT to best support the organization** – directors should:
- **consider** opportunities for better business practices arising from IT
- **assess** their current activities
- **direct** the development and implementation of plans to address the gaps.

The equipment component of IT has changed dramatically over recent years. It has become smaller and much more affordable. The Internet has established Standards which have made equipment from different suppliers much more compatible and inter-operable. This has increased competition between vendors and created new business opportunities to reach and source products from wider markets.

However, business practices can take time to evolve. Early adoption has sometimes turned out to be a costly exercise, with little or no business benefits or the ability to create and claim a lucrative new market. Prospective users and customers can take longer to adopt new systems. For example, the switch from ATMs to Internet banking has not been instantaneous.

The third principle – **Valid Acquisition of IT** – covers the assessment of the risks and value of proposed and current investments in IT. Directors need to implement policies and procedures to ensure that checks and balances are in place to ensure ongoing investment is justified. Where an investment – an allocation of resources – ceases to be justified it needs to be reassigned in a timely manner.

The **Performance of IT** encompasses the integrity of information, the capacity and capability of systems. It extends to the decommissioning and disposal to ensure that the organization's environmental and data management obligations are met.

The fifth principle covers **internal policies** covering the use of technologies such as email and web browsing as well as **meeting obligations** in relation to record keeping, financial reporting, protection of personal information collected by the organization and business continuity.

The sixth principle – **Ensure IT respects human factors** – encompasses the people aspects of IT such as:
- the **usability** and **accessibility** of user interfaces
- **needs of people** affected by changes to business processes brought about by IT.

With IT having such a direct and immediate effect on the performance of organizations, directors should monitor, evaluate and direct their organizations' use of IT as carefully as they do the financial and human resources of the organization.

AS 8015 is short and readable. The AS 8015 framework provides useful guidance on effective governance of IT in any organization large or small.

10.5 Relevance to IT management

AS 8015 provides a governance framework in which the use of IT can be managed and aligned to the organization's priorities.

The basis of the framework is to establish a framework for informed and timely decision making on the use of IT, at the highest level of the organization.

For this to happen, appropriate measures and mechanisms need to be established for reporting and responding to the risks arising from the current or planned use of IT.

10.6 Strengths and weaknesses

The published Standard is a short readable document. It provides an overview of the scope of issues in governing IT effectively, as well as a glossary which assists technologists and the business to communicate.

It should be noted that while the document is only twelve pages, the concepts are quite complex.

The objective in developing a brief concise Standard was to provide a description of a general framework for effective governance of IT that would be read at every level and across organizations.

10.7 Cross-references/relationships

AS 8015-2005 provides a framework that directors of any organization can use to effectively govern the use of IT within their organization. AS 8015-2005 complements existing Australian Corporate Governance and Risk Management Standards:

- **AS 8000-2003 - Corporate governance** - good governance principles
- **AS 8001-2003 - Corporate governance** - fraud and corruption control
- **AS 8002-2003 - Corporate governance** - organizational codes of conduct
- **AS 8003-2003 - Corporate governance** - corporate social responsibility
- **AS 8004-2003 - Corporate governance** - whistle blower protection programs for entities
- **AS 3806-1998** - compliance programs
- **AS/NZS 4360:2004** - risk management.

In addition to the above Standards, AS 8015-2005 refers its readers to two information security management Standards:

- **ISO/IEC 17799:2005 - IT** - Code of practice for information security management
- **AS/NZS 7799.2:2003 : Information security management** - Specification for information security management systems.

It is anticipated that detailed advice on the governance of operational IT and proposed uses of IT (subject of IT Project) will be provided in two subsequent Standards.

In adopting BS15000 as AS 8018 IT Service Management Parts 1 and 2, it is clear that this Standard, along with ITIL, provides useful detailed guidance on the management of IT services. The Standard for governance of operational IT should enable directors/members of executive committees to govern the management of IT in accordance with AS 8018.

At the time of writing no equivalent project management Standard has been adopted as an Australian Standard.

10.8 Links and literature

The Australian Computer Society Governance of IT Committee www.acs.org.au/governance

Ramin Communications IT Governance Website www.ramin.com.au/itgovernance

AS 8015 is available from Standards Australia Standards.org.au

11 CoBiT – Control Objectives for Information and related Technology

Control Objectives for Information and related Technologies (CoBiT 4.0) is a high-level process model that organizes a broad range of IT activities in 34 processes. As a single source of good practice it provides a uniform structure to understand, implement and evaluate IT capabilities, performance and risks with the primary goal of satisfying business requirements. CoBiT consists of a selection of popular management tools and techniques described in an IT management context. It sets out the scope and defines what IT activities in a particular area of IT should be accomplished and this is largely harmonized with other popular frameworks that cross-reference to the same subject area.

Owner of the copyright:	IT Governance Institute (ITGI, www.itgi.org), owned by Information Systems Audit and Control Association (ISACA, www.isaca.org).
Distribution:	A very large number of organizations around the world currently use CoBiT. This is likely to include every entity that is expected to address Sarbanes-Oxley requirements, including their service providers.
Origin/history:	A few members of the EDP Auditors Association (EDPAA, now known as ISACA), in the 1990s developed the CoBiT Control Framework in response to the publication by COSO (Committee of Sponsoring Organizations of the Treadway Commission) of *Internal Controls - An Integrated Framework* as this publication did not address internal controls for IT.
When:	First version published in 1994.
Participants in the development:	Main driving force was Erik Guldentops, executive professor at the Management School of the University of Antwerp. CoBiT publications are now under the responsibility of the CoBiT Steering Committee within the IT Governance Institute, a legal entity affiliated to ISACA.
Certification bodies?	None, though for individuals wishing to improve their knowledge of the CoBiT framework, an online CoBiT Foundation course and examination is available from ISACA. This may be used by individuals wishing to obtain and test their basic understanding of the components of the CoBiT documentation set.

By Peter Hill

11.1 Origin/history

As a result of corporate governance scandals in the 1980s, a working group was established with the aim of identifying the essential internal controls for business processes that ought to prevent similar problems re-occurring. The result was a publication by the Committee of Sponsoring Organizations of the Treadway Commission in 1992 titled *Internal Controls – An Integrated Framework*. These internal controls were largely business process oriented and did not provide much guidance where IT was involved.

The EDP Auditors Association (now known as Information Systems Audit and Control Association, or ISACA) had a publication known as *Control Objectives* that was widely used by its members at the time. A handful of these EDPAA members in Europe recognized the need for something better and set about developing a much improved and more harmonized control framework for IT with the initial purpose of assisting auditors perform their work. COBIT has grown substantially from this point to a framework for better IT management.

The development of COBIT is led by the vision and driving force of Erik Guldentops, executive professor at the Management School of the University of Antwerp. As the COBIT initiative evolved from its first publication in 1994, a much larger body of contributors has participated at various stages and in a range of roles that include research, development, review and quality assurance.

COBIT publications are now under the responsibility of the COBIT Steering Committee within the IT Governance Institute, a legal entity affiliated to ISACA. The COBIT Steering Committee exercises quality control over all related publications. Since the first publication in 1994 there have been new releases of the main publication in 1996, 2000 and most recently COBIT 4.0 in 2005. A number of complementary publications have been released by ISACA over this period, including:
- **1998** - COBIT Implementation Toolset
- **2003** - IT Governance Implementation Guide
- **2003** - COBIT Quickstart
- **2003** - COBIT Online.

Other related publications from ISACA have included a number of Board Briefings and specialist documents addressing a range of topics that fall under IT governance.

Ownership and copyright is vested in ISACA's IT Governance Institute. Usage of the material for commercial purposes is restricted by ISACA to licensed organizations. It is an infringement to distribute the material outside the legal entity that originally obtained it from ISACA. However, the cost is small and the publications are easily obtained by members, in most cases free of charge and by non-members at a nominal fee.

11.2 Where is COBIT used?

As a high-level framework with generic descriptions of IT process areas and activities it provides guidance useful to a broad audience that includes:
- **business executives** looking for a dashboard or Balanced Scorecard to better understand their IT organization or service provider
- **IT management** seeking to communicate performance achieved or direct their subordinates' activities in line with business needs

- **IT staff** building capability to perform their daily tasks in a way that is adequate to deliver against business' expectations.

The CoBiT framework has also been widely adopted by the external and internal audit community seeking to better understand IT and the controls essential to satisfy an ever growing number of statutory, regulatory and contractual requirements that include financial reporting, Sarbanes-Oxley, Basel II and many more.

As an open framework for IT in its fourth version, it is now widely accepted across the globe as the preferred umbrella process model for good practices in IT. Its status as the *de facto* Standard arises from having achieved a balance in the detail of the content provided. This balance is between information sufficient to provide useful guidance but concise enough to focus primarily on **what** is required rather than **how** to undertake the activities themselves. The CoBiT framework is heavily weighted towards understanding the business requirements for IT and is less reliant on references to best practices for IT. This makes the framework particularly attractive to corporate executives, business leaders and senior IT management, but less so to novices in IT more interested in how-to work instructions that provide specific guidance.

Consequently a very large number of organisations around the world currently use CoBiT. This is likely to include every entity that is expected to address Sarbanes-Oxley requirements. This extends beyond the legal entity itself and includes in many instances their service providers.

11.3 Description and core graphics

The CoBiT framework organizes IT activities in thirty four processes split into four domains that follow the Deming structure of Plan, Do, Check and Act. Related IT activities are collected within individual processes that are cross-referenced to provide an integrated set of IT processes with which to manage IT in line with business expectations.

At the process level there is a description of the outcomes to be expected (process goals) together with details about the minimum controls (detailed control objectives) to be considered in countering the inherent risks of that particular process, as well as a model to assess current capabilities (maturity model) to support the entity's business activities and described in relation to the people, technology and process details. CoBiT 4.0 has included additional information about roles and responsibilities at the process level and the relationships between processes.

The framework shows how IT processes and resources, including application systems, information, infrastructure and people are used to provide the business with information that has the essential characteristics to be of value in satisfying quality, fiduciary and security requirements.

Guidance is provided on mapping individual processes to IT goals, and then on mapping IT goals to business goals. This provides for the alignment of IT processes with business objectives. Consequently, the CoBiT framework can be used to establish a Balanced Scorecard that communicates to business how the IT organization delivers value. For enterprises new to Balanced Scorecard concepts or struggling to develop their first version, the CoBiT documentation

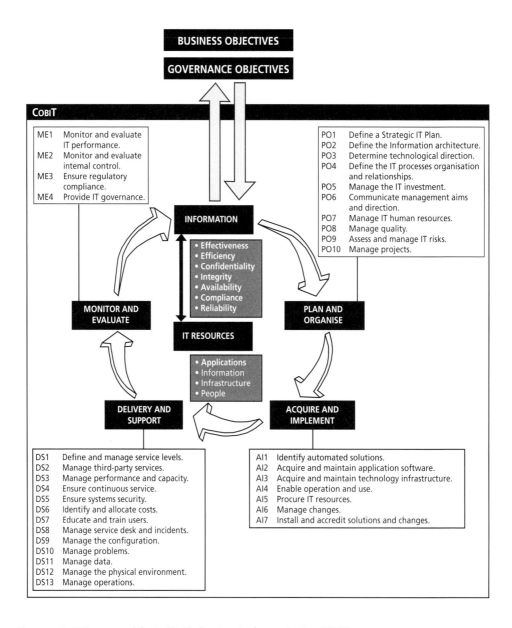

Figure 11.1 CoBiT IT processes defined within the four domains (source: CoBiT 4.0, ISACA)

provides a Balanced Scorecard that sufficient to assist the entity to get started within days rather than months or years.

With knowledge about the business goals and the IT processes that support the production of information about the business requirements, the framework describes how IT processes are to be controlled and the control practices that will be essential, together with audit guidelines to be used when undertaking a review.

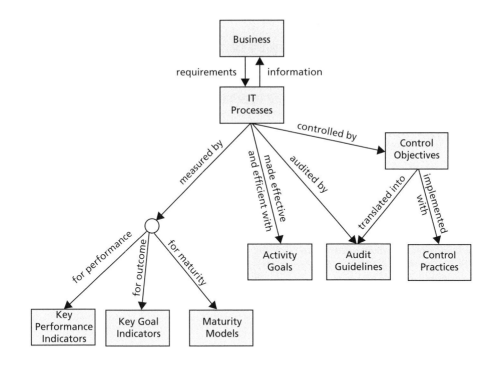

Figure 11.2 CobiT detailed control objectives (source: CobiT 4.0, ISACA)

The detailed control objectives for each process provide some understanding of flow within the process and the essential controls. This can be used to understand the basic process and its controls. Additional detail about the process can be derived from the process specific maturity model and the more detailed Control Practice Statements – a separate publication from the main CobiT documentation set. The IT control practices expand the capabilities of the CobiT framework by providing the practitioner with an additional level of detail about **how** and **why** controls are needed by management, service providers, end users and control professionals.

At the activity level there are stated activity goals with the aim of making the process effective, key goal indicators to focus on the business expectations as well as key performance indicators for managing the day to day activities.

Of primary interest to management and staff are:
- *Framework* – this explains how CobiT is structured in four domains for IT and thirty four processes, each linked to business requirements
- *Control objectives* – these provide generic guidance on good practices for the management IT activities
- *Control Practices* – these describe why controls are worth implementing and how to implement them
- *IT Assurance Guide* – a generic audit approach and supporting guidance for audits of all CobiT's IT processes

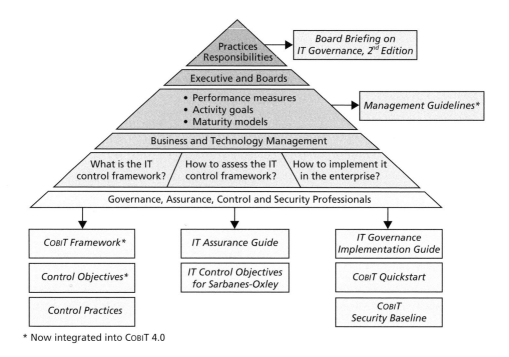

* Now integrated into CoBiT 4.0

Figure 11.3 List of CoBiT publications (source: CoBiT 4.0, ISACA)

- *IT Control Objectives for Sarbanes-Oxley* – providing guidance on how to ensure compliance for the IT environment based on the CoBiT control objectives
- *IT Governance Implementation Guide* – a generic road map for implementing IT governance using a dedicated project team
- CoBiT *Quickstart* – the baseline of control for smaller organizations and a possible first step for the larger enterprise
- CoBiT *Security Baseline* – essential steps for implementing information security within the enterprise.

CoBiT is a framework designed to guide both large and small enterprises in a broad range of industries and at different stages of organizational maturity but, most importantly, with stakeholders who have different business goals and therefore different expectations of IT management.

To be relevant to a wide audience, the content of the CoBiT framework is generic in nature and therefore is most useful as a guideline rather than as a standard.

There is no intention to implement a certification scheme. CoBiT, like ITIL and other process frameworks, is a guideline that is useful as a source of good practice. Best practice is something internal to the organization and this is driven by the business needs of IT. For example, in an organization currently implementing an ERP solution, the business might expect the IT function, its consultants and the vendor to have suitable, but different levels of capability in the relevant IT processes. CoBiT would be a useful tool to understand their respective capabilities, but this capability should be measured against the organization's needs, rather than some notion of universal best practice. Compliance is sought first and foremost with business expectations and hence performance should be understood using tools such as the Balanced Scorecard and key goal indicators.

Best practice is not the ultimate goal. The CoBiT framework drives an organization towards understanding **what** is sufficient for the business to be successful and allows the organization and the staff to determine **how** best to arrange and perform the activities necessary for the business to succeed.

For individuals wishing to improve their knowledge of the CoBiT framework, however, an online CoBiT Foundation course and examination is available from ISACA.

11.4 Approach/how to

There is no single approach to implementing CoBiT. The framework has multiple applications with the most common being assessments related to the preparation of annual financial statements.

Corporate governance compliance requirements such as those for Sarbanes-Oxley have increased the popularity of CoBiT through the necessity to implement adequate controls over financial reporting at the operational level within IT. Future compliance requirements will continue to drive the need for adequate operational risk management activities in IT; consequently, controls need to be implemented in a sustainable way.

Interest is growing in understanding the IT organization's capability to deliver. CoBiT has started to play a more significant role in planning IT capability improvement, performance measurement and developing Balanced Scorecards. Through the analysis of specific IT processes, conclusions can be reached about an organization's capability to outsource or successful manage a large-scale ERP environment. Bespoke improvements in areas such as desktop management, software license optimization and contracting can be planned and directed with the aid of CoBiT to focus on both the processes needed and performance delivered.

Implementing IT governance based on CoBiT is frequently done in one of two ways. The first is usually triggered by a gap analysis with a measurement of what is in place being compared to a blueprint of what is expected – subjective in outcomes.

The second (and more reliable) approach is based on a business needs analysis that may include the review of the particular business' value chain and linking this to the underlying IT support processes for service delivery and business process performance.

Costs associated with a full-scale IT governance implementation can range from two per cent to ten per cent of the IT capital spend and operational budget. This will depend on the initial maturity of the IT organization, the goals set for the initiative and the availability of resources both internally and externally.

Many organizations choose something less than a full-scale IT governance implementation, preferring to focus on a few core processes that address specific themes such as value delivery, IT alignment, resource optimization or risk management.

Knowing what success will look like and who will make this assessment must be agreed upon before an initiative to improve IT governance begins. Simply improving IT systems and processes is meaningless, but improving systems and processes that result in the business achieving its goals adds real value. Any improvement initiative using COBIT must be focused on the outcome to the business.

COBIT certification is not available and is not appropriate, since the primary goal is for IT processes to satisfy business requirements.

11.5 Relevance to IT management

IT management can derive direct benefit from using the COBIT framework to implement better governance in three areas – building capability, directing IT activities with a view to achieving specific process outputs and measuring performance in successfully achieving outcomes that meet business goals.

Risk management, strategic alignment, value delivery, resource management and performance measurement will be improved through making use of the COBIT framework. COBIT can also be used to establish a foundation for information security management or undertaking exercises such as cost optimization and projects such as desktop management. Before outsourcing or implementing a large ERP solution, IT management could make use of the COBIT framework to better understand their own organizational readiness and its specific process capability in this regard. This will direct the organization's preparations, which will be essential for success. Many ERP and outsourcing failures to succeed could have been prevented if IT management and business executives better understood the true capability of the third party solution and service providers. Management should make use of COBIT to better plan the engagement of third parties and better prepare contracts and service level agreements to avoid possible disaster.

11.6 Strengths and weaknesses

COBIT's strength in being concise and easily understood is countered by the limited guidance provided to those who are seeking more details about **how** processes should be implemented. Consequently COBIT is better suited as an assessment tool rather than an implementation tool. Its content is broad but the details are not comprehensive. To implement IT governance based on COBIT requires sufficient process experience or other sources of good practice available to fill the gaps in the sequences of activity that can be derived from the detailed control objectives and maturity model.

COBIT 4.0 has introduced the Responsible/Accountable/Consulted/Informed (RACI) technique to address roles and responsibilities in each process, but does not describe the mechanics to fully define and assign responsibility across the entire process. Performance measures that link KPIs and activity, process, IT and business goals are dealt with superficially, with often no more than three or four measures described for what is a complex IT process, with many key process areas falling outside the current measures.

However, CobiT does provide concepts not used very often elsewhere, such as process maturity, generic process objectives, detailed control objectives and control practices. These will provide considerable help since most organizations around the world are at maturity Level One, that is:

- few process owners are defined for effective performance in all process areas
- responsibility is not formally allocated to all participants in the process
- sufficiently well-defined processes are not in place
- process goals and outcomes that will satisfy the business are not being achieved
- policies, plans and procedures are not adequate to support those with responsibilities in individual process areas.

CobiT mentions process ownership in the process PO4 but does not deal with overcoming the challenges at implementation time such as the IT 'silos' supporting the business, the inter-process relationships and loose-coupling required between processes, the extent to which processes should be defined to be meaningful while avoiding the danger of being overly detailed, the need for staff to be empowered to get what is required done, the clash between hierarchical management styles and the process based approach. Nor does CobiT address the challenge of sustainable improvement well into the future. Consequently a practitioner's perspective is missing and the guidance about actual implementations is weak, with existing processes and the staff performing these tasks completely ignored.

Using CobiT to plan and direct process improvement, if done correctly, will ensure that an appropriate balance is maintained in investing in people, process and technology resources. Too often the people resource is overlooked and the technology resource over-emphasized as the way to achieve maximum business value. The CobiT maturity model, control framework and performance measures set out a preferred sequencing of activities that starts with people who understand the process at a particular organization, defining that process and taking decisions about automation to drive efficiency and improve process quality while seeking competitive advantage.

Pitfalls that frequently occur in a CobiT implementation include basing improvement initiatives on best practice, rather than business need, overlooking the current staff employed (the people resource who need to be developed side by side with the process improvement), and expecting technology alone to overcome shortcomings if there currently are no well defined processes to support the business and no people sufficiently skilled to execute the improved processes.

11.7 Cross-reference/relationships

CobiT has been harmonized and various mappings between CobiT and other widely used frameworks exist, some formally researched and published and others informally prepared and shared over the Internet.

ISACA has two publications: *CobiT Mapping* that includes **ISO/IEC 17799:2000, ITIL, ISO/IEC TR 13335, ISO/IEC 15408:1999, Common Criteria/ITSEC, TickIT, NIST 800-14 and COSO,** and *Mapping between CobiT, ITIL and ISO 17799.*

In most instances the process models are complementary. CobiT frequently provides the high level umbrella framework for **what** is required across all IT areas, while individual process models such as ITIL provide more detail about **how** to perform process related activities in specific process areas.

The CobiT framework groups IT activities in thirty four processes. Each CobiT process has a similar structure and content that addresses key management activities, controls to manage inherent risks and performance measurement. As a framework, CobiT covers the broadest scope of IT activities. To treat each process consistently, CobiT must be fairly generic. The ITIL framework focuses primarily on service management. It provides further process definition and guidance to address the areas of service support and service delivery. These two frameworks are therefore largely complementary, with one or the other being more useful to audiences depending on the area of interest. For example, CobiT provides a single approach to performance across all areas of IT activity; ITIL does not. But ITIL will provide more specific information that could be useful to the performance measurement of service support and service delivery.

The **IT Balanced Scorecard** is one of the core concepts that is integrated in the CobiT 4.0 framework; see Chapter 9 on the IT Balanced Scorecard for more on this.

11.8 Links and literature

11.8.1 Publications
From ISACA, the following publications are available (see www.isaca.org):
* *Board Briefing On It Governance* - the *Board Briefing on IT Governance* is based on CobiT. It addresses executive management and provides an understanding about why IT governance is important, what the issues are and what their responsibility is for managing IT.
* *CobiT Quickstart* - CobiT *Quickstart* is a baseline for control over IT in small to medium enterprises (SMEs) and other entities where IT is less critical and not strategic to success. It contains a checklist of the minimum issues that ought to be directed and controlled in IT because of the typical characteristics of SMEs.
* *CobiT Security Baseline* - this survival kit card for Information Security lists important questions to ask and actions to be taken by Boards of Directors/Trustees.
* *IT Governance Implementation Guide* - the objective of this implementation guide is to provide readers with a methodology, using CobiT, for implementing and improving IT governance. The guide is focused on a generic methodology for implementing IT governance, covering the following subjects:

  – why IT governance is important and why organizations should implement it
  – the IT governance lifecycle

– the CobiT framework
– how CobiT is linked to IT governance and how CobiT enables the implementation of IT governance
– the stakeholders who have an interest in IT governance
– a road map for implementing IT governance using CobiT.

There also is a **Pocket Guide** available, which was written with the co-operation of ITSMF-NL, ISACA-NL and EXIN-NL:
• Koen Brand and Harry Boonen, *A Pocket Guide for IT Governance based on CobiT* (Van Haren Publishing 2005)
  ISBN: 9077212191

Website IT Governance Institute: www.itgi.org

11.8.2 Training:

• **ISACA** – online courses for beginners (see www.isaca.org).
  – CobiT Awareness Course (two hours, self paced e-learning)
  – CobiT Foundation Course (eight hours, self paced e-learning)
  – CobiT Foundation Exam (one hour, online forty questions)
  – CobiT for Sarbanes Oxley (four hours, self paced e-learning)
• **IT Governance Network Limited** (www.itgovernance.com) provides a wide range of regular and advanced CobiT related training at venues in Copenhagen, London, New York, Singapore and Zurich.
• **InfoGovernance** (www.infogovernance.com) provides training in conjunction with ISACA chapters in Europe, Middle East and Africa.
• **ez**CobiT**.com** – an online CobiT tutorial.

12 M_o_R – Management of Risk

> *Management of Risk (M_o_R®) is the overall process to assist in the effective control of risks. Risk can be defined as uncertainty of outcome, whether positive opportunity or negative threat, of actions and events. The risk has to be assessed in respect of the combination of the likelihood of something happening, and the impact which arises if it does actually happen.*

Owner of the copyright:	Office of Government Commerce (OGC), United Kingdom: www.ogc.gov.uk
Distribution:	With new legislation such as Sarbanes-Oxley, Management of Risk is increasingly used within the public and private sectors alike.
Origin/history:	Management of Risk (M_o_R®) was originally designed for use by the UK Government, but since its development as a commercial offering, it is used within both the public and private sectors.
When:	2002
Participants in the committee:	OGC
Certification bodies?	APM Group Ltd
Number of certified organizations	13

By Rubina Faber

12.1 Origin/history

There are various approaches to risk management, including Management of Risk (M_o_R®) which was originally designed for use by the UK Government and is owned by the Office of Government Commerce (OGC). Since its development as a commercial offering, it is now used in the public and private sectors alike with UK accredited examinations available.

12.2 Where is Management of Risk used?

Risk is managed by all individuals and all organizations in one form or another throughout daily life, whether it be crossing the road, moving house, or transacting a multi-million currency deal.

Ultimately within business, the directors of a company or corporation are responsible for risk; however all staff within a business have a part to play.

Historically, elements of corporate risk have been managed in specialist areas such as health and safety, information security, business continuity, but became more prominent and focused following a number of high profile corporate frauds and accounting scandals in the early 1990s.

In the UK, the London Stock Exchange (LSE) introduced new regulations for listed organizations, covering various aspects of corporate governance, director responsibilities etc. The regulations are based on the Cadbury Committee's code of best practice for financial aspects of corporate governance.

While this was targeted at listed organizations on the LSE, the principles have been applied to SMEs (small to medium sized organizations) and within all major industries.

Since the Cadbury Committee, a number of other reviews have been undertaken in the UK. Recent development in the US, in the form of Sarbanes-Oxley Act of 2002 has been driven by the collapses of Enron and WorldCom. The Basle Accord is also very influential within the banking sector affecting capital requirements relating to credit and market risk and subsequently including operational risk within Basle II.

12.3 Description and core graphics

Management of Risk is enterprise-wide and can be applied to the three core elements of a business, namely:

- **strategic** – business direction
- **change** – turning strategy into action, including program, project and change management
- **operational** – day-to-day operation and support of the business.

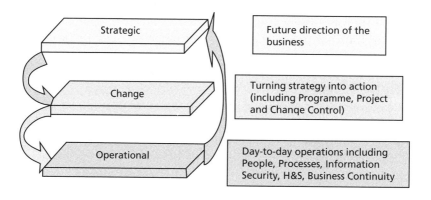

Figure 12.1 The three core elements of business where Management of Risk can be applied (source: OGC)

In this way, the strategy for managing risk should be led from the top of the organization while embedded in the normal working routines and activities of the organization.

While it is often misunderstood, even by risk managers, the aim of managing risk is not necessarily to simply reduce or eliminate risk within business, but to identify and manage risks to best effect for protecting and increasing shareholder value within the business. It has been stated that, paradoxically, better management of risk can allow an organization to take greater risks, but in a more controlled way, to the ultimate benefit of the organization and its shareholders.

12.4 Approach/how to

For Management of Risk to be successful it requires board level sponsorship, but must also fit into the corporate culture of the business.

An overall strategic framework, including a policy document, is also key and needs to include the following elements:

- **risk identification** – this is the process involved with identifying the key risks to achieving business objectives, whether at a strategic, change or operational level
- **risk evaluation** – is concerned with assessing the probability or likelihood of the risk occurring, the potential impact the risk could have on the business should it materialize and the proximity (timing of the risk)
- **setting acceptable levels of risk** – known as tolerance or 'risk appetite', should measure the amount of risk your organization is prepared to accept
- **identifying suitable responses to risks** – once the risks have been identified and evaluated, decisions will need to be taken on how to respond to the specific risk. Responses to risk will involve one of the four Ts, namely:
  - *transfer* – sharing risk with third party e.g. insurance
  - *tolerate* – to accept the risk, but continue to monitor it
  - *terminate* – doing things differently
  - *treat* – taking steps to control the risk by either a containment action to lessen the likelihood, or a contingent action, to reduce the impact should it occur
- **risk ownership** – while probable risk owners could be identified early in the process, the actual allocation should only come once the response has been agreed, so that the most appropriate owner is given the responsibility to manage the risk
- **implementing responses to the risks** – prepare and implement plans associated with applying the agreed response
- **gaining assurance about the effectiveness of the responses** – to confirm that the chosen action, once implemented, is effective and that any residual risk is noted
- **embedding, reporting and review** – to enable the overall framework to be fully effective, it needs to embedded within the business operation, reported appropriately to all levels of the business and continually reviewed to assure the effectiveness of the risk control and of the overall management process.

Once a framework is in place, a common approach can be used across the business, bringing together disparate risk disciplines and functions into a consolidated and consistent approach.

Often, a business case for implementing a Management of Risk framework is based on regulatory requirement. However, true business benefits can be achieved in terms of demonstrating the quality of an organization, winning new business and ultimately improving shareholder value. These positive aspects should be considered where possible when looking at the business case and associated costs.

12.5 Relevance to IT management

Within IT, risk is managed every day in relation to day-to-day operations and services to the business, programs and projects, disaster recovery and IT security.

By embedding the approach within the IT operation, IT management is more able to manage its risks through the visibility and reporting that would be in place.

One main challenge can be to ensure a 'no blame culture' within the organization where staff and management are more willing to report on risks associated with their area of responsibility.

12.6 Strengths and weaknesses

Value for this approach is obtained through the control, visibility and consistent handling of risks within the organization.

Its ultimate success will be achieved through the buy-in of senior (and preferably board level) personnel within the organization, the embedding of the framework of risk management within the day-to-day operation of the business and with a good understanding throughout the business delivered by an education and training program. For it to be fully effective it also needs to take account of the corporate culture of the business; the change in understanding and mode of operation will need to be handled with care.

Another challenge to the success of M_o_R® will come in ensuring that all risk related disciplines and resulting work are captured within a consolidated view of risk, as there can be a tendency to work in 'silos', such as information security, business continuity, health and safety, credit and market risk (in the finance sector), which could result in the business not being able to establish, at the highest level, its true exposure to risk.

12.7 Cross-reference/relationships

Management of Risk is a fundamental part of corporate governance, effectively linking elements such as information security, business continuity and health and safety.

Risk needs to be managed in all that an organization does and is reflected in other approaches, including PRINCE2, (project management) where it is a fundamental element to be considered throughout the life of a project and MSP (program management).

12.8 Links and literature

Management of Risk guidance can be obtained in book form from the TSO – reference ISBN 0113309090 (www.ogc.gov.uk) "and in the book from Jane Chittenden, "Risk management based on M_o_R - A Management Guide" (Van Haren Publishing, 2006).

A recognized course and qualification in M_o_R® including foundation and practitioner examinations is available through Approved Training Organizations (ATOs).

Other information relating to this subject can be found at the following websites:
• Corporate governance reports and guidance from around the world, and including the UK's Turnbull, Combined Code, Hampel, Greenbury and Cadbury documentation can be found via the European Corporate Governance Institute (ECGI) at www.ecgi.org/codes/all_codes.php

- Details of the FSA's Integrated Prudential Sourcebook (PSB) can be found at www.fsa.gov.uk/psb
- The Sarbanes-Oxley reference website can be accessed at www.sarbanes-oxley.com
- Further details on Basle II can be found through the Bank for International Settlements (BIS) website on www.bis.org/publ/bcbsca.htm
- The Office of Government Commerce (OGC) provide a risk toolkit that can be found via www.ogc.gov.uk/sdtoolkit/workbooks/risk/index.html
- The APM Group provides accreditation for the OGC Management of Risk qualifications and can be accessed through www.m-o-r.org/web/site/home/home.asp
- The Institute of Operational Risk www.ior-institute.org
- The Institute of Risk Management www.theirm.org
- Global Association of Risk Professionals www.garp.com
- The National Forum for Risk Management in the Public Sector www.alarm-uk.com

13 Generic Framework for Information Management

This information management framework consists of three domains through which information problems can be considered: activity or 'business', information and communication, and technology. There are also three layers: strategy, structure and operations. They enable a more fine-tuned positioning of organizational problems. It mostly concerns the distinction between the various strategic, structural and operational problems faced by information managers, and the distinction in technology, the significance of this technology and its application.

Owner of the copyright:	University of Amsterdam
Distribution:	The framework is used in Dutch IT management consultancy.
Origin/history:	The Generic Framework for Information Management is a re interpretation of the Strategic Alignment Model by Henderson and Venkatraman and has been produced in PrimaVera: the Program for Research in Information Management at the University of Amsterdam (Abcouwer, Maes and Truijens, 1997).
When:	1997
Participants in the committee:	University of Amsterdam

By Rolf Akker

13.1 Origin/history

The Generic Framework for Information Management was first published in August 1997 in the article *Contouren van een generiek model voor informatiemanagement*, by A.W. Abcouwer, R. Maes and J. Truijens. It is a re-interpretation of the Strategic Alignment Model by Henderson and Venkatraman. The framework has been produced in PrimaVera: the Program for Research in Information Management at the University of Amsterdam (Abcouwer, Maes and Truijens, 1997).

13.2 Where is the Generic Framework for Information Management used?

The Generic Framework for Information Management is a model for interrelating the different components of information management. It is used in the area of business-IT alignment and sourcing. It can be useful to consider IT governance issues as well. It is a high-level view of the entire field of information management; its main application is in the analysis of organizational and responsibility issues.

KPN, the Royal Dutch Telecom company, uses the framework in its approach to IT governance. The framework is being used more and more in Dutch IT management consultancy, offering a high-level framework for analysis.

The framework is used to support strategic discussions in three different ways:
- **descriptive, orientation** - the framework offers a map of the entire information management domain, to be used for positioning specific information management issues that are being discussed in the organization, avoiding technical jargon
- **specification, design** - the framework is used to re-organize the information management organization, e.g. specifying the role of the Chief Information Officer (CIO), or determining the responsibility of the retained organization in the case of outsourcing
- **prescriptive, normative** - the map is used as a diagnostic instrument to find gaps in an organization's information management, specifically aimed at identifying missing interrelationships between the various components of the framework.

13.3 Description and core graphics

The Generic Framework for Information Management was derived from the Strategic Alignment Model from Henderson and Venkatraman (Figure 13.1).

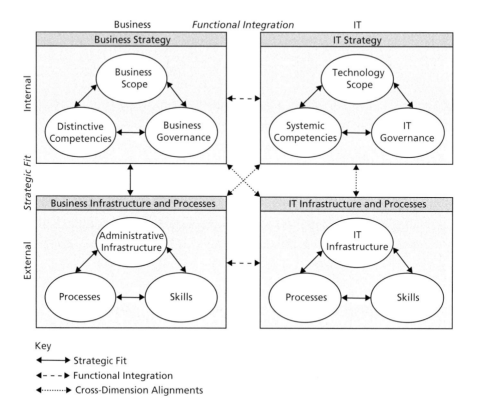

Figure 13.1 Strategic Alignment Model from Henderson and Venkatraman

This framework extends this model from a 2x2 matrix into a 3x3 matrix, by:
- replacing the External domains of (infra)structure and processes with the two tiers of Structure and Operations, resulting in a three-row framework: Strategy, Structure and Operations
- adding a middle column representing the internal and external information and communication aspects, resulting in a three-column framework: Business, Information/Communication and Technology.

The resulting Generic Framework for Information Management is shown in Figure 13.2.

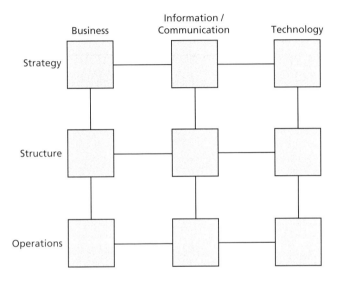

Figure 13.2 The Generic Framework for Information Management

The Generic Framework for Information Management defines Information Management as follows.

Information Management is the balanced management of the elements represented by the central components of the map, including their internal and external relations.

This is shown in Figure 13.3.

Business-IT alignment, sourcing and IT Governance are strategic issues and they are the responsibility of senior business and/or IT management. Strikingly, the middle column (Information and Communication) seems to attract little attention in world literature. This is remarkable because the model is very generic and abstract, and can be used in all situations and in all regions where business-IT alignment and IT governance are major issues.

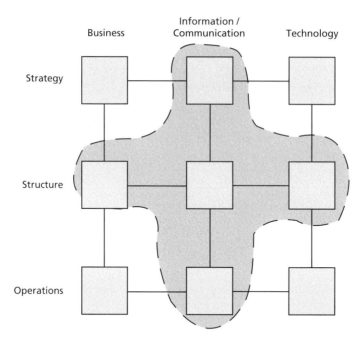

Figure 13.3 Central components of the framework

13.4 Approach/how to

To apply the framework three aspects need to be considered.

1. **The content of the cells** - *which* activities are carried out in the individual cells, *who* is carrying out the activities, and *what* is the *result* of the activities.
2. **The relationship between the cells** - the framework is balanced due to the relations between the cells in the framework. Managing all of the relationships between cells in the framework establishes a well balanced business-IT alignment. The relationships can be formalized by a formal handover of information and/or activities, but also by a committee of representatives of both cells involved in the relationship. This is the area of IT governance.
3. **The relative position of the Information and Communication (I&C) domain** - There are three archetypes of positions for I&C:
    a. *stuck-in-the-middle* - I&C is positioned at equal distance from the business and the technology domain, in many instances emblematic for organizations trying to implement I&C as a liaison function. The result is fairly often an I&C function 'stuck in the middle': missionaries talking to a brick wall at the business side, renegades for the IT side, and peacekeeping troops in the middle, missing a clear identity in their own mindset
    b. *extension of the IT function* - The responsibilities of the business side have been delegated to the technology domain, where the IT services are produced. This is a disastrous approach: management tends to be expressing itself in terms of technology, not in terms of business values. The information service provider is now controlled by itself, which leaves the business vulnerable in its relationships with suppliers

c. *extension of the business function* - here, information is considered to be a business asset, and the relationship with IT can be a contractual one: IT is a supportive function, to be managed as such and conceivably governed via outsourcing. Moreover, I&C is a shared business responsibility, where I&C as a separate function is only accommodating and stimulating, but never leading.

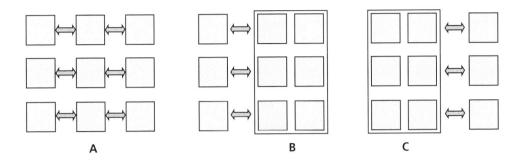

Figure 13.4 Stuck-in-the-middle (A), extension of the IT function (B) and extension of the business function (C)

13.5 Relevance to IT management

The framework is especially important in the area of business–IT alignment. The intermediate structure row and information/knowledge/communication column are key to a successful alignment of business and IT. Hence, they should be considered as independent variables in their own right.

The framework primarily provides a reference frame for the positioning of information management issues at organization and/or business unit levels. From a normative point of view, the framework states that each of the nine areas and their mutual relations should be addressed. The central axes of the framework are core to information management.

The framework contributes to the role of the CIO. The authors position the CIO (and the information manager) as the primary role responsible (the navigator) for the area highlighted in Figure 13.5, including the relationships with the adjacent areas. The framework further helps to make the different roles of the CIO explicit; the natural operating base of the CIO is the strategic information/communication component (top level of middle column). The following global roles for the CIO can be derived (see Figure 13.5).

1. **Information strategist** – this is the direct area of responsibility for the CIO. Central to this role is the definition and control of the information strategy, taking into account the business requirements and the IT opportunities. Here, fully exploiting information as a business resource is vital. Outlining the organization of information management itself is also part of this sub-role.

2. **Co-creator/advisor business strategy** - the CIO is a member of the board of an information-intensive organization. He/she co-defines and co-structures the business strategy, where his/her primary line of approach is to make strategic decisions about most of the information

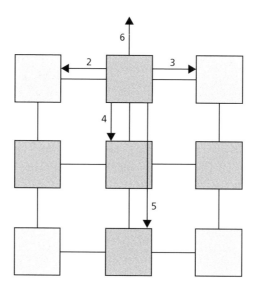

Figure 13.5 The CIO's roles

factor and of the business opportunities and risks of IT. In less information-intensive organizations, the CIO is advisor to the board.

3. **IT portfolio manager** - the CIO is responsible for the relationship with the (external or internal) IT provider(s). To this end, he/she defines a long-term strategy for IT services and is in charge of the control of performance and costs of the existing suppliers. He/she also keeps up with developments in the IT supply market.

4. **Organization architect** - The CIO and his/her team develop the overall, integrated organizational architecture covering the three columns of the map. The information architecture, a blueprint for the information/communication power of the organization, needs special attention. They ensure a flexible and scalable infrastructure and steer migration planning.

5. **Business advisor** - quite often, this role is neglected. The success of a CIO, however, is to a high degree dependent on their peer relationship with the business unit managers and their inspiring and coordinating power towards the information managers at business unit level. Together, they assist in redesigning business processes, developing business cases, roll-out, training and so on. The CIO and his/her team should be considered as part of the business, not as separate entities with separate agendas.

6. **Trend watcher** - The CIO keeps himself/herself informed about the external world: he/she keeps a close track of developments in the use of information, both at the organizational level and at the level of society as a whole; he/she assesses IT developments for their true value, and so on.

The framework provides some clarifying interpretations of information management:
*   from the right to the left information is **produced**, **interpreted** and **used**. In the column at the right **data** is recognized, in the middle column **information** is recognized *('the interpretation of*

data) and in the left column **knowledge** is recognized (*'Making decisions based on information'*). Information Management relates to all three

- for each of the three columns distinctive expertise is required (from the left to the right: **business domain** expertise, **information** expertise and **technology** expertise). Information management is primarily concerned with information expertise, but cannot do without the other two areas of expertise
- **technology** introduces a new **syntax**, while the business column represents **pragmatism**. Therefore, it is the task of information management to provide practical **meaning** to this **technology**.

13.6 Strengths and weaknesses

The model proves its value the most in the area of business-IT alignment and in IT governance. It is also very useful in the positioning of other frameworks, such as BiSL, ASL and ITIL into one coherent framework for information management (see section 1.6 about cross-references).

The greatest strength of the Generic Framework for Information Management is that it is very helpful in discussing information management at enterprise level, illustrating how different aspects of an organization fit together.

The weakness of the Generic Information Management Model is that it does not provide an instant solution and that it always requires more detailed frameworks, to support any implementation.

13.7 Cross-references/relationships

Although the Generic Framework for Information Management is not necessarily an instrument that can be applied to organizations in the way that ITIL does, the other management frameworks in this book can be related to it. In this case the Generic Framework for Information Management can be used as an umbrella-framework. It helps to position the other frameworks within an organization. Together, this can be visually depicted as in Figure 13.6.

13.7.1 ITIL

ITIL is primarily known as the ITIL Service Support and ITIL Service Delivery books; ITIL belongs to the technology domain. From the two core books, ITIL Service Delivery can be mainly positioned at the structure level and ITIL Service Support at the operations level.

13.7.2 ISO 27001

Information management is also about information security. Determining the necessary level of information security, planning to implement and pursuing the right level of information security are important issues in information management. ISO 27001 can be positioned at the strategy, the structure and the operations level in the Information/Communication domain of the framework.

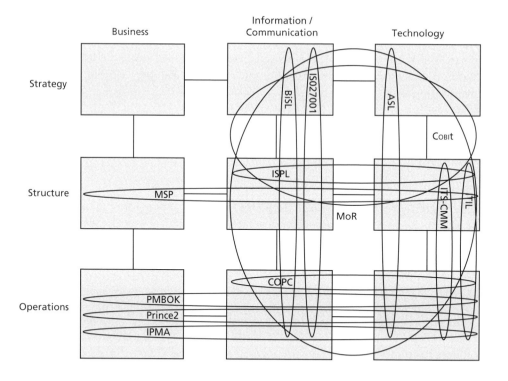

Figure 13.6 Graphical representation of the cross-references with other frameworks

13.7.3 PRINCE2

PRINCE2 is all about how projects are handled. Although primarily intended for the technology domain, it can be applied to the business and information/communication domains as well. PRINCE2 is an instrument used on the operations level in the three domains of the framework.

13.7.4 IPMA Competence Baseline

IPMA Competence Baseline is about the competences necessary for handling projects. IPMA can be used at the operations level in the three domains of the framework.

13.7.5 PMBoK

The PMBoK describes how projects need to be carried out; it is an instrument that can be used on the operations level of all three domains in the framework.

13.7.6 CoBiT

CoBiT enables clear policy development and good practice for IT control throughout organizations. Because CoBiT covers both the technology and the information/communication domains, it can be used in the strategy and structure levels of these domains.

13.7.7 MSP

MSP describes how programs need to be carried out. It is an instrument that can be used on the structure level of all three domains in the framework.

13.7.8 M_o_R

'Management of Risk' involves all the activities required to identify and control the exposure to risk that may have an impact on the business. Strategy, structure and operations activities are required in the information/communication and technology domains.

13.7.9 COPC

COPC is a standard for all contact center operations. Although the business domain may have its own contact center, COPC in regards to the Generic Framework for Information Management is limited to the operations level in the information/communication and technology domains.

13.7.10 ISPL

The Information Services Procurement Library (ISPL) is a practical approach to the procurement of IT services in the broadest sense of the word. This instrument can be used at the structure level of the information/communication and technology domains.

13.7.11 ITS-CMM

The ITS-CMM enables IT service providers to assess their capabilities and provides them with direction and steps for further improvement in the delivery of IT services. It can be positioned at the structure and operations level of the technology domain.

13.7.12 ASL

ASL offers a framework for application management. Because ASL covers the strategy, structure and operations level, it can be positioned at all three levels of the technology domain.

13.7.13 BiSL

BISL can be positioned at the strategy, structure and operations level of the information/communication domain, because it manages the provision of functionality into the business processes.

13.7.14 MIP: Managing the Information Provision

MIP was published in the annual Best Practices collection of ITSMF in the Netherlands (MIP: Van der Hoven, Hegger and Van Bon, 1998). MIP is a framework that looks quite similar to the Generic Framework for Information Management, but it has some essential differences. It uses different descriptions for the additional row and column in the framework. The vertical dimension uses the traditional three-tier management paradigm: Strategy - Tactics - Operations, or Aim - Specify - Operate. The horizontal dimension uses the SOD principle (Separation of Duties): the middle column represents the business in translating the business requirements into information technology specifications. This middle column manages the contract with the IT service provider, and manages the specifications of (integrated) information systems.

The MIP framework was developed in the same year that the Generic Framework for Information Management was created. It was published in Dutch in 1998, and in English in 2000 and 2002. These publications show the inputs and outputs of each of the nine cells, emphasizing the relationships between these cells in an integrated approach of information management.

Both MIP and the Generic Framework for Information Management are used to support strategic discussions on information management issues. The most important difference is in the way that the additional row/column is defined and specified, and the more practical way that MIP addresses Information Management issues (Figure 13.7).

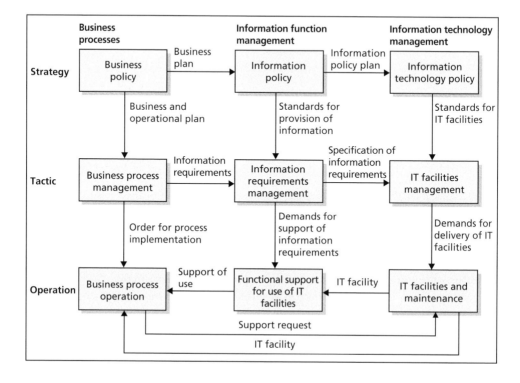

Figure 13.7 The 3x3 matrix for Management of Information Provision (MIP)

13.8 Links and literature

- Abcouwer, A.W., R. Maes and J. Truijens, "Contouren van een generiek model voor informatiemanagement, Tijdschrift Management & Informatie, 5 (3)", 1997, pp. 92-102 (in Dutch).
- Akker, R., M. Paulissen and E. Roovers, "Informatiemanagement als basis voor IT-Governance, Best Practices in IT Service Management", Volume 3, 2006, Van Haren Publishing.
- cms.dordrecht.nl/Dordrecht/up/ZqbpoxxGC_IMdordrecht031112.pdf
- imwww.fee.uva.nl/~pv/html/working_papers.cfm
- imwww.fee.uva.nl/~pv/PDFdocs/99-03.pdf
- www.rikmaes.nl
- www.tongatapu.net.to/compstud/mmedia/local_issues/ITAlignment.pdf
- Maes, R., "A Generic Framework for Information Management". PrimaVera Working Paper 99-03, April 1999, Amsterdam University.

- Van der Hoven, D.J. , G. Hegger and J. van Bon, 1998, in the IT Beheer Jaarboek 1998 (Ten Hagen & Stam, 1998, in Dutch), in the World Class IT Service Management Guide (Ten Hagen & Stam, 2000, English), and in The Guide to IT Service Management, 2000 (Addison Wesley, 2002, English).

14 BiSL – Business Information Services Library

The Business Information Services Library (BiSL) has a focus on how business organizations can improve control over their information systems: demand for business support, use of information systems and contracts and other arrangements with IT suppliers. BiSL is a public domain approach that offers guidance in the field of business information systems management: support of the use of information systems in the business processes, operational IT control and information management. BiSL consists of a framework of processes, supplemented by various publications and a periodically updated library of best practices that are available on the website of the supporting ASL Foundation. This foundation also provides a platform for organizations that are interested in improving their IT demand organization. BiSL is used as a management tool to improve the performance of processes and departments in the field of business information systems management.

Owner of the copyright:	ASL Foundation
Distribution:	It is estimated that BiSL has been adopted by about 150 organizations in the Netherlands, and over 1800 people in the Netherlands have followed a foundations course. The Dutch approach is attracting increasing attention from organizations from abroad.
Origin/history:	In order to shape the customer role in IT management, from 1998 on BiSL was developed by PinkRoccade, now part of Getronics. This resulted in the publication of the book *BiSL, een framework voor functioneel beheer en informatiemanagement* (by Remko van der Pols, Ralph Donatz and Frank van Outvorst) in February 2005. BiSL was then transferred to the public domain and adopted by the ASL Foundation.
When:	February 2005
Participants in the committee:	Organizations participating in the BiSL section of the ASL Foundation are, amongst others: Interpolis, Fortis, UWV, Dutch Ministry of Defence, Getronics PinkRoccade, LogicaCMG, Dutch Police, ISES, EXIN.
Certification bodies?	Since the beginning of 2006 a certificate can be obtained on an individual basis.

By Frank van Outvorst and Ralph Donatz

14.1 Origin/history

The advantages of having a structured method for performing the customer role in the field of IT management began to be considered in the 1980s. Although IT suppliers tried their utmost to meet their customers' expectations, the customers still were not satisfied. This situation gave food for thought about the customers' role in the whole field of IT management. Many customer organizations had no idea of the importance of their own role and depended on their IT suppliers to interpret their requirements. It became evident that the customer role is a crucial factor in enabling IT to deliver value. It became clear that a structured approach towards shaping the customer role was needed.

As a response to this need BiSL was developed by PinkRoccade, one of the oldest IT companies in the Netherlands and now part of Getronics. Several articles on the subject were published in Dutch yearbooks on IT management (*IT Beheer Jaarboek* editions 1998 to 2004). With the publication of the book *BiSL, een framework voor functioneel beheer en informatiemanagement* (by Remko van der Pols, Ralph Donatz and Frank van Outvorst) in February 2005, BiSL was transferred to the public domain. BiSL has been adopted by the ASL Foundation. Organizations participating in the BiSL section of the ASL Foundation are, amongst others: Interpolis, Fortis, UWV, the Dutch Ministry of Defence, Getronics PinkRoccade, LogicaCMG, the Dutch Police, ISES, EXIN.

14.2 Where is BiSL used?

BiSL is primarily aimed at both business management and professionals who wish to improve the support of their business processes by realizing better performance and output of their business information systems management. Business information systems management refers to the way in which organizations can realize added value from a business perspective through adequate deployment and use of information systems. Demand management, information management and operational IT control are aspects of business information systems management. BiSL mainly focuses on IT demand processes in administrative automation; however, the number of examples where BiSL is used in process automation environments is growing.

In the Netherlands BiSL is rapidly becoming an industry standard for business information systems management. It is estimated that BiSL has been adopted by about 150 organizations in the Netherlands; since the publication of the Dutch version of the book in 2005 over 1800 people in the Netherlands have followed a foundation course. Since the beginning of 2006 it is also possible to obtain a certificate on an individual basis. The Dutch approach is attracting increasing attention from organizations from other countries.

At present there are no plans for a major revision; however, the ASL Foundation hosts some very active workgroups that produce supplementary materials and best practices.

14.3 Description and core graphics

14.3.1 Objectives

The aim of the BiSL framework is to build bridges between the business processes and IT and between operational business information administration and high level information management. An overview of all relevant processes within the field of business information systems management is given. All relationships between these processes are tackled as well. BiSL offers guidance for improvement of these processes as well as a uniform dictionary. This enables professionals and organizations to exchange good practices and to learn from each other.

Use of BiSL is intended to lead towards effective and efficient processes in the field of business information systems management. Primary targets are:
- adequate IT support of the business processes
- outstanding support of end-users who make use of the information systems, both during daily operations and after implementation of major or minor changes to these information systems
- adequate control over internal and external IT suppliers
- realization of an appropriate cost/benefit ratio (both in financial and qualitative terms) related to information systems
- allowing timely adaptation of information provision to changing business needs, business processes, the user organization and business environment.

14.3.2 Structure of the BiSL framework

BiSL identifies processes at the following three levels (see Figure 14.1):
- **operations** – the implementation or operational processes involve the day-to-day use of information provision, and determining and effecting changes to the latter
- **management** – the management processes involve income, expenditure, planning, the quality of information provision and making arrangements with IT suppliers
- **strategy** – as part of the processes at the strategic level the nature of information provision is determined for the long term and how its management should be structured.

Within these three levels the various processes are grouped into seven process clusters, three at the operational level, one at the managerial level and three at the strategic level. These clusters are discussed in more detail in the following section.

Process clusters at the operational level

The following three process clusters can be found at the operational level:
- **use management** – the purposes of the processes in these classes is to provide optimum, ongoing support for the relevant business processes. The utilization management processes focus on providing support to users for the use of information provision, the operational management of IT suppliers and the control of operational data administration. The key question about utilization management is: *Is the operational information provision being used and managed properly?*
- **functionality management** – the aim of the processes in this cluster is to structure and effect changes in information provision. The key question about functionality management is: *What will the modified information provision look like?*

- **linking processes at the operational level** – the goal of the processes in this cluster is decision-making about which changes need to be made to information provision and their actual implementation in information provision within the user organization. The key question about the linking processes at the operational level is: *Why and how should we modify information provision?*

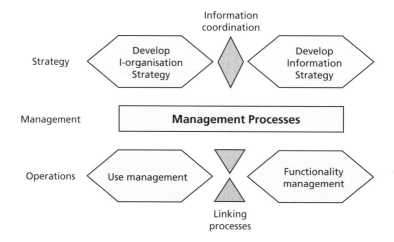

Figure 14.1 Process clusters within the BiSL framework

Process clusters at the management level

The management processes are umbrella processes: they are situated above the operational processes. These managerial processes act as a bridge, linking the strategic and operational processes.

The processes at the management level ensure comprehensive management of the implementation of information provision. Four different aspects of managing are dealt with:
- planning of time, timelines and capacity
- cost-effectiveness
- demands and needs
- contracts and service level agreements.

The key question about the managerial processes is: *How do we manage the information provision?*

Process clusters at the strategic level

There are also three clusters of processes at the strategic level. These clusters involve the formulation of policy concerning information provision and the organizations involved in this.
- **Develop information strategy** – the purpose of the processes in the information strategy cluster is to translate developments affecting business processes, the organization's environment, and technology into a view of the nature of information provision in the future. The key question

about formulating the information strategy is: *What will information provision look like in the medium and long term?*

- **Develop information organization strategy** – the processes in this cluster focus on organizing all parties involved in business information systems management. That means: coordinating the communication, management, structures and methods of all the parties involved in making decisions about information provision. The key question about determining a strategy for structuring information provision is: *How will the management of information provision be structured?*

- **Linking process at the strategic level** – the aim of the linking process at the strategic level is the coordination of all parties involved. It also plans the various subsidiary elements of the information provision. The key question about this cluster of processes is: *How can all parties influencing information provision act together?*

Figure 14.2 shows all the processes of the BiSL framework within the clusters that are described above. For a detailed description of all processes, refer to the BiSL book.

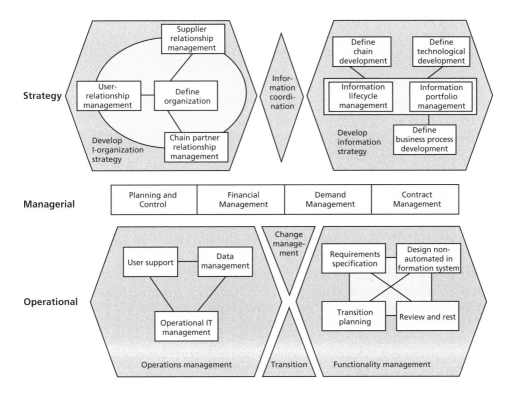

Figure 14.2 The overall BiSL framework

14.4 Approach/how to

The BiSL framework can be used as guidance within all organizations where (automated) information provision plays a significant or a less significant role. How BiSL is used varies by individual organization; each has its own unique combination of processes, structures and information needs. Which BiSL processes are used and to what extent is dependent on unique organizational characteristics. In every case the BiSL framework provides a checklist of all the processes that need to be executed in the field of business information management. The underlying best practices can be used to fit these processes to specific organizational needs. The uniform dictionary provides lessons learned and best practices to be shared with organizations or different parts of organizations.

When using the BiSL framework it is essential to be aware of the practical opportunities and possibilities within the internal organization. BiSL is not an aim in itself, but only a means of making business information systems management more professional.

Some frequently encountered pitfalls when improving business information systems management with the help of BiSL are:

- **focusing on the model instead of the best practices:** it is not the formal descriptions of the model that achieves results, but proven experiences in real practice
- **being too ambitious and avoiding an incremental approach:** a 'big bang' improvement very seldom delivers the desired results
- **failing to analyze the perceived problems:** improvement with the help of BiSL should be problem-driven; this creates commitment to the changes and solves actual problems.
- **not using the 'experience from the floor':** trying to improve changes without knowing what is really going on in practice almost guarantees failure.

14.5 Relevance to IT management

In the last few years attention for business information systems management has risen. The most important reasons for this are the following:

- **growing importance of information provision** - the business processes and information provision become more and more intertwined. Information provision becomes an important aspect of managing the business processes
- **an increasing number of situations where IT is outsourced** - when outsourcing IT services the business organization needs to take control. It has to act like any other customer: stating demands, determining a fair price to pay for these demands and setting a long term view on information provision
- **organizations are constantly changing** - given the fact that organizations change continuously, it is essential to monitor the alignment of IT to the changing business.
- **different parties involved and different demands** - most organizations consist of several departments, business units or other organizational parts that make use of common IT infrastructures and common information systems/applications. However, these different departments may have different and sometimes even opposing information demands. A clear and transparent structure is needed that is responsible for decision-making about information provision.

As the examples above show, business information systems management is becoming more and more important. The BiSL framework helps organizations to put their business information management processes in place.

14.6 Strengths and weaknesses

14.6.1 Strengths
- **Stable framework** - although BiSL is relatively new, it already has a stable framework. In the development of the framework (which took several years), many practical experiences were taken into consideration. A review board that consisted of representatives of several branches was active during development of the model.
- **Usable in various organizations** - use of BiSL need not be limited to only one kind of organization or one branch. BiSL states that the way in which business information systems management is shaped is highly dependent on the specific organization business characteristics. The BiSL framework gives guidance via a generic framework that can be applied in all sorts of situations.
- **Public domain** - BiSL is part of the public domain and is not owned by one single corporation. Anybody can make use of BiSL.
- **Supported by a foundation with a growing number of participants** - BiSL is adopted by the BiSL program of the ASL Foundation. The ASL Foundation has set its goal on improving application management and business information systems management; It has grown since adoption of BiSL and continues to grow. Membership of the Foundation is open to corporations and professional organizations as well as individual persons.
- **Fills a gap** - the BiSL framework recognizes and supports a management topic that is becoming more and more important. With BiSL, more and more recognition is given to this management topic and BiSL enables organizations to increase their IT customer role's professionalism.

14.6.2 Weaknesses
- **Relatively new and therefore unknown** - BiSL is relatively new and therefore not well known. In the Netherlands most organizations recognize the need for something like BiSL, but not all organizations are aware of its existence yet.
- **No use of existing terminology** - BiSL focuses on a newly discovered management topic that was addressed by terms such as the retained IT organization, demand management and IT customer role. It has proven to be quite difficult both in the Netherlands and internationally to use common terminology.
- **No predetermined implementation** - one of the strengths of BiSL is by some perceived as a weakness. BiSL can be used in many different organizations and situations. Improvement with BiSL is problem driven; there is no predetermined implementation.

14.7 Cross-references/relationships

14.7.1 EFQM, TQM
Implementation of BiSL within an organization will enhance the maturity of the processes and improve several areas of the EFQM model, especially Partnerships and Resources, Policy and Strategy and Results (primarily Customer Results and Key Performance Results).

With the TQM model as an umbrella, BiSL can contribute to adequate information provision to improve overall organizational performance.

14.7.2 ISO 9000:2000

When BiSL-processes are implemented within a business information management organization at maturity Levels 2 to 3, this organization is well on its way in complying to the criteria for an ISO 9000 certificate. Only the 'soft' skill criteria are not met.

14.7.3 CobiT

CobiT supports IT governance by providing a framework to ensure that IT is aligned with the business, enables the business and maximizes benefits, IT resources are used responsibly and that IT risks are managed properly. CobiT can be used to give guidance on how to execute the processes that BiSL addresses. This means that CobiT is complementary.

14.7.4 ISPL

ISPL (Information Services Procurement Library) deals with procurement of IT services. It gives guidance on how to execute procurement processes within the BiSL framework.

14.7.5 TiCKIT, ITS CMM, CMMI, ITIL, eTOM and ASL

Where the BiSL framework focuses on the demand/customer link of the information provision chain, there are other models (like TiCKIT, ITS CMM, CMMI, ITIL, eTOM and ASL) that are more suited for the IT vendor/ IT services processes. BiSL can be combined with any of the models mentioned above in order to achieve improvements in the overall information provision chain. For adequate cooperation it is crucial that all the different process models should connect to one another.

14.7.6 MSP, PRINCE2 and PMBoK

MSP. PRINCE2 and PMBoK are methods for program and project management that can be used within BiSL when projects – for instance a major change to the functionalities of an existing business information system – are of a degree of complexity that requires extra attention.

14.8 Links and literature

At present most information is only available in Dutch. However, the book and some other publications are currently being translated into English and will become available through 2006.

The core Dutch information and best practices can be found on the internet: www.bisl.nl, or the website of the ASL Foundation: www.aslfoundation.org. The ASL Foundation frequently organizes events that are open for both participants and the general public.

15 ISPL - the Information Services Procurement Library

> *The Information Services Procurement Library (ISPL) is a systematic approach to tendering and delivering IT projects and services. Its main purpose is to professionalize customer-supplier relationships.*

Owner of the copyright:	ISPL Consortium, presided over by EXIN.
Distribution:	Several organizations have adopted ISPL as a standard; hundreds of organizations have used the approach.
Origin/history:	The ISPL project (1998 – 1999) was part of the SPRITE S2 program of the European Commission and was fifty per cent funded by the Commission. ISPL has been developed out of Euromethod with the permission of the European Commission The European Committee has created the ISPL Consortium to develop ISPL to be a *de facto* standard.
When:	Version 1.0 was launched in 1999.
Participants in the ISPL Consortium:	European Commission, EXIN. ISPL's primary editors are Marcel Franckson (Atos Origin, France) and Denis Verhoef (Ordina, the Netherlands)
Certification bodies?	At EXIN, the Netherlands, individual examinations can be taken to become ISPL Foundation Manager or ISPL Procurement Manager. (www.exin-exams.com)

By Denis Verhoef

15.1 Origin/history

The ISPL project (1998 – 1999) was part of the SPRITE-S2 program of the European Commission and was fifty per cent funded by the Commission. ISPL has been developed out of Euromethod with the permission of the European Commission. Its primary editors are Marcel Franckson (Atos Origin, France) and Denis Verhoef (Ordina, the Netherlands). The copyright of ISPL rests with the ISPL Consortium, which is presided by EXIN.

In the first years after its launch, users and authorities provided the following statements, based on their experiences.

> *ISPL is a magnificent method which helps and guides you to get in control of your suppliers. ISPL has formed the basis of our strategy to implement an organization that will excel in procurement.*
> *Jacques van Wijk, Postbank, 1999*

> *Some of the recommended strategies and measures have been implemented and show better mitigation of the applicable risk and uncertainty areas. Some of the recommended strategies have deliberately not been implemented and show continuation of the associated risks and uncertainties.*
> Ben van der Zon, Ministerie van Verkeer en Waterstaat, 2000

> *Contractual relations seldom fail because of the quality and comprehensiveness of contracts. They often fail because of the lack of managing these contracts in a proper way. ISPL enables organizations to manage their contracts effectively.*
> Swier Jan Miedema, Belastingdienst/AutomatiseringsCentrum, 2001

> *Besides its unique and well known capability of supporting the management of customer-supplier relationships, ISPL is also an essential component of the tool box used for planning and managing IT programmes and projects consistently with business and IT strategy; moreover, its decision focus and risk management approach are very appealing to business executives.*
> Marcel Franckson, Sema Group, France, Primary editor ISPL

> *Failing to plan is planning to fail. ISPL helps organizations to formulate an acquisition strategy, to organizate decision making processes and to manage risks overall.*
> Denis Verhoef, Ordina Institute for Research and Innovation, Primary editor ISPL

> *We have benchmarked more than 200 European procurement organizations and found that many do not adequately manage the risks associated with IT procurements. ISPL provides an important methodology for better managing these risks and getting more consistent and improved results for IT procurement projects.*
> Scott Hansen, European Procurement Forum, The Open Group

15.2 Where is ISPL used?

Within customer and supplier organizations, ISPL is used at senior management level. ISPL helps organizations to understand the services to be acquired and delivered in large-scale settings, in the private as well as in the public sector, and to structure their acquisition and delivery.

Several organizations have adopted ISPL as a standard; hundreds of organizations have used the approach. The European Committee has created the ISPL Consortium to develop ISPL as a *de facto* standard. Version 1.0 of the approach was launched in 1999.

15.3 Description and core graphics

15.3.1 Scoping

In the uncertain and complex world of outsourcing, a robust process is essential to support the customer of IT services. Understanding the requirements, negotiating and complying with clear agreements, organizing, planning: all need to be addressed. If not addressed, the outsourcing initiative will fail.

ISPL is an example of an approach that is supported by practical application experience. The approach is based on *best practices* from large-scale IT service contracts in the European private and public sector; the design of the approach is based on the philosophy that 'one set of rules works for all' approach does not exist. Instead, this particular approach contains heuristics and practical advice that be adapted to different situations. Each heuristic contains a description of relevance in specific situations. ISPL offers many methodical building blocks for creating a customized approach. A thorough approach cannot be described in one page of short simple instructions, and ISPL does not attempt this. The ISPL approach offers various management instruments for understanding and controlling fast-changing outsourcing arrangements.

15.3.2 Benefits
Against this background, ISPL helps customers and suppliers to build a professional and businesslike relationship during an outsourcing initiative.

The following benefits concern customers. The most important responsibilities of the customer are formulating a clear requirement and making appropriate and transparent decisions. ISPL encourages customers to follow an outsourcing strategy that is designed to identify and control the major risks. During tendering they are encouraged to make use of market competition, for example by making the proposals of suppliers comparable. During delivery, ISPL supports them in using the contract as an effective control instrument and organize decision-making.

By following ISPL, suppliers are able to propose solutions that address the specific customer requirements in their proposals. During the tendering process, they are encouraged to make the responsibilities of the customer organization more explicit and based upon its control of service delivery. Because the roles of both parties in joint control are explicit, it is much easier for the supplier to build a good relationship with its customer.

15.3.3 Processes

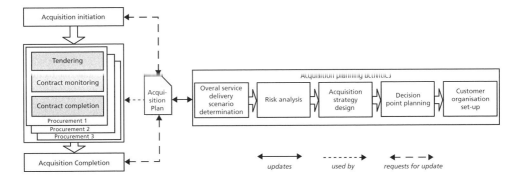

Figure 15.1 The acquisition process (source: ISPL consortium)

Two processes are focal within ISPL: the acquisition process and the procurement process. Acquisition processes aim at acquiring IT related systems and services, see Figure 15.1. The customer organization initiates the acquisition process by determining:
• **the acquisition goal**: which systems and services to be acquired
• **the acquisition strategy**, for example: how many suppliers, which procurement procedure (e.g. in Europe, the Open, Restricted and Negotiated procedures), how to engage with suppliers (for example is the Request for Proposal preceded by a Request for Information?), how flexible should the contracts be and so on.

Initiation of the acquisition process is followed by one or more procurement processes. Finally, the acquisition process is completed.

Procurement processes aim at preparing a contract and subsequently acquiring the deliverables and services defined in that contract, see Figure 15.2. Procurement processes consist of a tendering process, a contract monitoring process and a contract completion process.

The right halves of both Figure 15.1 and Figure 15.2 show a set of activities that can be executed throughout acquisition and procurement processes, emphasizing risk analysis, strategy design and decision point planning. ISPL provides guidance and heuristics for these activities.

To be in control of these processes, two deliverables have been designed; the acquisition plan and the delivery plan. ISPL offers guidance to produce these deliverables, among others, by a number of predefined activities. Risk analysis, the design of the delivery strategy and the planning of decision points are examples of those activities.

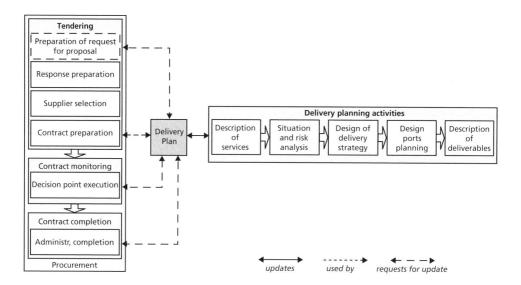

Figure 15.2 The procurement process (source: ISPL consortium)

15.3.4 Deliverables
The ISPL deliverable model is depicted in Figure 15.3.

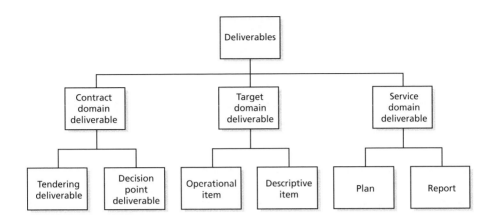

Figure 15.3 The ISPL deliverable model

15.3.5 Key concepts
All of these benefits are based on the key concepts of the approach: decision, role, deliverable, strategy option, risk, success factor and service requirement.

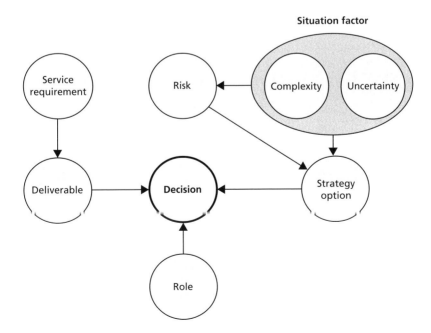

Figure 15.4 Key concepts of the ISPL model

15.4 Approach/how to

Several scenarios are available for the implementation of ISPL.

- assessment of individual existing IT programs and services, following the risk management techniques from ISPL
- organization of individual new IT programs and services, following ISPL techniques
- training of IT purchasing and management departments.

15.5 Relevance to IT management

Target groups for ISPL are: acquisition managers, program managers, contract managers, procurement managers, service level managers and project managers in the IT area.

This instrument is specifically relevant to IT management as there is a strong focus on understanding and managing large-scale, complex, uncertain IT requirements.

The major benefits of using ISPL for customer organizations are:

- formulating clear IT requirements
- designing a delivery strategy that is customized to the critical risks
- designing an acquisition strategy that is customized to the critical risks
- organizing decision making processes in a transparent way
- receiving comparable suppliers' responses
- gaining advantage from a competitive market.

The major benefits of using ISPL for supplier organizations are:

- formulating clear IT requirements
- designing a delivery strategy that is customized to the critical risks
- designing an acquisition strategy that is customized to the critical risks
- organizing decision making processes in a transparent way
- understanding customers' responsibilities.

All these benefits contribute to professional customer-supplier relationships.

15.6 Strengths and weaknesses

The major strength of ISPL is in its large body of the knowledge required to be in control of complex and uncertain IT situations. This body of knowledge is structured according to a sound conceptual framework in which the key concepts are:

- **decision** - it is made clear how decision making should be planned and structured
- **role** - it is made clear how authorities and responsibilities should be defined, related to decision making processes
- **deliverable** -deliverables are agreed only as they support decision making processes
- **strategy option** - strategy options are offered for the specification, construction and installation of IT systems and services, and for the management of IT projects and services. Hundreds of

guidelines are offered on the design of a delivery strategy which is tailored to the characteristics of a particular IT requirement

- **situation factor** – dozens of situation factors are offered to help understand the complexity and the uncertainty of an IT requirement, in a variety ranging from the attitude of the business actors and the complexity of the business processes to the adequacy of time schedules and budget. For each of these factors, the likely risks are identified
- **service requirement** - a language is offered for specifying requirements for IT systems and services, also helping to clarify expectations about analysis and design reports.

The major weakness of ISPL is related directly to its major strength. To understand and control complex and frequently changing situations, one page of short simple instructions would not be adequate. ISPL is a thorough approach and to take full advantage of its benefits, it is necessary to invest time in understanding its methodical building blocks.

15.7 Cross-references/relationships

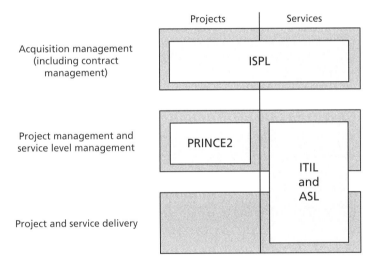

Figure 15.5 Position of ISPL

To relate ISPL to other approaches, see Figure 15.5. In this figure there are three levels of organizing projects (left column) and services (right column):

- **project and service delivery** – this provides the customer with the required services and systems. For this purpose, resources (skills, products, knowledge, etc.) are used. ITIL and ASL structure and support the delivery of services. Many systems development approaches such as Unified Modelling Language (UML) support the delivery of projects
- **project management and service level management** – this plans and monitors the services and projects. Teams are organized, resources are allocated to tasks, the required quality is

ensured within timescales and budget. ITIL and ASL support the management of service delivery. PRINCE2 supports the management of projects

- **acquisition management (including contract management)** – the acquisition and its various contracts are controlled. Service and systems requirements are documented in Requests for Proposals, responses and contracts. It controls whether requirements are met, measures are taken when they are not. ISPL supports the acquisition of systems and services, the specification of requirements and the monitoring of service and project delivery, in terms of requirements and results rather than resources.

15.8 Links and literature

The first publications were delivered in 1999. Together these books constitute the first version of the Information Services Procurement Library:

1. Introduction to ISPL (Ten Hagen & Stam 1999), ISBN 90.76304.85.8
2. Managing Acquisition Processes (Ten Hagen & Stam 1999), ISBN 90.76304.81.5
3. Specifying Deliverables (Ten Hagen & Stam 1999), ISBN 90.76304.82.3
4. Managing Risks and Planning Deliveries (Ten Hagen & Stam 1999), ISBN 90.76304.83.1
5. Dictionary (Ten Hagen & Stam 1999), ISBN 90.76304.84.X

Today, the Library has been translated into the Dutch language:
Denis Verhoef e.a., *IT Services Procurement op basis van ISPL, een introductie* (Van Haren Publishing), ISBN 90.77212.34.5.

A pocket guide in the English language has been published:
Johan C. Op de Coul, *IT Services Procurement, Based on ISPL - a Pocket Guide* (Van Haren Publishing 2005), ISBN 90.77212.50.7.

The ISPG, the Information Services Procurement Group, is considered as the ISPL User Group (though its scope is somewhat broader). Web site www.ispg.nl, e-mail bestuur@ispg.nl.

16 ITIL - the IT Infrastructure Library

ITIL (The IT Infrastructure Library) provides a framework of best practice guidance for IT service management that has become the most widely used and accepted approach to IT service management in the world. It has provided a universally accepted framework for establishing a set of integrated processes for delivering high quality IT services.

Owner of the copyright:	Office of Government Commerce (OGC), United Kingdom: www.ogc.gov.uk
Distribution:	ITIL is the worldwide *de facto* standard for IT service management.
Origin/history:	Originally developed by the Central Computers and Telecommunications Agency (CCTA, later to become part of the UK Office of Government Commerce (OGC)). The original three books were revised and consolidated into its current seven core books. ITIL Version 2 is the current version.
When:	First books in the late 1980s and 1990s, revisions from 1999 onwards, Version 3 expected to be available end of 2006.
Participants in the committee:	OGC
Certification bodies?	EXIN (www.exin-exams.com) and ISEB (www.bcs.org) offer individual examinations at Foundation level as well as practitioner level.

By Colin Rudd

16.1 Origin/history

ITIL was originally developed by the Central Computer and Telecommunications Agency (CCTA, later to become part of the UK Office of Government Commerce (OGC)), in the late 1980s and early 1990s. The library originally consisted of approximately forty books providing guidance to all areas of local and central UK government. It was subsequently adopted and used by many organizations within the private sector as well. The contents of the library were revised in a period from 1999 onwards and consolidated into its current seven core books to bring it in line with modern practices, distributed computing and the Internet.

16.2 Where is ITIL used?

ITIL provides best practice guidance in almost all areas of IT; all areas of IT should have an awareness and knowledge of the library and its contents. The successful implementation of service management within an organization depends upon vision, direction and commitment from the very top, so the contents of the library should be used and applied from heads of IT and CIOs through to practitioners, IT support technicians and administrators.

The guidelines contained within ITIL are applicable to all IT organizations whether they are internal IT service providers, outsourcing or hosting service providers providing IT services to external customers.

16.3 Description and core graphics

The challenge for IT managers is to co-ordinate and work in partnership with the business to deliver high quality IT services. This generally has to be achieved while reducing the overall Total Cost of Ownership (TCO) and often increasing the frequency, complexity and the volume of change. The main method of realizing this goal is the operation of effective, stable processes and the provision of appropriate, value for money services. The correct processes need to be developed and implemented with built-in improvement. Good IT management is all about the efficient use of the four Ps (Figure 16.1):

- people
- processes
- products (tools and technology)
- partners (suppliers, vendors and outsourcers).

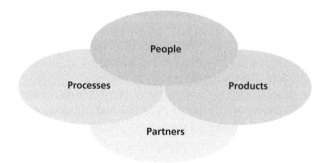

Figure 16.1 The Four Ps (source: OGC)

Though management needs to develop joint strategies and plans for all the Ps, many organizations recognize them but do not use them to maximum advantage. All too often products are bought to manage areas of technology and then the processes, partners and people roles are engineered to fit the technology and its limitations. The people and process issues must be addressed first and this is one of the core principles of ITIL.

The main objective of ITIL is to enable IT service provider organizations:

> "to improve the overall quality of service to the business within imposed cost constraint, while improving the overall effectiveness and efficiency of IT."

ITIL provides comprehensive ***best practice*** guidelines on all aspects of ***end-to-end*** service management and covers the complete spectrum of people, processes, products and the use of partners. It is scoped and developed within an overall framework (Figure 16.2). This illustrates the relationship that each of the modules has with the business and the technology. The Business Perspective module is more closely aligned to the business and the IT Infrastructure Management module is more closely aligned with the technology itself. The Service Delivery and Service Support modules provide the heart of the process framework. Together these seven modules constitute the core of ITIL:

- Service Delivery
- Service Support
- IT Infrastructure Management
- Planning to Implement Service management
- Application Management
- The Business Perspective
- Security Management.

Section 1.3 provides further detail on each of these modules.

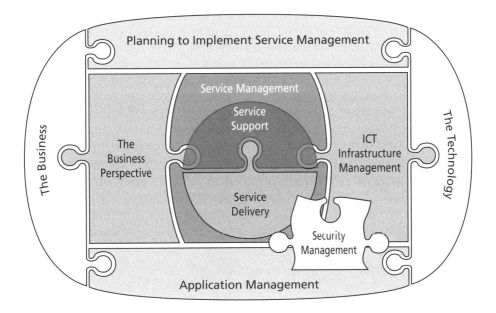

Figure 16.2 The ITIL Framework (based on OGC source)

16.4 Approach/how to

There is no universal answer to the implementation of service management solutions. Each organization is unique in terms of its business, people and culture. ITIL provides best practice guidelines and should be adopted and adapted to fit specific situations. The framework should be adopted as the process guidance, to use within an organization. Specific content should then be adapted to implement processes that are effective and efficient for the unique requirements for each organization. The only approach to the implementation of effective service management processes is to establish continuous improvement to ensure that processes are regularly developed and improved (Figure 16.3)

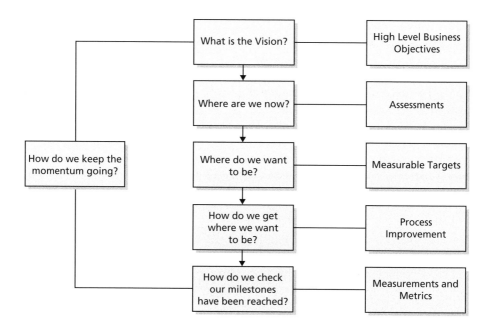

Figure 16.3 Continuous improvement (source: OGC)

This involves continuous assessment and review of the current situation, setting new targets, identifying improvement actions and measuring the effect of those completed actions. Business driven metrics, Critical Success Factors (CSFs) and Key Performance Indicators (KPIs) need to be established to measure the success of the process implementation and ongoing improvement.

16.4.1 Service Delivery

The Service Delivery module of ITIL is concerned with developing plans for improving the quality of the IT service delivered and covers the more forward-looking delivery aspects of IT service provision, including:

- Service Level Management (SLM)
- Financial Management for IT
- Capacity Management
- IT Service Continuity Management
- Availability Management.

The *SLM* process provides the major interface to the business and customers, and negotiates, documents, agrees and reviews business service requirements and targets, within Service Level Requirements (SLRs) and Service Level Agreements (SLAs). These relate to the measurement, reporting and reviewing of service quality delivered by IT to the business. The SLM process also negotiates and agrees the support targets contained in Operational Level Agreements (OLAs), with support teams and underpinning contracts with suppliers, to ensure alignment with business targets contained within SLAs. Other roles of the SLM process are:

• production and maintenance of the Service Catalog
• development and management of the Continuous Service Improvement Program (CSIP).

The Service Catalog provides essential information on the complete portfolio of IT services provided. The CSIP is the overall improvement plan for continuously improving the quality of IT services delivered to the business.

Financial Management for IT provides the basis for running IT as a business within a business and for developing a cost conscious and cost effective organization. The principal activities consist of understanding and accounting for the cost of provision of each IT service or business unit, and the forecasting of future expenditure within the IT Financial Plan. Another optional, but preferred activity, is the implementation of a charging strategy and processes, which attempt to recover the IT costs from the business, in a way that is fair and equitable.

The *Capacity Management* process ensures adequate capacity is available at all times, to meet the requirements of the business by balancing business demand with IT supply. To achieve this, a Capacity Plan closely linked to the business strategy and plan is produced and reviewed on a regular basis. This covers the three principal areas of Business, Service and Resource Capacity Management (BCM, SCM and RCM). These three areas comprise the activities necessary for ensuring that the IT capacity and the Capacity Plan are kept in line with business requirements. The common activities used within these areas are performance management, Workload Management, Demand Management and Application Sizing and Modeling.

IT Service Continuity Management produces recovery plans to ensure that, following any major incident causing or potentially causing disruption of service, IT services are provided to an agreed level, within an agreed schedule. It is important for each organization to recognize that IT Service Continuity is a component of Business Continuity Planning (BCP). The objective of IT Service Continuity is to assist the business and BCP to minimize the disruption of essential business processes during and following a major incident. To ensure that plans are kept in line with changing business needs, Business Impact Analysis, Risk Analysis and Risk Management exercises are undertaken on a regular basis together with the maintenance and testing of all recovery plans.

Availability is a key aspect of service quality. *Availability Management* is responsible for ensuring that the availability of each service meets or exceeds its availability targets and is proactively improved on an ongoing basis. To achieve this, Availability Management monitors, measures, reports and reviews a set of key metrics for each service and component, including availability, reliability, maintainability, serviceability and security.

16.4.2 Service Support

The Service Support component of ITIL deals with the day-to-day support and maintenance processes of:

- Incident Management
- Problem Management
- Change Management
- Configuration Management
- Release Management
- Service Desk function.

The *Service Desk* provides the single, central point of contact for all users of IT within an organization, handling all incidents, queries and requests. It provides an interface for all of the other Service Support processes and is the principal user of the *Incident Management* process, which is responsible for the management of all incidents through their lifecycle, from instigation and recording through to resolution and closure. The objective of Incident Management is to restore normal service as soon as possible.

The goal of *Problem Management* is to minimize the adverse impact of incidents and problems on the business. Problem Management supports Incident Management by determining the route cause of incidents and problems, while recording all workarounds and 'quick fixes' as known errors where appropriate and raising changes to implement permanent structural solutions wherever possible. Problem Management also analyses incidents and problems and their trends to proactively prevent the occurrence of further incidents and problems.

A single centralized *Change Management* process, for the efficient and effective handling of changes, is vital to the successful operation of any IT organization. Changes must be carefully managed throughout their lifecycle from initiation and recording, right through to their eventual review and closure. One of the key deliverables of the process is the Forward Schedule of Change (FSC), a central program of change agreed by all areas, based on business impact and urgency.

The *Release Management* process takes a holistic view of changes to IT services, considering all aspects of a release, both technical and non-technical. Release Management is responsible for all legal and contractual obligations for all hardware and software in use within the organization. To achieve this and protect the IT assets, Release Management establishes secure environments for hardware in the Definitive Hardware Store (DHS) and software in the Definitive Software Library (DSL).

Configuration Management provides the foundation for successful IT service management and underpins all other processes. The fundamental deliverable is the *Configuration Management Database* (CMDB), consisting of a single database detailing the entire organization's IT infrastructure components and other important associated assets. It is these assets that deliver IT services and they are known as *Configuration Items* (CIs). What sets a CMDB apart from an ordinary asset register are the relationships, or links, that define how each Configuration Item is interconnected and interdependent with its neighbors. These relationships allow activities such as impact analyses and 'what if?' scenarios to be carried out. Ideally the CMDB should also contain details of any incidents, problems, known errors, changes, contracts and any other necessary records associated with each Configuration Item.

16.4.3 IT Infrastructure Management

IT Infrastructure Management (IT IM) looks at the management of the IT infrastructure on which the IT services run. It covers:

- management and administration
- design and planning
- technical support
- deployment and operations.

These processes are about managing the four Ps (see Figure 16.1) but also concentrate on those areas of IT most closely related to the actual tools and technology. They are responsible for managing a service through each of the stages in its lifecycle, from requirements, through design and feasibility, through to development, build, test, deployment, operation and optimization and disposal.

The goal of *Management and Administration* is to improve the effectiveness and efficiency of the IT infrastructure, while maintaining the overall quality of the IT services provided. The *design and planning* function is responsible for all of the strategic issues associated with the running of an IT function. The *Deployment* process deploys new and changed IT solutions to the business to agreed quality, cost and timescales. *Operations* manages the operational IT services and environments and uses the management tools available to ensure that all services and components meet all operational targets, as agreed with the business and other teams in SLAs and OLAs. *Technical support* ensures that the necessary support, skills and knowledge are available to underpin the overall service delivered by IT IM.

16.4.4 Planning to Implement Service Management

This module addresses the task of implementing or improving ITIL within an organization and considers aspects such as where and when to start, organizational change, cultural change, project and program planning, process definition and performance improvement. Initially an IT service management vision is produced expressing a mutually agreed objective between the business and IT and describing the aim and purpose of service management.

Once the vision has been determined it is important to establish **Where we are now.** This can be assessed using an overall IT organizational growth model that determines the current maturity of the IT organization in terms of:

- vision and strategy
- steering
- processes
- people
- technology
- culture.

The business and IT must then agree the future role and characteristics of the IT organization and understand *'Where do we want to be?'* This involves a gap assessment report, together with a business case for the CSIP. Wherever possible, 'quick wins' must be identified, provided they do not inhibit the achievement of long term objectives.

A plan must then be produced for the CSIP project of *'How do we get where we want to be?'* This considers:
- how the changes are going to be achieved
- where to start
- which elements are essential to address within the CSIP.

The answers to these questions determine the approach, final scope and terms of reference for the CSIP project.

A set of measurable milestones, deliverables, CSFs and KPIs must be agreed to assess the progress and performance of the CSIP, that is *'How do we check objectives have been reached?'* All of these areas need to be measured, monitored and reviewed at each stage. They should relate directly to business benefits and quality business improvements.

Having started a CSIP, one of the hardest issues to address is maintaining the focus and commitment, that is *'How do we keep the momentum going?'* Sustaining improvement is made more difficult by the continued acceleration in the rate of IT change. The success of 'quick wins' can be used to maintain the momentum during the project. Each improvement, once achieved, must be consolidated into everyone's everyday activity, in job roles and job descriptions.

Throughout all CSIP activities, the key messages of maintaining business focus, priority, impact and alignment must be emphasized and re-emphasized to ensure that all improvements realize true business benefits.

16.4.5 Application Management
A key issue is the problem of integrating application developers and IT service management more closely. The lack of service management considerations within all phases of the application lifecycle has been evident for some time. Applications need to be deployed with service management requirements included, that is:
- designed and built for:
  - operability
  - availability
  - reliability
  - maintainability
  - performance
  - manageability
- tested for compliance to specification.

It is essential that the requirements of all areas of the business and service management are considered at each stage of the application lifecycle. Development of joint IT and business strategies, as a mutual effort, needs to be a precursor to beginning any application development or deployment project. This ensures that IT and the business agree to objectives that are clear, concise and achievable. Then, the required number of applications should be appropriately documented. An application portfolio could be used for this, providing a mechanism for reviewing and evaluating the entire suite of applications in the business enterprise.

Organizations need to assess their ability to build, maintain, and operate the IT services needed by the business. A readiness assessment provides a structured mechanism for determining an organization's capabilities and state of readiness for delivering a new or revised application to support business drivers. The information obtained can be used to determine the *delivery strategy* for an application, IT service, or IT system. This is the approach to move an organization from a known state, based on the readiness assessment, to a desired state, as determined by the business drivers.

Application Management sees application development and all areas of service management as interrelated parts of a whole, which need to be aligned. The implication of this is that Application Development, Service Management and IT information management units need to co-operate closely to ensure that every phase in the lifecycle dedicates the appropriate attention to service creation, delivery and operational aspects. The emphasis must be on the importance of dealing early in the lifecycle with these issues as this can have a major impact on the effectiveness and efficiency of service delivery and operation.

16.4.6 Business Perspective

It is essential for IT organizations to align their organization, delivery and culture as closely as possible to that of the business. Close alignment can achieve significant benefits for the business, especially in areas such as continuity, risk, change and SLAs, bringing improved delivery focus and achievement of key business objectives. Alignment needs to start at the top, with alignment of IT strategies, governance and culture to those of the business. IT management needs to review its organization and services against the business and improve business alignment through CSIPs.

Effective processes ensure that IT services are aligned to business requirements and that the supplier elements also underpin and support that alignment. The Business Perspective approach to the delivery of IT services focuses on the key principles and requirements of the business, and how they relate to the provision of IT within all areas of service management. It consists of a number of processes, (Business Relationship Management (BRM) and Supplier Relationship Management (SRM) being the most important ones), aimed at aligning the current and future business and IT activities at strategic, tactical and operational levels.

IT service providers need to develop relationships with their customers and business managers, and with their major suppliers. This is particularly important where aspects of the overall service are outsourced to these suppliers and they have a direct interface to and direct impact upon the quality of service delivered to the customers and the business. Establishing BRM and SRM processes is the preferred method of achieving this.

It is crucial that the people working within the BRM process appreciate the value of IT and its role within the business value chain, and continually publicize this and reinforce the message of business and IT alignment. They need to have synergy and empathy with the business units and represent their views to the rest of IT.

SRM needs to ensure that supplier relationships are maximized to business advantage. This includes recognizing the need for different types of suppliers together with:
• appropriate relationships
• Service Catalog
• contract lifecycle
• integration of suppliers into the end-to-end service management processes
• supplier performance management.

Effective relationships can also ensure effective and innovative use of IT for business advantage, for example:
• identifying new technologies
• facilitating business transformation
• meeting ever increasing, rapidly changing business demands.

16.4.7 IT Security Management

IT Security Management defines and enforces an Information Security Policy and manages a defined level of security for information, IT services and infrastructure, in line with the policy. It enables and ensures that:
• security controls are implemented and maintained to address changing circumstances such as:
  – changed business and IT service requirements
  – IT architecture elements
  – threats
• security incidents are managed
• audit results show adequacy of security controls and measures taken
• reports are produced to show the status of information security.

IT security management needs to be part of every IT manager's job description. Management is responsible for taking appropriate steps to reduce the chances of a security incident occurring to acceptable levels. This is risk and vulnerability assessment and management. Corporate executive management is responsible for defining the corporate security policy. Every organization must have such a policy, governing IT security management by providing guidelines and direction regarding what is allowable and what is not, in the use of IT systems and data. This policy should be widely circulated, committed to by everyone within the organization and actively enforced and reviewed.

16.5 Relevance to IT management

ITIL enables and encourages IT management to recognize that no matter how good an organization is at providing IT services it can always improve. It gives a robust framework for relating and aligning with the business and its requirements on an on-going basis. It also recognizes that there are many problems associated with the delivery of high quality IT services and gives advice on how these can be avoided. It provides solutions to many problems including:

- a lack of vision, direction and senior management commitment
- poor business alignment and focus on business requirements, impacts and priorities
- poor relationships and communication
- poor quality of service
- low levels of customer satisfaction
- repeated disruption and failure of it services
- poor track record of delivering it solutions and changes.

16.6 Strengths and weaknesses

The strength of ITIL is that it is the only universally accepted best practice guidance on the implementation of IT service management. Unlike many other frameworks, architectures and standards, ITIL is the only one that provides comprehensive and extensive guidance on how service management processes can be implemented within an IT organization. Its great strengths are:

- a simple and flexible structure
- a process driven approach, scalable to any size of organization
- the breadth and depth of experience and knowledge embedded within the guidance
- the business benefits derived from its adoption and implementation
- the worldwide, universal adoption of the library and its contents
- the number of management tools that have been produced to support the implementation of ITIL-based solutions
- the breadth of publications and White Papers on ITIL and its implementation.

However, care must be taken when developing IT service management within an organization. It is easy to view and interpret ITIL as bulky and bureaucratic and as a result implement processes that inhibit change rather than facilitate it. *'Adopt and adapt'* should be the adage. Then, ITIL provides an ideal guide and framework from which each IT service provider can engineer and implement a unique and appropriate set of processes for their own specific situation.

ITIL could be improved by greater integration and consistency between the individual modules. These issues will be addressed in the current redevelopment of ITIL within the ITIL Refresh project, currently underway, which should see the publication of a new version of the library at the end of 2006 or early 2007.

16.7 Cross-references/relationships

ITIL was the first comprehensive set of guidance to be produced within the service management area. It has provided the basis for many other frameworks, architectures and standards that have subsequently been produced. The most recent of these was the international Standard for IT service management, ISO/IEC 20000. This important development has provided a key set of controls against which an organization's service management process implementation can be assessed and audited. These two publications are strongly aligned to each other in their content and application. ITIL is closely linked with several quality frameworks, such as TQM and is also aligned with CobiT.

16.8 Links and literature

The core books and CDs, as well as many other complementary publications can be purchased from OGC or the IT service management Forum (ITSMF). The ITSMF provides a worldwide community of ITIL and service management users and expertise committed to the promotion, adoption and implementation of best practice within all areas of IT service management:
www.itsmf.com
www.itil.co.uk
en.itsmportal.net/books.php?id=35

17 eTOM – the Enhanced Telecom Operations Map

> *The enhanced Telecom Operations Map (eTOM) is the most widely used and accepted standard for business process in the telecom industry. The eTOM describes the full scope of business processes required by a service provider and defines the key elements and how they interact, creating a guidebook that is fast becoming the common business language of the telecom industry.*

Owner of the copyright:	TeleManagement Forum (TM Forum): www.ogc.gov.uk
Distribution:	Used throughout the telecommunications business as the prime industry standard.
Origin/history:	Product of the TeleManagement Forum, founded in 1988 as the OSI/Network Management Forum, that was responsible for the introduction of the SNMP/CMIP interworking package reflecting multi-protocol management environments across computing and telecom environments in 1994 and for the first version of the eTOM in 1998.
When:	First version published in 1998.
Participants in the committee:	The OSI/Network Management Forum was founded by Amdahl Corp, AT&T, British Telecom PLC, Hewlett-Packard Co, Northern Telecom, Inc, Telecom Canada, STC PLC and Unisys Corp. Currently, over 400 communications service providers, network operators, their hardware suppliers and their software suppliers participate in the development of the industry, through the forum.
Certification bodies?	The TM Forum's many seminars and training opportunities can now lead to the status of a TM Forum certified engineer, through the NGOSS accreditation program that was announced in November 2005.

By Jan Hendriks

17.1 Origin/history

The eTOM is the product of the TeleManagement Forum, founded in 1988 as the OSI/Network Management Forum by Amdahl Corp, AT&T, British Telecom PLC, Hewlett-Packard Co, Northern Telecom, Inc, Telecom Canada, STC PLC and Unisys Corp. This organization was responsible for the introduction of the SNMP/CMIP interworking package reflecting multi-protocol management environments across computing and telecom environments in 1994 and for the first version of the eTOM in 1998. TM Forum organizes many conferences and training sessions worldwide and hosts a large number of working groups, where members can contribute to the development of the standards. Currently, over 400 communications service providers, network operators, their hardware suppliers and their software suppliers participate in the development of the industry, through the forum.

The primary goals for the eTOM and the associated instruments are the following:
• establishing operational guidance on the shape of business processes
• agreeing on information that needs to flow from one business activity to another
• identifying a realistic systems environment to support the interconnection of operational support systems
• enabling the development of a market and real products for integrating and automating telecom operator processes.

There are several initiatives associated with the eTOM model that address different challenges for the industry. These range from specifying the information/data model in addition to the function model of the eTOM (SID), to defining a model for the integration of IP (internet protocol), IN (intelligent networking) and IT, to defining a model for SLA management with respect to the customer to service provider interface. Of these initiatives, the eTOM is among the more mature ones, while NGOSS (next generation OSS) is the TeleManagement Forum initiative to drive efficiency in and cost out of the operation of telecom networks. NGOSS enables service providers to change the way they think about their business and operations. The eTOM is incorporated into the NGOSS initiative.

As with any tool, the eTOM model is quite frequently misused by vendors who use the terms to suggest that their solutions fit today's challenges. The TM Forum's many seminars and training opportunities can now lead to the status of a TM Forum certified engineer.

This NGOSS accreditation program is quite new (it was announced in November 2005) and aims to ensure that industry consultants deliver high-quality services that are up to date on standards and have access to assistance. Considering the wide range of professionals involved in standardization activities, this quality measure is vital.

17.2 Where is eTOM used?

The eTOM framework is widely used throughout the telecommunications business as the prime industry standard. An earlier version (R4.0) has been accepted by the International Telecommunication Union, an international organization within the United Nations System, ITU-T and is now published as part of the ITU-T TMN (Telecommunication Management Network) set of recommendations as M.3050 (2004). It is not only used by the traditional wireline operators, but also by mobile operators and in the rapidly evolving IP-based communication services sector.

Because of its layered approach, the broad eTOM picture is widely used at the board level, while at the same time the more detailed specifications support the interaction between business partners and both hardware and software vendors. As a result of the radical changes for the telecommunications market, both in the domains of commerce and technology of government regulations, the eTOM is continually being updated.

An example of this is the extension of IP-services specifics into the (details of) the model, which is becoming vital to the market, as the traditional networks are starting to migrate towards IP-only networks. Currently (April 2006) the latest released version of the eTOM is v6.0, which dates back to March 2006.

The eTOM framework is not only used by the telecommunication services providers themselves, but also by most of the vendors active in the industry. They use it to tune their product offerings to match business requirements, even before receiving these requirements. This shared use of the eTOM framework not only leads to a better match between requirement and offering, but also facilitates offerings that meet as yet unformulated requirements, thus yielding a better time to market for future developments.

Although developed for and by the combined players in the telecommunications market, the eTOM framework is sometimes even used outside the telecommunications domain, for example in the energy sector. Here customers, commercial services and network resources are also recognized, who need IT provision and management and whose usage will lead to billing. The need for separation between the enterprise, customer-oriented, service-oriented and network-oriented processes and the different dynamics of the fulfillment, assurance and billing end-to-end processes, makes it possible to generalize many of the details in the eTOM framework.

17.3 Description and core graphics

Figure 17.1 shows what is referred to as the Level One process map. It shows a set of business processes, grouped in various ways.

The oval labeled 'Customer' at the top depicts the focus for the upper levels, whereas the box at the bottom labeled 'Enterprise Management' depicts the focus of the lower levels in the diagram. The left hand side shows processes in the box labeled Strategy, Infrastructure and Product, which is aimed at strategic changes, while the box on the right hand side, labeled Operations contains operational processes. The Enterprise Management processes are not aimed directly at supporting the customer, but rather at supporting enterprise continuity. The vertical grouping in the Operations part of the map shows one set of support processes and the three main end-to-end processes: Fulfillment, Assurance and Billing for the industry. The horizontal grouping in the Operations section of the map shows the four focus areas:
• Customer Focus for the Customer Relationship Management group
• Service Focus for the Service Management and Operations group
• Infrastructure Focus for the Resource Management and Operations group
• Partner Focus for the Supplier/Partner Relationship Management group.

Figure 17.2 shows the end-to-end process flows for the three main operational processes: Fulfillment, Assurance and Billing. It visualizes the overlap between processes, where business functions play a role in multiple end-to-end processes.

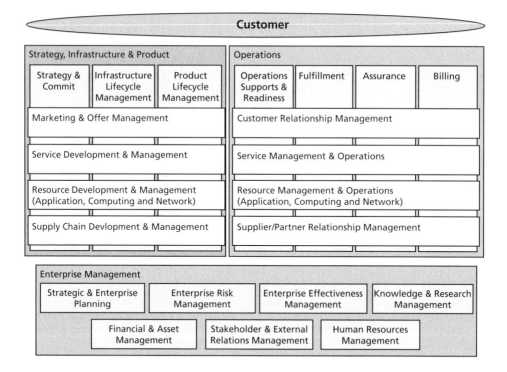

Figure 17.1 The eTOM Level One process map

All end-to-end processes begin and end with the customer. Initial fulfillment of a telecommunications service typically requires resource provision. Service requests could refer to problems with resources, while billing often depends on resource usage.

In some cases, a partner provides part of the service, which introduces a dependency on this partner for all end-to-end processes.

Diagrams such as Figure 17.3 break down the Level One process map shown in Figure 17.1 into Level Two processes. The example in Figure 17.3 breaks down the Level One process Customer Relationship Management into nine Level Two processes, which are then broadly described. These Level Two processes in turn are further detailed as a total of 270 Level Three processes, which are really business activities. These are then described in some detail.

This description specifically lists information that is vital to the activity or that is generated by it. In addition, processes from or to which the information flows are named.

This Level Three process description should not, however, be mistaken for a process flow diagram. Despite the suggested information flows, the chaining of activities into process flows is left to the user, as business-specific tuning of their organization.

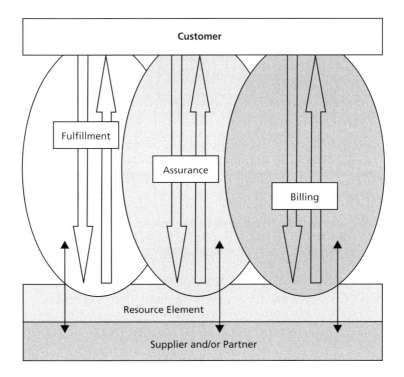

Figure 17.2 End-to-end processes

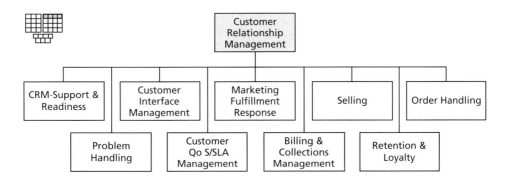

Figure 17.3 Process decomposition

17.4 Approach/how to

As a business process framework, the eTOM is particularly useful, when setting up or changing the business processes and their associated support. The main end-to-end operational and support processes are defined and specified in some level of detail. Mapping the relevant business model to these processes will help the interaction with partners. The terms in which these processes are specified are common across the industry, which facilitates vendor interaction. In a broad sense the processes themselves are common across the industry, which helps vendors provide ready-made rather than bespoke solutions. Not only does the eTOM help in communicating with various parties, it also functions as a checklist: have we covered all aspects that are relevant to our business? As with any model, it should be used as a aid, not as a solution in itself. Every business is unique and a framework should not be considered as more than a framework. It should never replace careful consideration and must always be adapted to fit the specific requirements of the organization's situation.

It is particularly useful in drafting or interpreting a (response to a) request for a proposal, since it so clearly defines common terminology for well defined business functions.

17.5 Relevance to IT management

The telecommunication services industry is highly dependent on IT. Over the past decades, telecommunications networks and systems and computer networks and systems have converged to the extent that currently a provider of telecommunications services is in fact a provider of (a specific class of) IT services.

IT is one of the main drivers for the next generation of telecommunication services, so that not only the network but also a significant amount of IT has to be managed, in order to provide innovative and new service offerings while maintaining a high level of flexibility and responsiveness to change. These changes are not only visible in the technology domain, but also in the commercial and in the regulatory domains; They require the flexibility of a modular approach for processes and the associated IT support, which can be found in the layers and in the end-to-end processes of the eTOM model. This process modularity provides clear separations between areas of responsibility, for example between business management logic and service management logic.

One way of looking at it is to say that the telecommunications industry runs IT as a business. Telecommunication services are sold directly to real-world customers. A service level agreement specifies the availability, performance and associated cost. Internal or external organizations are responsible for actually delivering the service and the IT/Telco service provider communicates to all parties involved and makes sure the service is delivered in line with the agreement, both now and in the future. eTOM tells us what is needed to make this happen for the telecommunications sector.

What the eTOM does in this market is to help define and support the business processes that can bring the business forward. It is a vital tool in requirements engineering and process design for all aspects of the organization. The eTOM plays a role in the planning phase of the organization lifecycle (cf. COBIT). In addition, vendors have widely adopted the framework, so that commercially available software packages readily support the business processes identified and specified in the eTOM.

17.6 Strengths and weaknesses

A particular strength of the eTOM as a business process framework is that it is positioned within the NGOSS program and links with other work underway in NGOSS (see section 17.7). In particular, the eTOM provides the Business Map for NGOSS and is a prime driver for business requirements to feed through from the NGOSS Business View to the System View and eventually into the NGOSS Implementation and Deployment Views.

The eTOM is aimed at supporting the planning and organization phase in the CobiT IT Control cycle. Used as a checklist, it helps an organization to cover all relevant aspects of the business. Used as a template, it yields a starting point for the process specification, both internal to the organization and, perhaps even more important, with respect to interfaces with external parties. These process specifications in turn function as the basis for the key performance indicators that are used for internal process performance management, or for external service level management. The eTOM process definitions are a first step towards process quality management.

In addition to defining processes, the eTOM can be used to help define requirements for IT support for these processes. Whenever a business can implement processes that are close to the eTOM process specifications, support for these processes becomes standard. The fit of available Commercial-Off-The-Shelf (COTS) software to the business thus improves dramatically, immediately lowering the associated costs. This is achieved through the close involvement of software and hardware vendors in developing the eTOM process framework itself.

One of the strengths of the eTOM lies in its broad scope; not only the business processes themselves, but explicitly the interfaces to the customer, the physical and logical resources, partners and the enterprise's management are included. The model is not limited to the operational processes, but includes the strategic and tactical processes needed to support the dynamics of a business. Thus, a broad range of processes and interaction with a broad range of stakeholders are incorporated into one comprehensive framework.

A possible weakness of the eTOM is that it defines business activities in isolation. The process itself, as a flow of business activities, is only sketchily defined. This could perhaps be remedied by mapping the eTOM to the ITIL framework, an effort that has recently received much attention.

Figure 17.4 shows a mapping of ITIL processes onto eTOM Level Two processes. This awareness allows IT service providers to combine the eTOM's business perspective and wide scope with ITIL's details and best practice definitions. It yields processes that both meet the internal requirements and closely match the customer's needs.

17.7 Cross-references/relationships

Internal to the TeleManagement Forum (see section 17.8), the eTOM links to various associated initiatives. Among these are the following:
- **NGOSS (Next Generation Operations Support Systems)** - NGOSS defines for service providers and their suppliers a comprehensive, integrated framework for developing, procuring

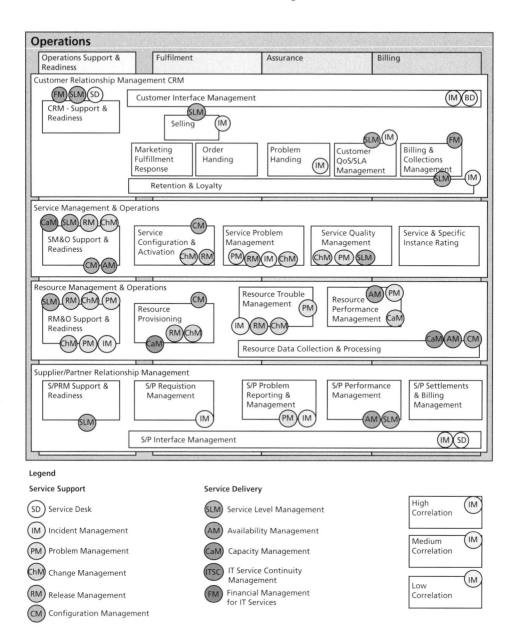

Figure 17.4 Mapping ITIL to the eTOM framework

and deploying operational and business support systems and software. NGOSS is provided as a set of documents that make up a toolkit of industry-agreed specifications and guidelines that cover key business and technical areas, and a defined methodology for use of the tools. NGOSS uses a lifecycle approach to the development of management systems, based on clear definition of business processes, specification and architecting software and systems to automate those processes, together with compliance of those systems against NGOSS test criteria. This includes a service framework, which shows how a service is modeled into its hierarchical constituent parts, SID (the NGOSS Shared Information/Data model) and NGOSS Architecture

- **MTNM (Multi Technology Network Management)** - a model for managing centralized and disparate network environments. The MTNM model provides a single, common solution for managing multi-technology networks (including SONET, SDH, DWDM, ATM, Ethernet and others) and new technologies and network capabilities emerging from ITU SG15 and OIF, including the Control Plane and Ethernet
- **IP Network Management** – a TeleManagement Forum initiative, aimed at creating solutions for the integrated management of multi-vendor IP networks. Solutions will enable a complete flow-through of IP network services from business management applications, service management and network management to the network itself.

Cross-references to other sections in this book:

- **CobiT** - links more directly to the strategic and tactical business processes. While the eTOM specifies the business activities that need to be performed, the strategic and tactical business process flows are less obvious, even in view of ITIL. The control layer on top of these tactical and strategic processes is described by the CobiT framework
- **ITIL** - has become widely accepted in the IT service management arena. Where the eTOM defines the telecommunication-specific operational business activities, ITIL can be used to chain these activities, in order to form business process flows. ITIL deals with the end-to-end process flows specifically for the assurance processes, touching also the fulfillment and billing areas.

17.8 Links and literature

More information on TM Forum and the official eTOM documentation can be found at www.tmforum.org. Here you can also find a list of members, a list of activities such as training events and more details on the various technical programs within the NGOSS framework.

18 ASL – Application Services Library

The Application Services Library (ASL) is a public domain approach for management, maintenance and enhancement/renovation of (business) applications. It consists of a framework of processes, supplemented by various publications and a periodically updated library of best practices that are available on the website of the ASL Foundation, which also provides a platform for application management organizations. Organizations use ASL as a management tool to improve the performance of application management services.

Owner of the copyright:	ASL Foundation: www.aslfoundation.org.
Distribution:	In the Netherlands, most of the major application management services providers and a number of IT departments of user organizations have joined the ASL Foundation. More than 250 Dutch organizations have adopted the ASL philosophy, and it is regarded as the de facto standard for application management in the Netherlands.
Origin/history:	ASL was developed in the late 1990s by the Dutch company PinkRoccade in order to complement the ITIL books. The ITIL books focused on IT service management, leaving room for additional best practices on application management to be documented in ASL.
When:	The first version was launched in 2002, and the intellectual property was transferred to the ASL Foundation.
Participants in the ASL Foundation:	Various organizations, both on the demand side and the supply side of IT, participate in the foundation.
Certification bodies?	On an individual level, there is an ASL Foundation examination available in English and Dutch, developed and administered by EXIN.
	Organizations will also be able to have their application management processes audited against an independent standard in future. The Netherlands Standardization Institute (NEN) is currently developing a standard for application management, based on ASL.
Number of certified people:	Over 2500 people have followed a Foundation course; approximately a third of them have also obtained a certificate.

By Mark Smalley and Machteld Meijer

18.1 Origin/history

ASL was derived from the first version of ITIL in the late 1990s. The service management processes that are recognized in ITIL were translated for the application management domain. This was needed because the ITIL books focused on IT services and not specifically on application management services, whereas the investments in application management services were growing. In addition, application managers did not recognize their own specific activities enough in ITIL.

ASL was developed by PinkRoccade in the Netherlands and based on the best practices of this IT service provider, one of the oldest IT companies in the Netherlands (now part of Getronics). ASL was donated to the public domain in April 2002 by transferring the intellectual property to the ASL Foundation. Various organizations, both on the demand side and the supply side of IT, participate in the Foundation.

18.2 Where is ASL used?

ASL is aimed primarily at both managers and professionals who wish to improve the maturity of the processes for delivering application management services. It is supported internationally, but the highest adoption rate is in the, the Netherlands, where most of the major application management services providers and a number of IT departments of user organizations have joined the ASL Foundation. More than 250 organizations have adopted the ASL philosophy. Since its introduction in 2002, over 2500 people have followed a Foundation course, approximately a third of whom have also obtained a certificate. ASL is regarded as the de facto standard for application management in the Netherlands and has also been included in various academic programs. There are no plans for a major revision of the framework, which was launched in 2002, but the ASL Foundation has active workgroups that regularly publish supplementary material and best practice.

18.3 Description and core graphics

ASL defines application management as follows:

> *Application Management* - the contracted responsibility for the management and execution of all activities related to the maintenance and evolution of existing applications, within well-defined service levels.

It is concerned with the management of the maintenance, enhancement and renovation of applications in an economically sound manner. A key principle is to support the business processes using information systems during the lifecycle of the business processes (as opposed to the life of the individual application).

This means managing and maintaining the software, databases and documentation. It entails programming, systems development, design and impact analysis and processes that ensure the optimum availability of the applications with a minimum of disruption in the operation. ASL is positioned according to the IT management model of Professor Maarten Looijen (Delft University, the Netherlands), who distinguished three forms of IT management: business information management, application management and infrastructure management:

- **business information management** deals with maintaining the functionality of information systems. It represents the user organization that benefits from the functionality and is the owner of the information system

• **infrastructure management** is responsible for maintaining the operational aspects of the information system, comprising hardware, software and databases. It is the organization that runs the information systems and maintains the infrastructure. This will often be the data center. ITIL is a widely adopted standard in this area.

ITIL introduced a concept that was new to Professor Looijen's model: service management, an overarching layer over the application management and infrastructure management domains. To a large degree, ASL is based on ITIL concepts, which is evident from the names and structure of many processes. ASL uses these concepts specifically for the application management domain: management, maintenance and enhancement of applications. This does not only tackle other issues but also requires different skills.

The ASL Framework includes generic process descriptions of all the 26 processes, including items such as goal, input/activities/output and relationships with the other processes. The purpose of the management framework is to be able to describe the breadth and depth of application management, so that readers can appreciate the activity domains and the aspects relevant to them or require management attention. It can also be used to facilitate awareness and understanding.

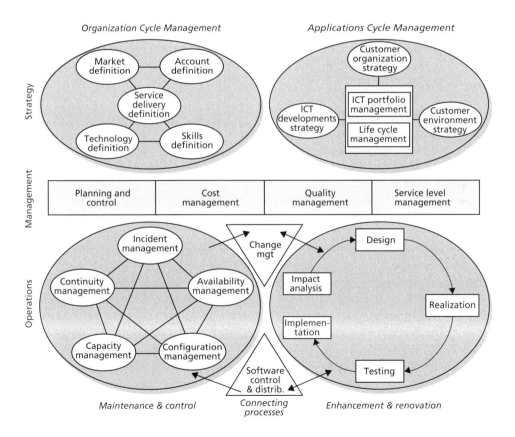

Figure 18.1 ASL Framework

The framework consists of six process clusters, divided into three levels: the operational and management processes have a short to medium term perspective whereas the governance processes look two years ahead.

The **Maintenance and control cluster** aims to ensure that the current applications are used in the most effective way to support the business processes, using a minimum of resources, and leading to a minimum of operational interruptions. The primary objective of application management is to support and ensure the applications are up-and-running.
The five processes are similar to ITIL processes with the same names and with similar objectives but different content, due to the different nature of application management:
- **incident management** registers and handles reported defects and questions and provides users with information about the implications of (changes in) the application and the application management services
- **configuration management** entails the identification, registration and management of the application and application management service components that are being used, such as the applications and documentation
- **availability management** is concerned with the availability and reliability of the application and the application management services
- **capacity management** manages the deployment of the required (non human) capacity and assets to provide the right application management services and performance
- **continuity management** ensures the continuity of the operation and support of the application and application management services and, for example with security, fraud prevention, fallback facilities and back-ups.

The **Enhancement and renovation cluster** ensures that the applications are modified in line with changing requirements, usually as a result of changes in the business processes, keeping the applications up-to-date. This is where the modifications to the software, data models and documentation are made. These processes are similar to activities performed during the initial development of applications:
- **impact analysis:** activities to identify and assess the impact of a request for change
- **design:** information analysis and functional design
- **realization:** technical design and programming of changes to applications, resulting in new releases
- **testing:** testing the new releases and transfer for acceptance
- **implementation:** final preparation for the introduction of the changed software and other service components, including conversion, acceptance tests, training, instruction and migration, followed by a sign-off.

Although the approach looks similar to application development, there are some fundamental differences between the initial development of applications and enhancement and renovation later on in the lifecycle. Unlike development, maintenance and enhancement are affected by a number of complications:
- **heavier demands:** a new release often has to be introduced at a set date in order to cope with changed legislation or because new products have to be introduced
- **shorter feedback cycle:** the designer and programmer will be quickly confronted with poor quality work, which will have to be tackled promptly

- **fewer options for improvement:** due to the restrictions imposed by choices made several years before; changes have to be made within the existing structure and the ideal solution often has to be sacrificed for a creative compromise.

The operational process clusters **Maintenance and control** and **Enhancement and renovation** are closely related as they deal with the same application objects. The two connecting processes deal with transferring software and data enhancement to maintenance in a controlled way:

- **change management** relates to the process that determines which requests for change are introduced in a 'release'. In consultation with the client, and validated by impact analysis, this process results in an agreement on the alterations that will be made on the scheduling, costs and completion dates. It monitors during the enhancement project whether changes to the release have to be made
- **software control and distribution** covers the processes involved with the control and distribution of software objects and additional objects (such as documentation) during development and testing and during the transfer to operation.

The **Management processes** ensure that all of the operational process clusters are integrally managed. Attention is paid to managing human resources, deadlines, revenue and costs, internal and external quality (service levels).

- **Planning and control** ensures that the agreed application management services are provided at the right time and with the right capacity, by deploying the right IT and human resources at the right time. This deals with both project-like activities (releases within Enhancement and renovation) and continuous activities (Maintenance and control). Balancing and managing both these aspects, usually within the same department and people, is one of the main challenges of the application management organization.
- **Cost management** deals with registration of costs, providing adequate financial data for decision making and billing for the agreed application management services.
- The objective of **quality management** is to assure the quality not only of the processes and organization but also of the application itself. It focuses on structural issues that cannot be dealt with in the day-to-day operation.
- **Service level management** aims to monitor and improve customer satisfaction and to improve the application management services provided to the customer. It covers the activities needed to define the service level required by the customer, as well as monitoring the actual service level.

Applications Cycle Management (ACM) deals with business and IT alignment, developing a long-term strategy for the information systems, in line with the long-term strategies of the (business) organization. It is approached from two perspectives: the individual applications and the application portfolio, looking at all the applications in relation to each other. ACM looks mainly at business issues – developments in both the sector in which the organization operates and the organization itself – so it has to be done together with business information management. The main task of application management is to ensure these issues are addressed.

Organization Cycle Management (OCM) looks at the long-term organizational development of the application management unit, whether this is an internal department or a commercial organization. Application management departments are often very conservative and this is a stimulus to get them thinking about the kind of application management services they want to provide. The services demanded by the users become so broad that it is difficult for both internal and external application management organizations to provide the full range. This forces a decision about the services that should be provided by the application management organization itself, and those where a partnership might be appropriate. OCM stipulates that the application management department or company considers not only its customers' future needs but also its own future.

Based on the ASL framework and best practice with application management, an ASL maturity model was developed, to measure the maturity of individual processes and of the application management services organization.

18.4 Approach/how to

ASL can be used to improve a broad spectrum of aspects of application management, varying from cost control and quality of service to staff motivation and strategic alignment. The overriding recommendation is that a pragmatic approach should be followed, starting with an analysis of problem areas. Then, part – not necessarily all – of ASL can be adopted, with a strong emphasis on utilizing the best practices that other organizations have developed and approaching the improvement as a continual process rather than a discrete project.

Due to the diversity of both the problem areas and the size, complexity and maturity of organizations, it is difficult to give an indication of the results and costs of adoption. In terms of days spent, the costs could vary between twenty to fifty days for improving the communication in a small organization, introducing the framework and uniform terminology, to several thousands of days for a major revamp of processes in a large organization.

Some frequently encountered pitfalls include:
- focusing on the model instead of the best practices
- being too ambitious and avoiding an incremental approach
- failing to analyze the perceived problems
- not utilizing the experience and insights of the team members involved in the management and execution of application management.

Training and certification of personnel plays an important role in implementing ASL. Most of the courses provided by various training institutes focus on preparation for the ASL Foundation examination (40 multiple choice questions, developed and administered by EXIN), which is available in English and Dutch.

In addition to this certificate, which is awarded to individuals, organizations will also be able to have their application management processes audited to an independent standard in future. The Netherlands Standardization Institute (NEN) is currently developing a standard for application management, based on ASL.

18.5 Relevance to IT management

IT management is faced with a number of major challenges: justifying the large proportion of IT spending, mitigating operational and other risks while coping with increasing technical and organizational complexity and the seemingly never-ending challenge of bridging the gap between IT and the business.

ASL can make a contribution to resolving these issues by providing more insight into the costs of application management, reducing risks by improving the reliability of both management processes and operational processes and finally improving the alignment with the business by initiating and feeding a strategic dialogue between application management and business information management.

18.6 Strengths and weaknesses

Organizations can benefit the most from ASL by adopting it where bespoke software is maintained and enhanced. Teams with combined responsibility for the operational management of the application and its enhancement and renovation will benefit more than teams where enhancement and renovation is performed by the organization that focuses on the initial development. Development organizations will benefit from the best practices for maintenance of existing systems, which is often neglected in most system development methodologies.

One of ASL's stronger points is that it provides an overview of all of the activities (from operational to strategic) that are needed to keep applications up-to-date with the changing needs of the business. Most other models only cover part of the spectrum. ASL can be improved by a better demarcation between application management and infrastructure management and by removing some minor conflicts in terminology.

18.7 Cross-references/relationships

- **EFQM** - Implementation of ASL within an organization for application management will enhance the maturity of the Processes and improve the areas of Policy and Strategy and Results (primarily Customer Results and Key Performance Results).
- **ISO 9000:2000** - when ASL processes are implemented within an application management organization on maturity Level three to three, this organization is well on its way to complying with the criteria to master an ISO 9000 certificate (about eighty per cent coverage at least). Only the soft skill criteria are not met.
- **ITS-CMM** - IT Service CMM does not cover software maintenance and is complementary to ASL. ITS-CMM offers more thorough management processes than ASL, so if this is an area that needs particular attention, it might be worth combining these models. ITS-CMM can be applied to all domains within an IT service organization, including part of the business information management domain. ASL, however, pays much more attention to strategic processes than ITS-CMMI and gives a more detailed description of the activities that need to be performed within the operational processes. This is supported by best practices.
- **CMMI** - CMM primarily looks at aspects dealt with by the ASL processes Quality Management and Planning and Control but not at the strategic level. ASL does not use maturity levels for

the Application Management organization as a whole but provides a way of determining the maturity of the ASL processes. This is similar to the continuous approach of CMMI. Where ASL focuses on how well the processes are implemented, CMMI focuses on how well these processes are managed.

- **CobiT** - CobiT supports IT governance by providing a framework to ensure that IT is aligned with the business, enables the business and maximizes benefits, IT resources are used responsibly and IT risks are managed appropriately. ASL also addresses the first two points, but does not contribute significantly to the last two; this means that CobiT is complementary. CobiT covers all aspects of IT, whereas ASL focuses on application management.
- **ISPL** - ISPL (Information Services Procurement Library) deals with procurement of IT services and has links with application services. It mostly addresses business information management issues and can enhance the quality of input for the ASL Service Level Management process.
- **MSP, PRINCE2, PMBoK and ICB** - methods for program and project management can be used within ASL when projects – for instance a major release or the renovation of an application – are of a degree of complexity that requires rigorous attention.

18.7.1 BiSL

BiSL (Business Information Services Library) is a relatively new model, with a structure similar to ASL, which targets management of business information systems. The most important subjects are:

- information management
- demand management
- end-user support
- defining new functional requirements
- managing the implementation of changed information systems.

It is generally acknowledged that of the three IT management domains in the Looijen model (which also is the context for the BiSL model), business information management currently is the weakest link. A more professional and mature business information management would enable both application management and infrastructure management to act at a higher level.

18.7.2 ITIL

ITIL and ASL are complementary frameworks. Where ITIL is usually applied to generic service management processes, ASL is used for the application management processes, which ITIL does not cover in depth.

As ASL was derived from ITIL, the superficial overlap between ASL and ITIL Application Management deserves particular attention and is addressed in the following two paragraphs by describing the major similarities and differences.

Similarities

Both ITIL Application Management and ASL address the alignment of IT with changing business needs. ITIL Application Management describes an approach based on the Henderson and Venkatraman Strategic Alignment Model (SAM), including control methods. In ASL, business and IT alignment is addressed by the Applications Cycle Management process cluster, developing a long-term strategy for information systems in line with the long-term strategies of the organization. The approaches are complementary.

Differences
- ITIL Application Management focuses on the manageability aspects of applications, whereas ASL focuses on how application management is executed.
- ITIL Application Management aims to improve the application development processes in order to deliver better IT services; ASL aims to improve the application management processes (service management processes as well as application maintenance and enhancement processes) in order to deliver better application management services.
- In order to benefit from implementing ITIL Application Management, the organization needs to have attained a certain degree of experience and maturity, whereas ASL can successfully be adopted by organizations of varying levels of maturity.

18.8 Links and literature

The main publication in English is:
- Remko van der Pols, *ASL: a Framework for Application Management* (Van Haren Publishing 2004).

Other experts who frequently publish and speak on ASL can be found via the ASL Foundation.

The core information and best practices can be found at the ASL Foundation website: www.aslfoundation.org. The Foundation frequently organizes events that can be attended by both participants of the foundation and the general public.

19 MSP – Managing Successful Programmes

> *The method 'Managing Successful Programmes' (MSP) is a systematic approach to manage successful programs to achieve outcomes and realize benefits that are of strategic importance.*

Owner of the copyright:	UK Office of Government Commerce (OGC)
Distribution:	MSP is accepted as a *de facto* best practice standard in the UK and rapidly becoming a best practice standard in the Netherlands and the other European countries.
Origin/history:	After developing the project management method PRINCE2, OGC considered developing a program management method as the logical next step.
When:	First edition published in 1999 by CCTA (now part of OGC). Second and revised edition published in 2003 by OGC.
Participants in the committee:	Best Practice Reference Group, MSP Review Group
Certification bodies?	Individual certification can be obtained via The APM Group Limited and by the accredited training organizations and overseas also by appointed examination bodies/ professional bodies.

By Bert Hedeman

19.1 Origin/history

Managing Successful Programmes (MSP) is a publication of the UK Office of Government Commerce (OGC). The first edition of the manual *Managing Successful Programmes* was published in 1999 by CCTA (now part of OGC). A second and revised edition was published in 2003 by OGC.

Program management is about achieving outcomes and realizing benefits and therefore considered by OGC as an automatic next step after the development of the project management method PRINCE2.

OGC is an office of the UK's HM Treasury, set up in 2000. OGC incorporates the Central Computer and Telecommunications Agency (CCTA), which no longer operates as a separate agency. MSP remains in the public domain and the Crown retains copyright. MSP is a registered trademark of OGC.

19.2 Where is MSP used?

MSP can be used as a fundamental reference for anyone interested in program management, such as:
- policy and strategy developers who are initiating change and need to build links to program delivery to ensure the policy or strategy has a feasible delivery route
- members of the executive management board who are responsible for commissioning programs
- program owners
- program and project managers
- business change managers
- business managers who are responsible for the realization of the benefits identified within the program
- functional managers involved in programs and business change
- people involved in the direction, steering or management of projects that are part of a program
- review team leaders and members involved is assessing programs
- people who are members of project teams or who make audit or assurance contributions to projects, if their projects are to be implemented within a program
- management consultancies and service providers, who may be employed to support or work within a program.

Senior executives, program owners, program managers and business change managers will find most added value in MSP, as it helps them to successfully fulfill their responsibilities within the program setting. However, all roles such as involved business and functional managers and other stakeholders may very well find it useful to understand the principles of program management.

Managers are likely to be interested in program management because it provides a structure to achieve outcomes and realize benefits. It integrates the changes to be implemented and focuses on strategic importance..

MSP can be used to deliver change in parts of an organization, across the entire organization, across more than one organization, or in the environment in which the organization operates. A program can be used to deliver a range of different types of change (see Figure 19.1):
- based on making and delivering of new facilities
- focused on changes the way the organization works
- focused on changes and improvements in society.

MSP is accepted as a *de facto* best practice standard in the UK and rapidly becoming a best practice standard in the Netherlands and the other European countries. MSP can be applied in public as well as private sector organizations.

There are no important revisions planned, apart from a review to integrate the terms of reference of the best practice methods of OGC, such as MSP, PRINCE2 and M_o_R.

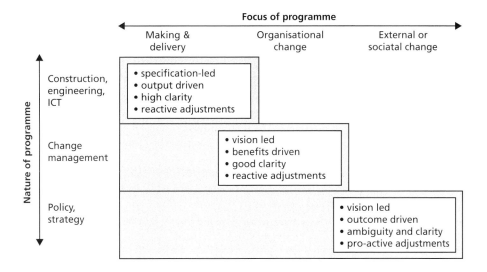

Figure 19.1 Types of change (source: OGC)

19.3 Description and core graphics

19.3.1 Project versus program management

> A **project** is a temporary organization created for the purpose of delivering one or more business products (outputs) according a specific business case.
>
> A **program** is a portfolio of projects and (business) activities that are co-ordinated and managed as a unit such that they achieve outcomes and realise benefits that are of strategic importance.

A program is not the same as a project. Projects delver outputs such as a new product or facility. The outputs contribute to a program, which achieves outcomes – a business responsibility.

Within the framework of a program a portfolio of projects will be carried out to deliver outputs needed to create the new situation. Based upon this, the program can achieve the planned outcome and can realize the expected benefits.

Differences between a project and a program are shown in Figure 19.3:
- in contrast to a project whereby pre-defined results are delivered, a program is intended to realize the objectives
- a project includes work packages and project activities to deliver the project result. A program uses products and services from projects and business activities in order to realize the objectives
- the closing of a program must thus be deliberately determined and initiated. The decision must be made as to how long the benefits of maintaining a separate program organization justify the extra costs. The time will come when a separate organization of the change is no

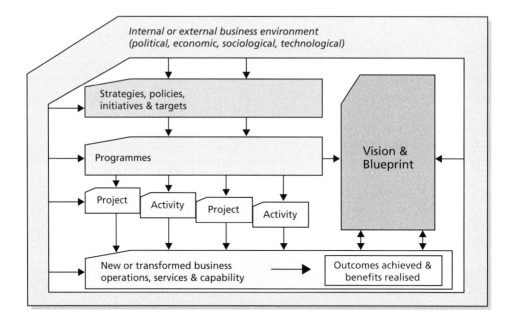

Figure 19.2 Program versus projects (source: OGC)

longer desirable via a program, and it is better to transfer this responsibility back to the business organization. This contrasts with a project, where the end of the project automatically follows the completion of the project delivery

- objectives and associated added value must not just be realized at the end of a program, but also during the program itself. These also fall within the responsibility of the program. The benefits of a project accrue at the end of a project or afterwards.
- a program runs longer than a project. The results of various projects are delivered while a program is underway.

Project	Program
• Delivery product of service	• Realizing objectives
• Co-ordinate work packages	• Co-ordinate projects & business activities
• Ends by handing over output	• Must be closed formally
• Benefits accrue at end or after the project	• Benefits realized during Program and afterwards
• Shorter timescale	• Longer timescale

Figure 19.3 Differences between projects and programs (Source: Programme Management based on MSP)

19.3.2 Program management based on MSP

MSP describes the best practice to manage programs. It adopts a process model of initiating, defining, governing and closing a program. It also contains seven knowledge areas, known as 'principles':
• organization and leadership
• benefits management
• stakeholder management and communications
• risk management and issue resolution
• program planning and control
• business case management
• quality management.

These principles represent the skills and practices that the program management team will need. The method is then supported by a glossary of program management terms, a risk identification checklist and product description outlines for the most important program management documents.

Organization and leadership contains the key principles of leadership, the terms of references for each role of the program management team and practices for designing and implementing a program organization. The other principles all describe the respective objectives, strategies, activities, practices, responsibilities, inputs, outputs and links.

The critical success factors to manage a successful program are:
• clear and consistent vision of the changed business or revised outcome
• focus on benefits and the internal and external threats to their achievement
• coordination of a number of projects and their independencies in pursuit of these goals
• leadership, influence, management and direction of the transition, including handling cultural change.

Organization and leadership

Effective leadership is indispensable for carrying out changes within an organization. Good management is not enough; someone must take the lead and give direction, instill enthusiasm and create the conditions necessary to actually carry out the changes. Here, leadership takes over from simple management.

Effective leadership requires:
• empowered decision-making, giving individuals the autonomy to fulfill their roles effectively
• visible commitment and authority with enough seniority to balance the program's priority with business-as-usual. There must be a focus on the realization of the business benefits and influence and engagement with stakeholders
• relevant skills and experience to provide active management of the cultural and personal aspects of the changes and other issues and risks.

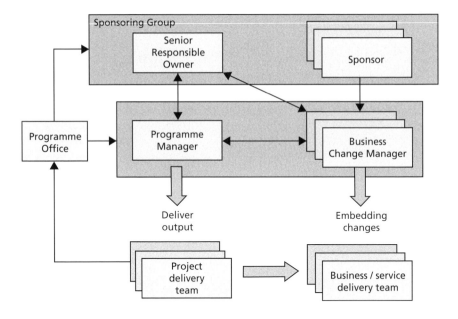

Figure 19.4 Program management structure (Source: Programme Management based on MSP)

MSP describes in detail the roles and the structure of the program management team, consisting of:

- **sponsoring group** - all managers who have final responsibility for the business units involved in carrying out the strategic change
- **Senior Responsible Owner (SRO)**- the program owner, the person who is accountable to the sponsoring group for the outcome of the program
- **program manager** - is responsible for daily management of the program under direct control of the senior responsible owner
- **business change managers** - individuals responsible for carrying out the changes and realizing the objectives in the individual business units
- **program office** - the organizational unit responsible for administrative and professional support of the program.

Benefits management

Every program starts with a vision. Whether the goal is solving or preventing a problem, or extending chances in the future, each change involves realizing benefits. It is the added value of the change that justifies the investment in the new future.

A program coordinates projects that deliver outputs, which deliver new or improved capabilities for the organization when the outputs are integrated into business operations. The new or revised capabilities enable the business to achieve its goals and to realize the envisaged benefits. The program has achieved the end goal if the organization has adopted this new way of working and realized the end goals and associated benefits.

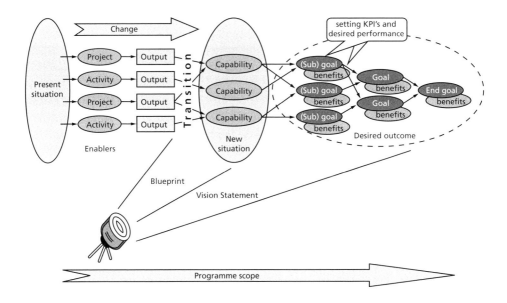

Figure 19.5 How a program achieves goals (Source: Programme Management based on MSP)

Program management lifecycle

The initiative to start a program can come from any level in the organization, but it is only viable if supported by senior management. This starts with the Program Mandate to the future SRO. In order to clarify the scope of the program, the SRO will first set up a Program Brief (for identifying the program) for approval by the Sponsoring Group (Identifying a program).

The program will start after the Program Brief has been approved, and the program has been authorized by the Sponsoring Group. Following approval, a program team, led by the program manager and based on the Program Brief, will prepare the program definition with the associated plans, strategies and risk and issues registers for managing the program (Defining a program).

Implementation of the program can start following review and approval of the program definition and all plans, strategies and risk and issues register by the Sponsoring Group at the end of Defining a program. First, program control and a Program Office must be set up. The program must be managed and its performance assessed throughout the entire process (Governing the program).

New projects are started up. Existing projects with program objectives are aligned. The program portfolio of projects is coordinated and monitored in accordance with the Program Plan and adjusted for the constantly changing environment (Managing the Portfolio).

The departments concerned must be prepared for the changes, and the new capabilities are implemented. The envisaged benefits are realized. The new way of working should be embedded into the organization in order to become the new 'business as usual' (Managing Benefits).

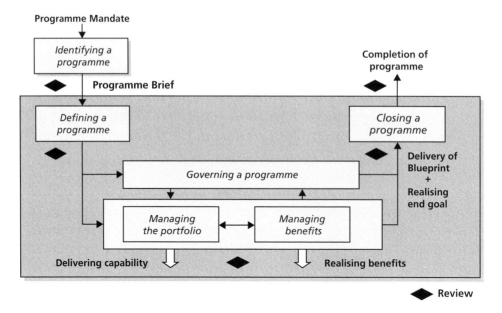

Figure 19.6 Program processes and main products (Source: Program Management based on MSP)

The program should be closed either once the end goals have been achieved or when the required new or revised capabilities described in the Blueprint have been delivered and it has been concluded that the remaining benefits to be realized do not require a separate program organization any more. The program is given a final assessment, the organization disbanded and the responsibility for the realization of the remaining benefits and the associated performance measurements transferred to the respective departments (Closing a program).

19.3.3 How program management helps
The objective of implementing program management is to achieve strategic outcomes and to realize the respective benefits effectively.

MSP provides organizations with an approach to program management that will:
• enable more effective delivery of change
• keep the focus on the business change objectives
• provide a framework for senior management to direct the change process
• encourage more efficient use of resources through project prioritization and integration
• provide better management of risk because the wider context is understood
• achieve business benefits during and after the program through a formal process
• improve control of costs, standards and quality
• enable more effective management of the business case
• provide more efficient control of a complex range of activities
• provide clear definition of roles and responsibilities
• deliver a smooth transition from current to future business operation.

MSP comprises a set of principles and processes for use when managing a program. It is founded on best practice although it is not prescriptive. It is very flexible and designed to be adapted to meet the needs of local circumstances.

19.3.4 Certification program

There are currently three qualifications available for MSP. The examinations are person focused:

- **foundation** - the first qualification consists of fifty multiple choice questions to be answered in forty minutes. This is a closed-book examination. The Foundation examination is designed to test the candidates general understanding of the fundamental principles of MSP based on the book
- **intermediate** - the second qualification is 120 minutes long. The examination is closed book, and consists of five questions, of which three must be answered. No reference material is allowed. The Intermediate examination is designed to test the candidate's comprehensive understanding of the principles and theory of the MSP book
- **practitioner** – the third qualification is also 120 minutes long. The examination is open- book, and consists of a case study with one or two questions which must be answered. Paper based reference material can be used. The Practitioner examination is designed to test the candidate's thorough understanding of the principles and theory of the MSP book supported by practical application and a good general level of understanding that comes from having worked within large programs.

Candidates must always take the Foundation Examination before the Intermediate and Practitioner Examinations, either on the same day or separately.

Accredited Training Organizations run and invigilate the MSP examinations. Open Centre Examinations are organized by The APM Group Ltd. Overseas examinations are organized by both Accredited Training Organizations and appointed examination bodies/professional bodies.

19.4 Approach/how to

The program management practice can be applied in many ways, but it always needs commitment from the top of the organization. Executive management needs to conclude that change is necessary and that it cannot be an incremental change. This management needs to take the lead to initiate and direct the program.

Effective leadership of a program can only be achieved through informed decision-making and a flexible management regime. The organization, structures and roles need to be tailored to suit individual programs. Program management is most effective when issues are debated freely and risks evaluated openly.

Program management should be considered as an instrument of top management of the organization to manage strategic change. With program management there will be a continuous focus on the costs, benefits and risks of the required change. The business retains control of the change and remains ultimately responsible to achieve the outcomes and to realize the defined benefits.

19.5   Relevance to IT management

Very often IT projects stand alone and are not integrated with the business. IT projects often miss business attention. Responsibilities for the implied change and the realization of the defined benefits are not clear. Business units are not ready and even not willing to implement the change and to make optimal use of the outputs of IT projects.

MSP gives the IT managers the opportunity to position their projects within a framework of change and within a business vision of the future organization. Responsibilities can become clear. A Blueprint of the new organization can be developed and agreed.

19.6   Strengths and weaknesses

MSP is becoming essential reading for people interested in program management. Some considerations of value are:
- MSP is a best practice in program management
- focus on achieving outcomes and realizing benefits
- characteristics and concepts of program management are well described
- focus on added value and management of risks
- clear terms of references for all roles within the program management structure
- focus on processes: describes all processes and activities within these processes of program management
- there are outlines for all program management products
- MSP can be seamlessly combined with the PRINCE2 project management method, as they both have been developed as a best practice by OGC and they have a similar, process based, management approach.

In addition:
- MSP is a framework: it can be applied with different tools and techniques
- MSP has a generic approach: it can be used in all types of programs
- MSP is not prescriptive: it is flexible and can be adapted to meet the needs of local circumstances
- open to all; no license to use
- certification programs all over the world
- continuous development by active user groups
- training via Accredited Training Organizations.

Some aspects that could be improved include:
- best practices for different areas of application
- integration of the terms of reference for MSP, PRINCE2 and M_o_R
- the description of the initiative to start up a program, incorporating an assessment of the sense of urgency and a SWOT-analysis[1]

---

1   An analysis that is widely used to consider the **S**trengths, **W**eaknesses, **O**pportunities and **T**hreats of a given product or idea.

19.7   Cross-references/relationships

Program management based on MSP is directly related to other best practices and those of OGC in particular:

- **Organizational Maturity Models (OPM3, PM3)** – these models measure the organization maturity of project and program management in organizations
- **performance managements (Balanced Scorecard)** – performance measurements are an essential part of managing benefits, which is the primary objective of any program
- **Management of Risk (M_o_R)** – risk is an essential aspect of managing programs. The method M_o_R describes and integrates risk management within programs, projects and business operations. M_o_R is therefore directly linked to MSP and is also a best practice of OGC
- **Generic Framework for Information Management** – this is a framework to support the coordinated management of a portfolio of projects
- **management frameworks in general** – implementation of management frameworks require an integral change within organizations. Program management is essential to apply these changes in the organization
- **Project management frameworks** - MSP can be used in conjunction with any project management framework, be it **PRINCE2**, **PMBoK** or **IPMA Competence Baseline**. However, as PRINCE2 and MSP are both methods designed by OGC, they are in certain ways comparable. Both frameworks are process based and both frameworks emphasize roles, responsibilities, authorities and tasks. It is an advantage if both frameworks are used in conjunction with each other. However, MSP is less prescriptive in its nature than PRINCE2. For instance PRINCE2 defines sub-processes for each process and describes these sub-processes in full detail. MSP has only processes and tasks and no sub-processes at all.

All best practices of OGC (PRINCE2, ITIL, MSP, M_o_R,) are process oriented and therefore fit with each other. However, it is not essential to use MSP with other best practices of OGC. MSP can be applied together with other managerial frameworks too.

19.8 Links and literature

19.8.1 Sites

- **www.get-best-practice.co.uk** - The site is a one-stop shop for all the official OGC publications, including MSP.
- **www.apmgroup.co.uk** - The APM Group provides accreditation and qualifications of OGC best practice products such as MSP on behalf of OGC. The website contains also a listing of all Accredited Training Organizations for MSP.
- **www.programmes.org** – The special website of the APM Group for the method Managing Successful Programmes (MSP)
- **www.usergroup.org.uk** – The best practice User Group provides high quality support services for users of OGC Best Practice products such as MSP and act as the central coordinator of general user feedback about them to OGC.
- **www.mspug.nl** - The website of the MSP User Group in Holland. Please note that this site appears in the Dutch language.

- **www.e-program.com** - The program management website. This site is dedicated to the promotion, discussion and exchange of information relating to the field of program management. E-program provides a world wide focus for knowledge exchange for those involved in managing programs of all kinds.

19.8.2 Books

- Office of Government Commerce, *Managing Successful Programmes* (The Stationery Office 2003)
  - This is the original manual of the method
  - ISBN: 0-11-330917-1
- Office of Government Commerce, *An Introduction to Programme Management* (The Stationery Office 1993)
  - ISBN: 0-11-330611-3
- B. Hedeman, G. Vis van Heemst, *Programme Management based on* MSP (Van Haren Publishing 2006)
  - ISBN: 90-77212-06-X
- J. Chittenden, *Programme Management based on MSP, a management guide* (Van Haren Publishing 2006)
  - ISBN: 90-77212-67-1
- B. Hedeman, G. Vis van Heemst, *Programmamanagement op basis van MSP, een introductie* (Van Haren Publishing 2005)
  - ISBN: 90-77212-51-5

20 PRINCE2 - PRojects IN Controlled Environments

PRINCE2 (acronym of PRojects IN Controlled Environments) is a project management method for any type of project.

Owner of the copyright:	Office of Government Commerce (OGC), United Kingdom: www.ogc.gov.uk
Distribution:	PRINCE2 is the *de facto* best practice project management standard in the UK and is widely used in the Netherlands and Australia. Spreading out from these centers examinations in the method have currently been taken in over fifty countries throughout the world.
Origin/history:	PRINCE2 is a development of a 1975 IT project management method called PROMPT II (Project Organization, Management and Planning Techniques), developed by a group of ex-IBM project managers. This was adopted by the CCTA (Central Computer and Telecommunications Agency, now part of OGC), in 1979. Additions were made in 1989 and it was renamed PRINCE. The method was revised in 1996 to be applicable to all types of project.
When:	Latest version 2005
Participants in the committee:	OGC, APM Group, ISEB, Accredited Training Organizations representative, APM, Chief Examiner, Chief Assessor
Certification bodies?	Two certificates are offered in the method, Foundation and Practitioner. Over 200,000 people have taken the Foundation examination in the UK alone and 180,000 people have taken the Practitioner examination, also in the U.K. Elsewhere in the world over 20,000 have taken the examinations.
Number of certified organizations	70+

By Colin Bentley

20.1 Origin/history

PRINCE2 is a development of a 1975 IT project management method called PROMPT II (Project Organization, Management and Planning Techniques), developed by a group of ex-IBM project managers. This was adopted by the CCTA (Central Computer and Telecommunications Agency, now part of OGC), in 1979. Additions were made in 1989 and it was renamed PRINCE. The method was revised in 1996 to be applicable to all types of project. Ownership rests with

OGC. Most U.K government departments have it as their standard project management method and a number of public and private companies insist on its project managers holding the two PRINCE2 certificates.

20.2 Where is PRINCE2 used?

The method is owned by the UK Office of Government Commerce, part of HM Treasury. It concentrates on the work of the project manager, team managers and those members of senior management involved in the decision-making activities of the project. It is the *de facto* best practice project management standard in the UK and is widely used in the Netherlands and Australia. Spreading out from these centers, examinations in the method have currently been taken in over fifty countries worldwide. An office has recently been set up in China to develop the growing interest there and elsewhere in the Far East.

20.3 Description and core graphics

PRINCE2 is a scalable, flexible project management method, suitable for use on any type and any size of project. It has been derived from professional project managers' experiences and refined over years of use in a wide variety of contexts.

There are two **key principles** of PRINCE2 that form the basis for an understanding of the method:
- **a project should be driven by its business case** - a project should not be started unless there is a sound business case for it. At regular intervals in the project lifecycle there should be a check to confirm that the project is still viable; the project should be stopped if the justification has disappeared
- **PRINCE2 is product-based** - PRINCE2 focuses on the **products** (documents) to be produced by the project, not the activities to produce them. This affects its method of planning, many of its controls and its approach to ensuring quality.

A key approach of the method is that it firmly distinguishes the **management** of the development process from the **techniques** involved in the development process. The method consists of eight **processes**, eight **components** and three **techniques** which will be discussed below. Figure 20.1 shows how they fit into the 'big picture' of the PRINCE2 method.

Figure 20.2 shows the standard PRINCE2 project organization. This should be tailored to individual projects, combining or sharing many of the roles where appropriate.

Two certificates are offered in the method, Foundation and Practitioner. Over 200,000 people have taken the Foundation examination and 180,000 people have taken the Practitioner examination in the UK alone. Elsewhere in the world over 20,000 people have taken the examinations.

20.3.1 Processes

PRINCE2 offers a set of **processes** that provide a controlled start, controlled progress and a controlled close to any project:
- starting up a project

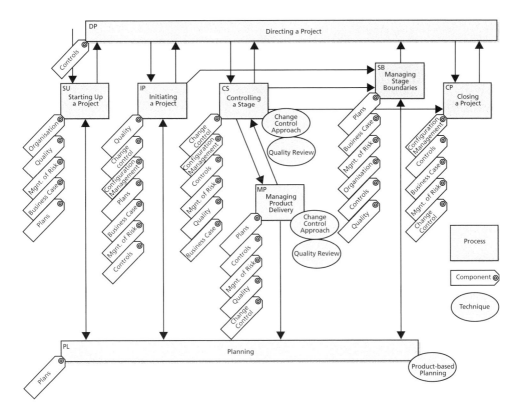

Figure 20.1 PRINCE2 processes, components and techniques (based on OGC source)

- initiating a project
- directing a project
- controlling a stage
- managing product delivery
- managing stage boundaries
- closing a project
- planning.

The processes explain what should happen, when it should be done and by which role. Any project run under PRINCE2 will need to address each of these processes **in some form**. However, the key to successful use of the process model is in tailoring it to the needs of the individual project. Each process should be approached with the question: 'How rigorously should this process be applied on this project?'

Directing a Project (DP)

This process is aimed at the senior management team responsible for the project, the key decision-makers. They are usually very busy people and should be involved only in the decision-making process of a project. PRINCE2 helps them achieve this by adopting the philosophy of management by exception. The DP process covers the steps to be taken by this senior management

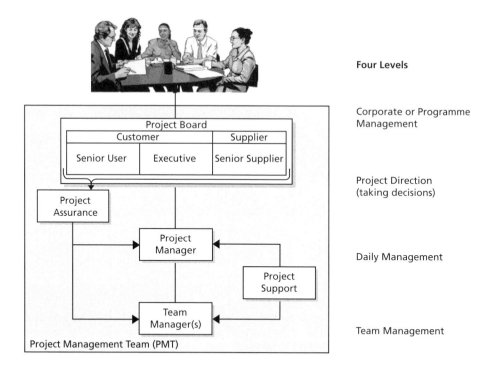

Four Levels

Corporate or Programme
Management

Project Direction
(taking decisions)

Daily Management

Team Management

Figure 20.2 Organizational structure of PRINCE2 (based on OGC source)

team (the project board) throughout the project from start-up to project closure and has five sub-processes:
- authorizing the preparation of a project plan and business case for the project
- approving the project go-ahead
- checking that the project remains justifiable at key points in the project lifecycle
- monitoring progress and giving advice as required
- confirming that the project comes to a controlled close.

Starting Up a Project (SU)
This is intended to be a very short pre-project process with five objectives:
- design and appoint the project management team
- ensure that the aims of the project are known
- decide on the approach which will be taken within the project to provide a solution
- define the customer's quality expectations
- plan the work needed to draw up the PRINCE2 'contract' between customer and supplier.

Initiating a Project (IP)
This process prepares the information on whether there is sufficient justification to proceed with the project, establishes a sound management basis for the project and creates a detailed plan for as much of the project as management are in a position to authorize. The management

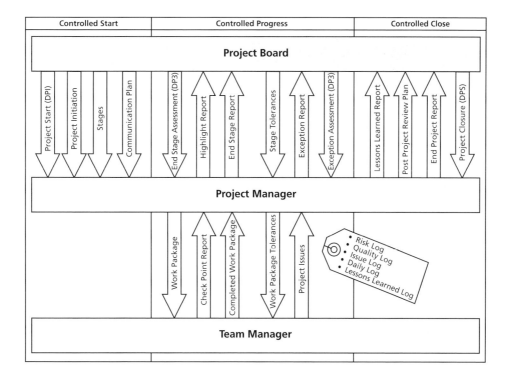

Figure 20.3 Project controls

product created is the Project Initiation Document, the baseline against which project progress and success will be measured.

Controlling a Stage (CS)

This process forms the core of the project manager's effort on the project, being the process which handles day-to-day management of the project development activity. It describes the work allocation, monitoring and control activities of the project manager involved in ensuring that a stage stays on course and reacts to unexpected events. Throughout a stage there will be many cycles of:

- authorizing work to be done
- gathering progress information about that work
- watching for changes
- reviewing the situation
- reporting
- noting useful lessons in the Lessons Learned Log
- taking any necessary action.

The process covers these activities, together with the ongoing work of management of risk and change control.

Managing Product Delivery (MP)

This process provides a control mechanism so that the project manager and any specialist teams can agree details of the work required. This is particularly important where one or more teams are from third party suppliers who may or may not be using PRINCE2. Each individual piece of work agreed between the project manager and the team manager, including target dates, quality and reporting requirements, is called a work package. The MP process covers:

- making sure that work allocated to the team is authorized and agreed
- planning the team work
- ensuring that the work is done
- ensuring that products meet the agreed quality criteria
- reporting on progress and quality to the project manager
- obtaining acceptance of the finished products.

Managing Stage Boundaries (SB)

The objectives of this process are to:

- report on the outcome and performance of the stage which has just ended
- plan the next stage
- update the project plan
- update the business case
- update the risk assessment
- obtain project board approval to move into the next stage.

If a major deviation from a Stage Plan is forecast, the project board may request the project manager to produce an Exception Plan (See the Controls component for an explanation). This process also covers the steps needed for that.

Closing a Project (CP)

This process covers the project manager's work to request the project board's permission to close the project either at its natural end or at a premature close decided by the project board. The objectives are to:

- note the extent to which the objectives set out at the start of the project have been met
- confirm the customer's satisfaction with the products
- confirm that maintenance and support arrangements are in place (where appropriate)
- make any recommendations for follow-on actions
- ensure that all lessons learned during the project are annotated for the benefit of future projects
- report on whether the project management activity itself has been a success or not
- prepare a plan to check on achievement of the product's claimed benefits.

Planning (PL)

Planning is a repeatable process, used by several of the other processes whenever a plan is required. The process makes use of the PRINCE2 product-based planning technique and covers:

- designing the plan
- defining and analyzing the plan's products
- identifying the necessary activities and dependencies

- estimating the effort required
- scheduling resources
- analyzing the risks
- adding text to describe the plan, its assumptions and the quality steps.

20.3.2 Components

PRINCE2 has eight **Components** to explain its philosophy about various project aspects, such as organization, risks and plans, why they are needed and how they can be used. The eight components include:
- Business Case
- Organization
- Plans
- Controls
- Management of Risks
- Quality in a Project Environment
- Configuration Management
- Change Control.

This philosophy is implemented through the processes.

Business case

PRINCE2 is based on the premise that a viable business case should drive a project. The essential contents are defined and linked with the points in the processes when the business case should be updated or consulted.

Organization

PRINCE2 provides the structure of a project management team, plus a definition of the roles, responsibilities and relationships of all staff involved in the project. Depending to the size and complexity of a project, some of the roles described can be combined or shared.

Plans

PRINCE2 offers a series of plan levels that can be tailored to the size and needs of a project, and an approach to planning based on products rather than activities.

Controls

PRINCE2 has a set of controls which facilitate the provision of key decision-making information, allowing the organization to pre-empt problems and make decisions on problem resolution. For senior management PRINCE2 controls are based on the concept of 'management by exception', that is if a plan is agreed, the project manager should be allowed to carry on with it unless something is forecast to go wrong.

Risk

Risk is a major factor to be considered throughout the life of a project. PRINCE2 defines the key points when risks should be reviewed, outlines an approach to the analysis and management of risk, and tracks these through all the processes.

Quality

PRINCE2 recognizes the importance of quality and incorporates a quality approach to the management and technical processes. It begins by establishing the customer's quality expectations and follows these up by laying down standards and quality inspection methods to be used, and checking that these are being used.

Configuration Management

Tracking the components of a final product and their versions for release is called configuration management. There are many methods of configuration management available. PRINCE2 does not attempt to invent a new one, but defines the essential facilities and information requirements for a configuration management method and how it should link with other PRINCE2 components and techniques.

Change Control

PRINCE2 emphasizes the need for change control and this is enforced with a change control technique plus identification of the processes that apply the change control.

20.3.3 Techniques

PRINCE2 offers three **Techniques**. The use of most of them is optional:
- product-based planning
- quality review technique
- change control technique.

The organization may already have a technique that is covering that requirement satisfactorily, such as quality checking and change control. PRINCE2 works effectively alongside such in-house techniques. The exception is the product-based planning technique. This is a very important part of the PRINCE2 method. Its understanding and use bring major benefits and every effort should be made to use it.

Product-based planning is fundamental to PRINCE2. There are two reasons for this; firstly, a project delivers products, not activities, so why begin at a lower level? The second reason is about quality. The quality of a product can be measured. The quality of an activity can only be measured by the quality of its outcome (the product).

Product-based planning has three components:
- Product Breakdown Structure
- Product Descriptions
- Product Flow Diagram.

Product Breakdown Structure

Most planning methods begin a plan by thinking of the activities to be undertaken, and listing these in a hierarchical structure called a Work Breakdown Structure (WBS). These activities, however, depend on what products (documents) are required to be produced by the project, so the correct start point for a plan is to list the products. In fact, by jumping straight to the lower level of detail of activities, it is possible to miss some vital products and hence vital activities from the plan.

A Product Breakdown Structure is a hierarchy of products, the production of which must be shown in the plan. At the top of the hierarchy is the final end product, for example a computer system, a new yacht, a department relocated to a new building. This is then broken down into its major constituents at the next level. Each constituent is then broken down into its parts, and this process continues until the planner has reached the level of detail required for the plan.

Product Description

For each significant product a description is produced. Its creation forces the planner to consider if sufficient information is known about the product in order to plan its production. It is also the first time that the quality of the product is considered. The quality criteria indicate how much and what type of quality checking will be required. The first step when planning a project should be to write a Product Description for the final product.

The purposes of this are, therefore, to provide a guide:
• to the planner on how much effort will be required to create the product
• to the author of the product on what is required
• against which the finished product can be measured.

These descriptions are a vital checklist to be used at a quality check of the related products.

Product Flow Diagram

The Product Flow Diagram (PFD) is a diagram showing the sequence in which the products have to be produced and the dependencies between them. It is produced after the Product Breakdown Structure.

A PFD needs only three symbols; a rectangle to contain the products to be created by the project, an ellipse for products that are either already available or are to be obtained from a source external to the project, and an arrow to show the dependency.

20.4 Approach/how to

The method can be used free of charge, although OGC retains ownership rights. The method does not attempt to cover techniques that are already in the public domain, such as network planning and the use of Gantt charts, but it does show the interface with such techniques. The method covers all sizes of project, but understanding of the method is required to be able to use its flexibility and scalability.

20.5 Relevance to IT management

As the method was originally devised for IT by a group of IT managers, it is still very relevant to the management of IT projects. It has an excellent approach to the planning and organization of a project and describes the production of a business case, often a weak area in IT projects. The 'Closing a Project' stage is also very relevant as many IT staff are more interested in moving on to the next innovative project, rather than formally closing down a project and tying up any loose ends. The concept of a Work Package 'contract' between the project manager and a team manager brings a discipline often lacking in IT projects.

20.6 Strengths and weaknesses

The method provides a disciplined approach to project management through the combination of its processes and components. It sets out what information is needed in order to begin a project and the appointment of the necessary decision-makers for the project, establishing the link between the project manager and senior management representing the finance provider, those who will use the final product and those who will supply that product.

The controls, risks and quality chapters of the method are particularly strong, as they provide details of timings, products, roles involved and a full structure of how to apply these aspects of the method. Controls are described for senior or program management, the project board and the project manager. A complete approach to the management of risk is given, covering the topic from identification of a risk to its assessment, formulation of a suitable response and then resourcing, monitoring and controlling action against that risk. Quality coverage begins before the project officially begins, covers the establishment of the required quality standards and roles, quality planning and monitoring, reaction to any quality problems, and links to change control, configuration control and lessons learned.

PRINCE2 gives:
- controlled management of change by the business in terms of its investment and return on investment
- active involvement of the users of the final product throughout its development to ensure the business product will meet the functional, environmental, service and management requirements of the users
- efficient control of project resources
- active management of risk and quality throughout the life of the project
- active control of all products and changes to those products
- a controlled start, controlled progress and a controlled close.

PRINCE2 is not a complete answer to project management. It does not contain techniques such as leadership or any 'soft skills', network planning or Gantt charts. The reason that it gives for these omissions is that such techniques are already widely available, subject to personal choice and can be incorporated with PRINCE2 without conflicting with the method or these techniques.

Some people claim that a weakness of PRINCE2 is that it does not cover programs, but this is deliberate, because PRINCE2 has a sister product, *Managing Successful Programmes (MSP)* that takes care of program considerations.
Although PRINCE2 rightly states that the business case is the key aspect of a project, the chapter on business case lacks detail on investment appraisal.

20.7 Cross-references/relationships

PRINCE2 is a sister product to the *de facto* best practice program management product, MSP (Managing Successful Programmes). There is no problem with using it in conjunction with PMBoK. They share the same beliefs. PMBoK states in general terms what should be done in a project. PRINCE2 provides more of a prescriptive way of the when, how and who of implementing these things.

PRINCE2 is a project management method and is normative in its nature. PMBoK is a body of knowledge and is descriptive by contrast.

In general where PMBoK describes the best practice inputs, outputs, tools and techniques, PRINCE2 limits itself to a general set of management products and does not refer to any specific tools or techniques besides the three general techniques they have included in their own manual. On the other hand, PRINCE2 gives much more body to the (sub-)processes and is in that way more structured than PMBoK. Further, PRINCE2 is prescriptive in which roles have to be defined and the responsibilities, authority and tasks for the individual roles (who has to do what) and the PMBoK is not. The PMBoK limits itself to the statement that roles have to be defined and agreed.

Both frameworks limit themselves to project management. Both frameworks define (sub-) processes and a number of knowledge areas (in PRINCE2 called competences). Both frameworks define input and output documents for each sub-process. Both frameworks give outlines of management products: in PMBoK in the knowledge areas, in PRINCE2 in the annex. Both frameworks describe a number of techniques: PMBoK in the knowledge areas, PRINCE2 in separate chapters. Both frameworks state that they are based on best practices, which is correct for both.

In PMBoK the *knowledge areas* are the heart of the method, in PRINCE2 the *processes* are the heart of the framework. In PMBoK the processes are described in 35 pages and the knowledge areas in 200 pages. In PRINCE2 the processes are described in 170 pages and the components in 90 pages.

PMBoK has five processes and PRINCE2 eight. Where the PMBoK processes will repeat themselves in each stage, PRINCE2 defines the processes for the total project, although some processes can be applicable more than once. Based on the given set of processes with PRINCE2, a process flow can be defined for the project.

In PMBoK the process chapter is limited to defining the processes and sub-processes and to list the respective input and output documents per sub-process. The rest is covered in the knowledge areas. In PRINCE2 the processes form the heart of the method. PRINCE2 defines for each sub-process the fundamental principles,
• context
• process description
• scalability
• responsibilities
• key criteria
• hints and tips
• input and output documents are described.

PMBoK has nine knowledge areas inclusive of Integration, Scope, Communications and Procurement. PRINCE2 has eight competences inclusive of Business Case, Controls, Change Management and Configuration Management. In PRINCE2 Communications is included in Controls, and Integration is included in the processes. Procurement is not described in PRINCE2 as PRINCE2 considers procurement as a specialist activity and not a management responsibility. The business case is the main control condition of a PRINCE2 project.

In the knowledge areas in PMBoK, sub-processes are also described and for each sub-process the inputs, outputs and used methods and techniques are described. In the competences of PRINCE2 the subject is described, more focused on what has to be done and by whom, as the input and output documents are already described in the sub-processes.[2]

20.8 Links and literature
The PRINCE2 manual and other publications on the method can be obtained from:
- The Stationery Office, PO Box 29, Norwich, NR3 1JN, book.orders@tso.co.uk
- The Stationery Office Bookshop, 123 Kingsway, London WC28 6PQ,
- The APMG bookshop, 6th Floor, Sword House, High Wycombe HP 13 6DGD

Information can be found on the following websites:
www.get-best-practice.co.uk
www.apmgroup.co.uk
www.prince2.com
www.prince2.org.uk
www.apmg-network2.com

There are several user groups around the world, for example
www.prince.usergroup.org.uk

There are many books on PRINCE2 apart from the official manual, such as:
- Colin Bentley, *Practical PRINCE2* (The Stationery Office 2005)
  - ISBN 0-11-703544-0
- Colin Bentley, *The Essence of PRINCE2* (Hampshire Training Consultants 2000)
  - ISBN 0-9539107-7-6
- Colin Bentley, *Managing Projects the PRINCE2 Way* (Hampshire Training Consultants 2000)
  - ISBN 0-9539107-6-8
- Colin Bentley, *PRINCE2 Revealed* (Butterworth-Heinemann 1997)
  - ISBN0-7506-6672-2
- Bert Hedeman, Hans Fredriksz and Gabor Vis van Heemst, *Project Management based on Prince2. An introduction* (Van Haren Publishing 2005).
  - ISBN: 90 7721266 3

---

2 We thank Bert Hedeman, author of the MSP chapter, for extending the cross- reference between PRINCE2 and PMBoK for us.

21 PMBoK – the Project Management Body of Knowledge

> *The Project Management Body of Knowledge (PMBoK®) is a document guide gathering knowledge, concepts, techniques and skills of the Project Management profession.*

Owner of the copyright:	Project Management Institute (PMI®): www.pmi.org
Distribution:	PMBoK has been translated into eleven languages, and approximately 1.773.338 original copies of PMBoK in its different versions have been distributed. It is recognized throughout the world as a standard for managing projects. The *PMBoK Guide* is approved as an American National Standard (ANS) by the American National Standards Institute (ANSI).
Origin/history:	The PMI was founded in 1969 in the USA and has become one of the principal professional non-profit organizations in the specialism.
When:	The PMBoK was first published in 1987. New editions followed in 2000 and 2004.
Participants in the committee:	The PMBoK was written by many carefully selected authors and reviewed by further experts from the project management field, under supervision of the PMI.
Certification bodies?	Besides professional certification on an individual level, with Project Management Professionals (PMP) and Certified Associates in Project Management (CAPM), the PMI provides a certification model to enterprises, OPM3® Organizational Project Management Maturity. This model consists of:

- **Knowledge**: Organizational Project Management, its maturity relevant to best practices and how to use the Model
- **Assessment:** methods for evaluating best practices and capabilities
- **Improvement:** sequence for developing capabilities aggregating to best practices.

The PMI certificates organizations that offer PM Education programs like PMI Registered Education Provided (REPs). These organizations are officially accredited to give project management courses based on the PMI.

Number of certified organizations:	At the official PMI page: tel.occe.ou.edu/cgi-bin/PMI Provider/research.cgi are published the following numbers of certified organizations: • 67 Charters • 609 Global Providers • 274 Providers • 256 Chapters • 30 Specific Interest Groups.

By Raúl Assaf

21.1 Origin/history

The PMBok is a publication of the Project Management Institute (PMI®), an entity that is recognized as governing the discipline. PMI was founded in 1969 in the USA and has become one of the principal professional non-profit organizations in the specialism. In November 2005, PMI had 207,066 members and 170,969 certificates as Project Management Professional (PMP) around the world.

Today there are 260 chapters in 67 countries, 28 Specific Interest Groups (SIGs) officers and 3.676 colleges. The chronology of the main landmarks is as follows:

- **1969** – PMI founded
- **1983** – PMI Special Report on Ethic, Standards and Accreditation. The Standards portion was the Project Management Body of Knowledge
- **1987** – PMBoK standard was published
- **1996** – A Guide to the Project Management Body of Knowledge (PMBoK® Guide) (First edition) was published
- **1999** – PMI accredited as a Standard Development Organization (SDO) by ANSI
- **2000** – The PMBoK® Guide - 2000 Edition (Second edition) was published and is recognized as standard ANSI/PMI 99–001-2000
- **2004** – The PMBoK® Guide - 2004 Edition (Third edition) was published and is recognized as standard ANSI/PMI 99–001-2004

21.2 Where is the PMBoK used?

The PMBoK can be used as a fundamental reference for anyone interested in the project management profession, such as:

- senior executives
- program and project managers
- project team members
- members of a project office
- customers and other stakeholders
- functional managers
- educators teaching project management and related subjects
- trainers developing project management educational programs
- consultants and other specialists.

Leadership roles will find most added value in the PMBoK, as it helps them to successfully deliver their projects. However, other roles like sponsors, analysts, users, customers and other stakeholders may well find it an invaluable tool to understand the activities involved during the lifecycle of their projects.

Currently, people are generally interested in incorporating project management knowledge, skills and techniques, because the discipline has strong application in their general activities. The principle can be applied to almost any activity where change occurs – for example, planning a holiday or buying a house. Additionally, it is accepted that any change implemented in an organization should be handled as a project.

Projects are the way of implementing changes, which happen every day. It is essential to learn to how to manage them effectively to make them achieve their objectives, in the stipulated time, in line with the budget and with the quality specifications.

The PMBoK can be applied in public as well as private sector organizations, especially:
• defense
• financial service organizations
• industries
• retail
• chemical
• construction
• agriculture
• oil
• technology
• marketing agencies
• infrastructure companies.

In many countries, universities have also successfully used education programs of PMBoK. Many organizations around the world have adopted the PMBoK.
It can be used to manage any project, and is not limited to any specific area: for example IT, construction and pharmaceuticals. As a fundamental reference, the PMBoK is neither comprehensive nor all-inclusive; there are extensions to each application area and lists of further information on project management in the appendices to the document.

According to *PM Today*, there are 1,773,338 original copies of PMBoK in its different versions, and it has been translated into eleven languages. The next PMBoK will be published in 2008, but there will be ongoing revisions until the document is released. Currently revisions to the Code of Professional Conduct are being made.

A Guide to the Project Management Body of Knowledge (PMBoK® Guide) is recognized throughout the world as a standard for managing projects in today's marketplace. The *PMBoK Guide* is approved as an American National Standard (ANS) by the American National Standards Institute (ANSI). There is commitment to the continuous improvement and expansion of the *PMBoK Guide*, as well as the development of additional standards.

21.3 Description and core graphics

The PMBoK is the sum of knowledge within the profession of project management. It includes traditional practices and innovative and advanced ones. It is an excellent source of information based on successful practices and provides a common 'world-class' vocabulary essential for this profession.

The PMBoK adopts a modern education model for project management. It is organized as a body of knowledge, containing nine knowledge areas:
• Project Integration Management
• Project Human Resource Management
• Project Scope Management
• Project Communications Management.
• Project Time Management
• Project Risk Management
• Project Cost Management
• Project Procurement Management
• Project Quality Management

These areas represent the skills and practices that the project manager should gather (Figure 21.1).

1. Project Integration Mgt.	2. Project Scope Mgt.	3. Project Time Mgt.
1.1 Develop Project Charter 1.2 Develop Preliminary Project Scope Statement 1.3 Develop Project Mgt. Plan 1.4 Direct and Manage Project Execution 1.5 Monitoring and Control Project 1.6 Integrated Change Control 1.7 Close Project	2.1 Scope Planning 2.2 Scope Definition 2.3 WBS Creation 2.4 Scope Verification 2.5 Scope Control	3.1 Definition of activities 3.2 Sequence of activities 3.3 Estimation of activities resources 3.4 Estimation of activities duration 3.5 The development of the Chronogram 3.6 The control of the chronogram

4. Project Cost Mgt.	5. Project Quality Mgt.	6. Project Human Resource
4.1 Estimation of Costs 4.2 Budget of Costs 4.3 Control of Costs	5.1 Quality Planning 5.2 Quality Security Planning 5.3 Quality Control Execution	6.1 Human Resources Planning 6.2 Staff Recruitment 6.3 The development of the Team Work 6.4 The Team Work Management

7. Project Communications	8. Project Risk Mgt.	9. Project Procurement Mgt.
7.1 Communications Planning 7.2 Distribution of Infomation 7.3 Reporting Performance 7.4 Stakeholders Management	8.1 Identification of Risks 8.2 Risk Management Planning 8.3 Risk Qualitative Analysis 8.4 Quantitative Analysis 8.5 Risk Response Planning 8.6 The Control of the Risks	9.1 Contracts Planning 9.2 Response Requirement Salesman 9.3 Selection of the salesman 9.4 Contract Administration 9.5 Contract Closing

Figure 21.1 The nine areas and their processes (source: PMBoK® Guide Third Edition 2004)

Each area of knowledge contains processes, and has defined forty four processes distributed in the areas of knowledge. Each process describes objectives, activities, inputs, outputs and links.

This last characteristic emphasizes the PMBoK process focus, putting it in line with modern quality management concepts. People can manage projects on behalf of the processes that are needed in each project in particular, and they can optimize their own quality measures according to the way the processes work.

Another PMBoK quality is the division into five groups, following a chronological order of the project's lifecycle: Beginning, Planning, Execution, Control and Closing a project (Figure 21.2).

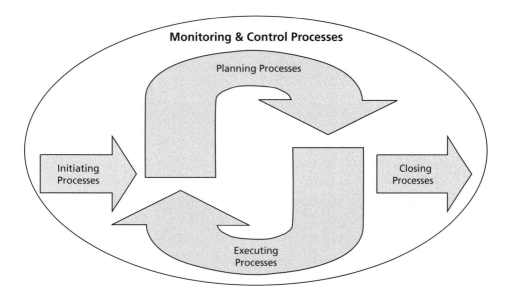

Figure 21.2 The five groups of processes (source: PMBoK® Guide Third Edition 2004)

This grouping of processes shows the application of them in a time line like the traditional Project Management methods do. These processes are connected by the results they produce; the output of one is the input for the next.

Thus, the ending of one phase becomes the beginning of the next. For example, closing the design phase requires the client's acceptance of the design document. This document describes the product for its forward implementation.

Figure 21.3 shows the concept of processes absorbed in phases - that is to say, the processes repeat in each one of the phases of the project, allowing the incorporation of the cycle **plan-do-check-act** described by Deming.

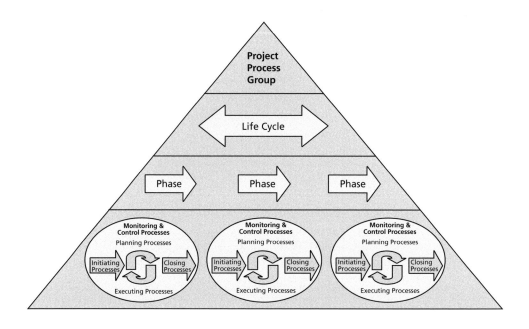

Figure 21.3 The triangle of the process groups (source: PMBoK® Guide Third Edition 2004)

For example, to repeat the Start process at the beginning of each phase helps to keep the project focused to the needs of business. The Planning process, for example, must not only provide details of the work to be done to bring the current phase of the project to successful completion, but must also provide some preliminary description of work to be done in later phases. This progressive detailing of the project plan is often called *rolling wave planning*.

The processes can be visualized with a double entrance, by knowledge area and by the groups of processes, as Table 21.1 shows. The first two numbers indicate which chapter of the PMBoK guide describes this action, the third what process group the action is a part of and the fourth describes what knowledge area this process is a part of.

The Project Management Institute (PMI) offers credentials to certificate as Project Management Professional (PMP) and Certified Associate in Project Management (CAPM). PMI's Project Management Professional (PMP) certification is the pre-eminent professional credential for individuals associated with project management.

Since 1984, PMI has been dedicated to developing and maintaining a rigorous, examination-based, professional certification program to advance the project management profession and to recognize the achievements of individuals. In 1999, PMI became the first organization in the world to have its Certification Program attain International Organization for Standardization (ISO) 9001 recognition.

Project Management Processes for a Project					
Knowledge Areas Processes	Initiating Process Group	Planning Process Group	Executing Process Group	Monitoring Process Group	Closing Process Group
1.Project Integration Management	Develop Project Charter 3.2.1.1. (1.1) Develop Preliminary Project Scope Statement 3.2.1.2 (1.2)	Develop Project Management Plan 3.2.2.1 (1.3)	Direct and Manage Project Execution 3.2.3.1 (1.4)	Monitor and Control Project Work 3.2.4.1 (1.5) Integrated Change Control 3.2.4.2 (1.6)	Close Project 3.2.5.1 (1.7)
2.Project Scope Management		Scope Planning 3.2.2.2 (2.1) Scope Definition 3.2.2.3 (2.2) Create WBS 3.2.2.4 (2.3)		Scope Verification 3.2.4.3 (2.4) Scope Control 3.2.4.4 (2.5)	
3.Project Time Management		Activity Definition 3.2.2.5 (3.1) Activity Sequencing 3.2.2.6 (3.2) Activity Resource Estimating 3.2.2.7 (3.3) Activity Duration Estimating 3.2.2.8 (3.4) Schedule Development 3.2.2.9 (3.5)		Schedule Control 3.2.4.5 (3.6)	
4.Project Cost Management		Cost Estimating 3.2.2.10 (4.1) Cost Budgeting 3.2.2.11 (4.2)		Cost Control 3.2.4.6 (4.3)	
5.Project Quality Management		Quality Planning 3.2.2.12 (5.1)	Perform Quality Assurance 3.2.3.2 (5.2)	Perform Quality Control 3.2.4.7 (5.3)	
6.Project Human Resource Management		Human Resource Planning 3.2.2.13 (6.1)	Acquire Project Team 3.2.3.3 (6.2) Develop Project Team 3.2.3.4 (6.3)	Manage Project Team 3.2.4.8 (6.4)	
7.Project Comunications Management		Communications Planning 3.2.2.14 (7.1)	Information Distribution 3.2.3.5 (7.2)	Performance Reporting 3.2.4.9 (7.3) Manage Stakeholders 3.2.4.10 (7.4)	

Table 21.1 Mapping of the Project Management Processes to the Project Management Process Groups and the Knowledge Areas

(source: PMBoK 2004)

Knowledge Areas Processes	Initiating Process Group	Planning Process Group	Executing Process Group	Monitoring Process Group	Closing Process Group
8.Project Risk Management		Risk Management Planning 3.2.2.15 (8.1) Risk Identification 3.2.2.16 (8.2) Qualitative Risk Analysis 3.2.2.17 (8.3) Quantative Risk Analysis 3.2.2.18 (8.4) Risk Response Planning 3.2.2.19 (8.5)		Risk Monitoring And Control 3.2.4.11 (8.6)	
9.Project Procurement Management		Plan Purchases And Acquisitions 3.2.2.20 (9.1) Plan Contracting 3.2.2.21 (9.2)	Request Seller Responses 3.2.3.6 (9.3) Select Sellers 3.2.3.7 (9.4)	Contract Administration 3.2.4.12 (9.5)	Contract Closure 3.2.5.2 (9.6)

Table 21.1 Mapping of the Project Management Processes to the Project Management Process Groups and the Knowledge Areas (source: PMBoK 2004) (continued)

Since 2002, PMI offers CAPM certification to people with less experience in project management, who are able to bring together project teams, to gain formal knowledge earlier in their professional development.

The PMI certificates organizations that offer project management education programs like PMI Registered Education Provider (REPs). These organizations are officially accredited to give project management courses based on PMI.

21.4 Approach/how to

The project management practice can be applied in many ways, but it always needs commitment from the management areas of the organization. Generally, qualifying staff is a primary activity when developing an organization's capability in project management.

The cross-character of projects generally means the involvement of different areas of the business and the participation of staff with different cultural characteristics, professional development and expertise.

That is why implementing project management should be done with a global vision, objectives clearly established and progressive development towards them. This last concept indicates that the implementation of project management in the organizations must be treated as a project in itself.

The basic steps to follow are:
- **business justification** – the scope of the projects, their significance, corporate decisions, main areas involved
- **objectives and intended outcomes** – application of the projects in specific areas such as IT, marketing and production; establishing a Project Management Office (PMO) and a portfolio of projects
- depending on the objectives and scope, different strategies can be defined for implementation, associated activities, resources, times and expected costs of implementation, intended results.

Typical implementation costs include:
- appointment of a project manager
- staff training: development of the course materials, study cases, laboratories, evaluation
- software training
- acquisition of project administration software.

When a project management office is established, these are other possible costs:
- setting up the project support office
- administrative staff
- infrastructure.

Implementation of the project management practice in organizations is not discussed in PMBok, as projects are part of everyday activities. However, where there is no formal knowledge of the discipline, this is one of the most significant challenges in implementation. Most university courses do not teach these skills; they require specialized training programs.

21.5 Relevance to IT management

In the last few years, the project management discipline has grown in strength, mostly due to the many IT projects and to the lack of formal knowledge in project teams. Since 1997, the number of members and project management professionals has grown very rapidly, as many organizations across the world have experienced. This is a clear sign of the profession's developing maturity.

Today the presence of IT in the business's activities, and therefore in its projects, is commonplace. This integration of IT in the business and its projects is making project management and its performance much more visible and has increased the quality requirements of the services.

However, there are statistics showing weak performance in the achievement of project goals, with projects running late, increased costs and failure to accomplish specific project goals.

The Standish Group recently published a study that included almost 365 interviews with executives who had managed over 8380 different informatics applications.[3] This investigation categorized the projects as 'successful', 'with problems' and 'canceled'. Those 'with problems' were not canceled but could not achieve the required functionality, timescales and costs. According to this study, 29 per cent of all projects succeed (delivered on time, on budget, with required

---

3 The Standish Group International, Inc. 2004 Third Quarter Research Report (West Yarmouth, Mass.) p.2

features and functions); 53 per cent are challenged (late, over budget and/or with fewer than the required features and functions); and 18 per cent fail (canceled before completion or delivered but never used). On average, only 61 per cent of the projects at risk were delivered.

Nicholas Carr, in his article *IT Doesn't Matter,* also states that the high failure rate of IT projects - estimated to be around 70 to 90 per cent - also proves how difficult it is for companies to harness the power of technology.[4] Figure 21.4 shows a study from KPMG of IT projects in 252 companies (Fortune 500), highlighting the most common weaknesses.

Causes	%
1. Project management, planning and control failures	32
2. Communication failures	20
3. Definition of the objectives failures	17
4. Insufficient knowledge of the business	17
Other causes:	
5. Hardware/Software	7
6. Project's dimension	2
7. Others	5

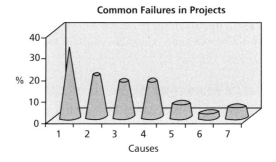

Figure 21.4 Common failures in projects

This graph shows the influence of project management on project success, in activities relating to planning, controlling, definition of objectives and scope (hard skills), communications with stakeholders (soft skills) and with the business knowledge to ensure the project will deliver business results and meet the users' needs (fitness for purpose).

The PMBoK is an instrument that tries to solve these common project problems, in an integral, consistent document, and a process of continuous improvement.

---

4 Nicholas G. Carr, "IT Doesn't Matter", *Harvard Business Review* May 2003 Issue.

IT must add value to an organization; it must develop its competence in areas such as team work, negotiation, resolution of conflicts, communication, risks and in the definition of effective processes. These competences are presented in the PMBoK in the form of a body of knowledge that unifies processes, knowledge, necessary skills and techniques for the management of projects.

IT projects are becoming of greater importance and visibility, for which professional project management is essential. The PMBoK with its modern approach, supported by specialist knowledge in all the major industry sectors contributes to this professional approach.

Another aspect to emphasize is that the recognition of PMBoK as an ANSI standard means that it can be referenced as the project approach in responses to Requests for Proposals (RFP) for IT projects.

21.6 Strengths and weaknesses

The PMBoK has become essential reading for people involved in project management. Some considerations of value are:
- extensive participation by the different industry sectors and organizations that are using project management all over the world
- recognized as a 'world class' standard in the profession
- generic: it can be applied to any project. There are documents associated with the PMBoK for many different areas and applications
- focus on process, similar to other frameworks in use (ITIL, CobiT, ISO)
- evolution and continuous improvement in line with modern concepts of quality management
- certification programs (PMP and CAPM) associated and guaranteed deployment of accreditation skills from all over the world (similar to ITIL)
- appropriate for IT projects.

Some aspects that could be improved include:
- incorporation of some aspects of implementation practice
- real-life examples of the use of the tools in practice.

21.7 Cross-references/relationships

Complementary practices and frameworks include:
- **ITIL** – Information Technology Infrastructure Library. The change management process is a clear example of this relationship, every time that a change takes place in a project
- **PRINCE2** - PRINCE2 describes a broader perspective on projects than PMBoK and is an open standard; however, the PMBok is the best known project management methodology in the world. Both have disadvantages as well: using everything from PRINCE2 for every project

can turn the organization into a bureaucracy; conversely, the Guide to the PMBok can lead to over-simplification of real-life project challenges[5]

- **OPM3** - Organizational Project Management Maturity Model. It allows measurement of the maturity of an organization's processes. Other maturity models are:
  - Capability Maturity Model Integrated (CMMI)
  - Organizational Maturity Model (OMM)
- **PMCD** - Project Management Competency Development. This framework was developed to improve the performance of project personnel. A development draft was released recently and this book is that draft in its entirety. PMI is now accepting comments on this development draft and a final version will be released soon based on feedback.

21.8 Links and literature

Many books, associations and sites exist that offer information about project management; some are listed below.

21.8.1 Sites
PMI : www.pmi.org
users : www.allpm.com
       www.gantthead.com
       www.pmblvd.com

PMI currently has cooperative agreements with the following organizations:
- **www.aacei.org** - Association for the Advancement of Costs Engineering
- **www.aeipro.org** - Asociación Española de Ingeniería de Proyectos
- **www.enaa.or.jp** - Engineering Advancement Association of Japan
- **www.aipm.com.au** - Australian Institute of Project Management
- **www.pma.india.org** - Project Management Associations
- **www.sovnet.ru** - Russian Project Management Association

21.8.2 Books
- Project Management Institute, *A Guide to the Project Management Body of Knowledge*, Third Edition (2004).
  - ISBN: 1-930699-45-X
- J. Davidson Frame, *Managing Projects in Organizations: How to Make the Best Use of Time, Techniques, and People*, 3rd Edition eBook (Jossey Bass Wiley 2003).
  - ISBN: 0787968315
- J. Davidson Frame, *Managing Risk in Organizations: A Guide for Managers* (Jossey Bass Wiley 2003).
  - ISBN: 0787965189
- Jack R. Meredith and Samuel J. Mantel, Jr., *Project Management: A Managerial Approach*, 6th Edition (John Wiley and Sons Inc 2006).
  - ISBN: 0471742775

---

5   Gerrit Koch, "ICB - IPMA Competence Baseline", chapter 22 in this book. For more on the cross-reference between PMBoK and PRINCE2, see section 20.7 in the PRINCE2 chapter 20 in this book.

- Harold Kerzner PhD, *Project Management: A Systems Approach to Planning, Scheduling, and Controlling*, 9th Edition (John Wiley and Sons Inc 2006).
  - ISBN: 0471741876
- Thomas R. Block and J. Davidson Frame, *The Project Office: A key to Managing Projects Effectively* (Crisp Publications, Inc. 1998).
  - ISBN: 156052443X
- Parviz Rad and Ginger Levin, *The Advanced Project Management Office: A Comprehensive Look At Function and Implementation* (CRC Press 2000).
  - ISBN: 1574443402
- Paul C. Dinsmore and Jeannette Cabanis-Brewin, *The AMA Handbook of Project Management* (Amacom 2006).
  - ISBN: 0814472710
- Milton D. Rosenau and Gregory D. Githens, *Successful Project Management: A Step-by-Step Approach with Practical Examples*, 4th Edition (John Wiley and Sons Inc 2005)
  - ISBN: 047168032X

In addition, there are other numerous organizations in related fields that can provide information about project management, for example:
- American Society of Quality Control (U.S.A.)
- Construction Industries Institute (U.S.A.)
- National Purchase Administration Association (U.S.A.)
- National Contract Administration Association (U.S.A.)
- Sociedad para la Administración de Recursos Humanos (U.S.A.)
- Sociedad Americana de Ingenieros Civiles (U.S.A.)

21.9 Acronyms
- **ANS** - American National Standard
- **ANSI** - American National Standards Institute
- **CAPM** - Certified Associate in Project Management
- **ISO** - International Organization for Standardization
- **PM** - Project Management
- **PMBoK Guide** - Guide to the Project Management Body of Knowledge
- **PMI -** Project Management Institute
- **PMP** - Project Management Professional
- **REP** - Registered Education Provided
- **SIG** - Specific Interest Groups

22 ICB – IPMA Competence Baseline

The IPMA Competence Baseline (ICB) is the competence standard for project management and is not restricted to any sector or branch. It was issued by the International Project Management Association (IPMA) as the common framework document all IPMA Member Associations and Certification Bodies conform to, to ensure consistent and harmonized standards for certification are applied. As such, the majority of its content focuses on the description of the project management competence elements.

Owner of the copyright:	International Project Management Association (IPMA): www.ipma.ch
Distribution/ How widely is the instrument used?	A large number of national and international organizations have adopted the IPMA certification to be the backbone of their project management competence development.
Origin/history:	IPMA started with the IPMA Competence Baseline Version 2.0. This was the first official version published in February 1999, with a small modification made in April 2001. The core team responsible for Version 3 which was accepted by the members in March, 2006.
When:	First version February 1999, latest version March 2006.
Participants in the committee:	Version 3: Gilles Caupin, Hans Knoepfel, Gerrit Koch, Klaus Pannenbäcker, Francisco Perez-Polo, Chris Seabury
Certification bodies?	The ICB is the basis for certification by the certification bodies of about forty national Member Associations, who use these competence elements in assessing candidates. The ICB, together with the IPMA Certification Regulations and Guidelines (ICRG), documents the IPMA four-level certification. The certification system complies with the relevant ISO-standards 9001: 2000, ISO 10006 and ISO/IEC 17024: 2003.
Number of certified organizations	50,000 certificates issued

By Gerrit Koch

22.1 Origin/history

IPMA started with the IPMA Competence Baseline Version 2.0. This was the first official version published in February 1999, with a small modification made in April 2001. The core team responsible for Version 3, which was accepted by the members in March 2006, consisted of: Gilles Caupin (France), Hans Knoepfel (Switzerland), Gerrit Koch (the Netherlands), Klaus Pannenbäcker (Germany), Francisco Perez-Polo (Spain) and Chris Seabury (Great Britain).

The IPMA member associations contributed with goal setting and reviews of the IPMA Competence Baseline Version 3. Copyright lies with IPMA.

22.2 Where is the IPMA Competence Baseline used?

The IPMA Competence Baseline (ICB) is of most use to individual project management personnel and assessors when undertaking an IPMA certification at any of the four certification levels. However, it can also be used as a guide for the preparation of training materials, for research purposes and as a general reference document for people seeking information about applied project management.

The primary interested parties are project, program and project portfolio personnel as well as general managers who play a role in directing them in project oriented organizations. The secondary target group consists of certification assessors, HR managers, universities, schools and trainers.

The ICB is the basis for certification by the certification bodies of about forty national Member Associations, who use these competence elements in assessing candidates. National cultural differences are addressed in National Competence Baselines by adding specific competence elements and content to the ICB. Validation of the National Competence Baselines by IPMA ensures their conformity to the ICB and the global recognition of certificates awarded by the national certification systems.

Up to 2005 these national associations have issued almost 50,000 certificates. A large number of national and international organizations have adopted the IPMA certification to be the backbone of their project management competence development.

The ICB, together with the IPMA Certification Regulations and Guidelines (ICRG), document the IPMA four-level certification. The certification system complies with the relevant ISO-standards 9001: 2000, ISO 10006 and ISO/IEC 17024: 2003.

The standard is based on *de facto* best practice in project management. The International Project Management Association (IPMA) is replacing the IPMA Competence Baseline (ICB) Version 2.0b from 2001 with the ICB Version 3.0, which has major changes to the content, during 2007. The ICB Version 3.0 was accepted by the Member Associations in March 2006 and also describes the basis for IRG Version 3. The IPMA project leading to this document is expected to be delivered early in 2007.

22.3 Description and core graphics

The cover presents the project manager's 'eye of competence' (Figure 22.1).

The 'eye of competence' represents the integration of all the competences of project management as seen through the eye of the project manager when evaluating a specific situation. The eye also represents clarity and vision. After processing the information received, the competent and responsible professional in project management takes appropriate action.

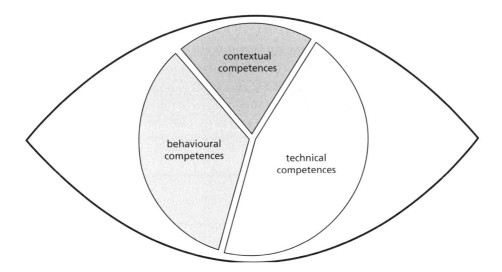

Figure 22.1 Project manager's 'eye of competence' (source: IPMA Competence Baseline, Version 3, 2006)

The ICB defines forty six competence elements covering the technical competence for project management (twenty elements), the professional behavior of project management personnel (fifteen elements) and the relationships with the context of the projects, programs and portfolios (eleven elements). The complete listing is shown in Table 22.1.

Each competence element consists of a title, a description of the content, a list of possible process steps and experience criteria required for each IPMA certification level. The key words and the key relationships to other elements are listed at the end of each element for comprehensive reading. The behavioral competences also contain pairs describing adequate behavior versus behavior that needs to improve.

The ICB does not recommend or include specific methodologies, methods or tools. The subject areas are described together with methods for determining tasks and, where they illustrate the latter well, some examples of methods. Methods and tools may be defined by the organization. The project manager should choose appropriate methods and tools for a particular project situation.

IPMA defines four levels of competence.
1. **At IPMA Level A** the candidate must have demonstrated successful use of the competence elements in the coordination of programs and/or portfolios. The candidate has guided program and/or project managers in their development and in the use of the competence elements. The candidate has been involved in implementing the competence elements or relevant methodology, techniques or tools in projects or programs. The candidate has contributed to the development of the project manager's profession by publishing articles or presenting papers on their experiences or by outlining new concepts. Specific knowledge or experience criteria and behavioral patterns for assessment are listed in the specific element in Chapter 4 of the ICB Version 3.

Competences					
	Technical		**Behavioral**		**Contextual**
1.01	Project management success	2.01	Leadership	3.01	Project orientation
1.02	Interested parties	2.02	Engagement	3.02	Program orientation
1.03	Project requirements and objectives	2.03	Self-control	3.03	Portfolio orientation
1.04	Risk and opportunity	2.04	Assertiveness	3.04	Project, program ad portfolio implementation
1.05	Quality	2.05	Relaxation	3.05	Permanent organization
1.06	Project organization	2.06	Openness	3.06	Business
1.07	Teamwork	2.07	Creativity	3.07	Systems, products and technology
1.08	Problem resolution	2.08	Results orientation	3.08	Personnel management
1.09	Project structures	2.09	Efficiency	3.09	Health, security, safety and environment
1.10	Scope and deliverables	2.10	Consultation	3.10	Finance
1.11	Time and project phases	2.11	Negotiation	3.11	Legal
1.12	Resources	2.12	Conflict and crisis		
1.13	Cost and finance	2.13	Reliability		
1.14	Procurement and contract	2.14	Values appreciation		
1.15	Changes	2.15	Ethics		
1.16	Control and reports				
1.17	Information and documentation				
1.18	Communication				
1.19	Start-up				
1.20	Close-out				

Table 22.1 The competence elements of ICB

2. **At IPMA Level B** the candidate must have demonstrated successful use of the competence elements in complex project situations. The candidate has guided (sub) project managers in their application and implementation of the competence.
3. **At IPMA Level C** the candidate must have demonstrated successful use of the competence element in project situations with limited complexity. The candidate might need to be guided in further development of the competence element.
4. **At IPMA Level D** only knowledge related to the competence element is assessed (by written examination).

Title	Capabilities		Certification process			Validity
			Stage 1	Stage 2	Stage 3	
Certified Projects Director (IPMA Level A)	Competence = knowledge, experience	A	Application, *Curriculum vitae*, project list, references, self-assessment	Projects director report		5 years
Certified Senior Project Manager (IPMA Level B)		B		Project report	Interview	
Certified Project Manager (IPMA Level C)		C			Written examination Options: work-shop, short project report	
Certified Project Management Associate (IPMA Level D) Knowledge	Knowledge	D		Application, *Curriculum vitae*, self-assessment	Written examination	not limited option: 10 years

Table 22.2 IPMA certification levels

Chapter 3 of the ICB Version 3 describes the certification process as an evolution from today's practice and compliant with the ICB Version 3. This description is the starting point for the ICRG project.

Enrolment in the certification programs is an incentive for the managers of projects, programs and portfolios and the members of the project management teams to:
• expand and improve their knowledge and experience
• continue their education and training
• improve the quality of project management
• achieve the project objectives more effectively.

The *benefits* of the certification programs are:
• **for project management personnel**: to obtain an internationally recognized certificate acknowledging their competence in project management
• **for the suppliers of project management services**: a demonstration of their employees' professional competence
• **for customers**: more certainty that they will receive high quality services from a project manager.

The IPMA four-level certification can be used as a requirement in the selection and/or professional development of project management personnel.

22.4 Approach/how to

Certification of project managers is only part of the work that has to be done to achieve maturity in an organization's project delivery. The organization has to decide on relevant standards for project management methodology, techniques and tools. Relevant stakeholders have to be trained in their roles in projects and the organization itself has to be organized to benefit from project management. Finally, information flow about projects, programs and portfolios has to be organized and formalized.

If an organization only invests in the certification and development of its project management personnel, the effect may be limited and produce disappointing results. Investment in mature projects in a mature project oriented organization always results in increased delivery of the right projects and better results from each project. The break-even of this investment may be expected within two years.

In the operation of any group of project managers the ICB can be introduced to assess each project manager. This gives an objective basis for the classification of the function along the four-level IPMA scale (D, C, B and A) as well as the road ahead. This indicates which kind of projects an individual should be able to manage and how to develop in the profession by education, training and coaching.

The ICB helps to assess and develop individual project managers as well as the whole group in an organization. The four-level certification helps to classify and build up career development in project management.

22.5 Relevance to IT management

Working in projects is a way of life in IT and almost every significant business project contains IT sub-projects. Investing in mature projects and project management is essential for survival in the IT industry. Projects contribute substantially to business and IT alignment.

22.6 Strengths and weaknesses

IPMA developed the ICB from National Competence Baselines, which were developed by the Member Associations, and then enhanced it into a continuous improvement process. A key benefit for customers is that the basis for the candidates' competence is not specific to particular organizations, disciplines, sectors of the economy or countries.

The different culture of organizations, disciplines, sectors of the economy and countries are taken into account in the interviews and assessment reports, as well as by choosing one assessor from the relevant sector (the second assessor is from another sector). The cultural aspects of a country can be included in a National Competence Baseline (NCB).

The official ICB language is English and every Member Association may decide to use the ICB directly for its certification. The Member Association can also decide to develop an NCB based on the ICB. At the end of 2005 every Member Association had its own NBC in operation.

As a result of the acceptance of the ICB by the Member Associations, every country has to develop the next version of its NCB within one or two years to continue to comply with the ICB.

The ICB as basis for IPMA four-level certification defines project management competences and offers the instruments for (self)assessment against these competences. Thus it provides answers to the questions of what project management personnel should know, how much and which experience is needed and the professional behavior required to be able to perform successfully in projects relevant to the different IPMA levels.

The ICB is not a textbook on how to deliver projects. Every mature project (management) methodology can follow IPMA's Competence Baseline. The ICB Version 2, which is in operation now, will be replaced by the ICB Version 3 in 2007. Improvements in the ICB Version 3 lie primarily in:
- the definition of the essential competences for project delivery, in relation to the project's context, as well as the major competences regarding project management behavior
- the definition of knowledge and experience required in each competence element for each IPMA certification level as well as the possible process steps in applying or assessing a competence
- broadening of the scope: from projects to include programs and (project and program) portfolios.

22.7 Cross-references/relationships

The ICB and the IPMA four-level certification are strongly related to quality standards such as **ISO 9000:2000**. It can be used together with standards on project management (**PRINCE2, Guide to the PMBoK**), programs (**MSP**) or risk management (**M_o_R**).

At the lowest level these standards are techniques to manage key aspects of a project. For instance, this can be to calculate the size of a system by applying Function Point Analysis (FPA) or to manage risks (M_o_R or an older standard like SBA (Sar Barchets Analysis)) or any other technique that supports the management of a project.

More recent and mature project management methodologies allow an organization to define which techniques are applied and how they should be used in relation to a specific project.

Because organizations run large numbers of projects and because they rely heavily on the performance of their projects, there is a strong need for the coordination of projects. This coordination includes (re)allocation of resources, prioritizing of projects and alignment to the organization's strategy.

There are two types of coordination identified:
- portfolio management
- program management.

If coordination is related to the projects of an organization or a business area within the organization, this is called *portfolio management*. The portfolio manager performs a line management role because projects come and go.

A program (according to MSP) is defined to achieve a strategic goal by coordinating a series of related projects and activities to achieve predefined business benefits. In a program the coordination of underlying projects is part of the management of the program.

The ICB and the IPMA four-level certification are not about methodologies or techniques so these standards are not related to the ones mentioned above. They are about determining competent project managers and their level of operation.

The ICB is a competence baseline. Besides the basic terms, it only names some tasks, practices etc, and does not describe these tasks, practices etc in detail. The listing is intended for scoping the nature of individual competences.

The required knowledge to be competent in technical competences can be found in PMBoK, PRINCE2 and MSP. For the behavioral and contextual competences, this information has to be found elsewhere as these elements are not described in the other frameworks.

The strength of the ICB is that it describes all the competences together with the behavioral and contextual competences expected from project managers and their staff where the other frameworks do not. The ICB also describes the different levels of competences for less and more experienced project managers. None of the other frameworks do so. The ICB is therefore most suitable as a reference model for development and assessment of individual project managers and of the organization's maturity in project management,.

The ICB is therefore complementary to the other frameworks.

The maturity and/or quality of project orientation can be measured by applying CMMI, EFQM or Six Sigma.

IPMA has developed an assessment model based on EFQM to assess the quality of project delivery at the end or after a project. This model is the basis for the annual project management excellence award issued by IPMA during its world congress for the best project of the year.

22.8 Links and literature

IPMA (www.ipma.ch) publishes professional literature references for the certification on its website.

Each certification body publishes a professional literature list which is useful for acquiring and updating knowledge in project management.

IPMA collaborates with the International Project Management Journal.

Several Member Associations publish regional or national journals and magazines on Project Management.

The different Member Associations and their certification bodies can be found through the IPMA website. At the end of 2005 over forty countries all over the world were member of IPMA. The number of members is still increasing.

The ICB contains a full list of existing NCBs.